CH00840375

UNLICENSED

Who's the Guv'nor

THE TRUE STORY BEHIND THE PHENOMENON OF UNLICENSED BOXING

The Men The Fights The History

JOSEPH ARNIE PYLE

Copyright © 2020 Joseph Pyle
Cover design MeanMachine Promotions
All rights reserved.
ISBN: 9798636842811

All rights reserved. No part of this publication may be reproduced, stored in a retrieval system, or
by any form or by any means, without prior permission in writing by the publisher, nor be
circulated in any form in binding or cover other than that in which it is published and without a
similar condition including this condition being imposed on the subsequent purchaser.

DEDICATION

To my father, Joseph Henry Pyle (The Guv'nor of them all)
Alex Steene
Roy Shaw & Lenny McLean

For my Father

If you are going to value a man, then don't value him by how much money he has, don't look at his cars or the house he lives in.
Look at those he loves and look at the love he gets back.
Value his heart, for it is the only true measure of a man.
Not just the courageous side of his heart, but the part which holds his empathy.
Value that he is strong enough to be strong for others,
See the strength of his heart that it is strong enough to break for others
Without empathy, there can be no humanity,
Only a man who has shed tears can hold others in comfort,
Only a man who has lived can tell you why not to die,
Value that which is pure, value that which stiffens the spine,
Men come and men go ... but a man with heart lives forever.

Joseph Arnie Pyle

Foreword

It is my pleasure to write a foreword for young Joe's book.

I have known young Joe for almost all his life, and even up to today, we keep in regular touch. He told me about his book, and it's from a great time in all our lives where we all shared some fantastic memories.

A great time in history when men were men with morals and principles, and a time which is very dear to my heart.

Joe's father, of course, was a very good friend of mine where we go back decades. I remember all the times of Roy and Lenny and how everyone was excited by the fights.

When Roy was fighting Lenny, I remember Joe's Dad had a car site in Peckham, where we would often pop in for a cup of tea and talk about the fights. It was a car site but more like a little clubhouse as everyone would pop in to say hello.

The Thomas a Becket gymnasium was just around the corner, and I would often see Alex down there with Roy Shaw, and some of the great fighters of the times. Back in those days, the Old Kent Road was a great little manor to be in.

Over the years, I have been to many boxing shows promoted by Joe and his father, and I can honestly say I have never been to a bad one.

The shows at Caesars were fabulous! Always a good laugh and always full of everyone we knew.

Joe Snr and Joe Jnr deserve to be acknowledged in this book as over the years, there are a lot of people who owe a big thank you to both of them.

They changed a lot of lives and paved the way for others to follow in their footsteps.

Good luck with the book, Joe

God Bless
Freddie Foreman

A word from Ori Spado

Author of The Accidental Gangster – The Mob Boss of Hollywood.

I believe it was 2006 when my son Anthony and my dear friend John Daly film producer and director of award-winning films flew to London to be with my best Mate Joey Pyle sr.

While there, we attended the fights at Caesars where young Joey was fighting, we were at our table drinking champagne. Joey sr was sitting next to me when young Joey fought a man named Burt Young, I was not only watching the fight, but I also was watching my dear mate as young Joey pounded Burt as you have never seen and I watched my mate's face fill with pride that only a father would have for his son that he loved so much. I have seen many fights in my life, but never did I enjoy one so much as this, John Daly, who also promoted the rumble in the Jungle with Muhammed Ali and George Foreman, was elated as my son Anthony was. We all celebrated, of course, and when the fight was over, we all went over to Joey' s house and celebrated more in his kitchen on Morden lane until the next morning.

It was not long after that we lost a real man, but that night I will never forget watching my best mates face full of pride for his son, and I know that today, he sits on his son's shoulder, giving him advice. Joey is now as we say my third son, and he is. Joey, I love you always, but always remember when you need your Dad, just look on your shoulder, and he is there for you, as I always will be also.

I wish you all the happiness and all the success you deserve.

Ori Spado your second father and your brother Anthony

CONTENTS

Introduction
UNLICENSED BOXING

GET READY FOR WORLD WAR 3

THE DISTINGUISHED title of the meanest, roughest, toughest, hardest, most brutal – not to say dirtiest – fighter in Britain will be awarded to one of two gentlemen tonight.

The runner up will very likely be on his way to the infirmary, an oxygen tent, the crematorium, or at least the title role in sleeping beauty.

Colin Dunne - The Sun newspaper (Sept. 11th, 1978)

The above was the write-up by the Sun newspaper's boxing columnist on the day of the third epic battle between Roy Shaw and Lenny McLean.

WHAT IS THE FASCINATION WITH UNLICENSED BOXING?

People have always been eager to watch men fighting, crowds all over the world gather in their thousands to see such a spectacle.

There is something about unlicensed boxing, something which hits a nerve in the male's primordial spirit.

It's raw and sexy. It has an entirely different atmosphere to its bigger brother (professional boxing) as soon as you arrive at the venue, you can feel the electricity in the air, taste the menace, sense the aura of danger.

Unlicensed boxing is legal, yet it feels like you are doing something naughty, it feels like you are part of a crime that is unfolding right in front of your face.

Lew Yates, who fought Roy Shaw once said, "It was gangsters promoting these events and not the Christian brotherhood."

Starting in the '70s, and now five decades later, thousands of young men all over the country are taking part in what is commonly known as … 'Unlicensed boxing.'

Often called the dark and dangerous side of boxing, it has evolved organically from the old days, creating variations like white-collar boxing and Semi-Pro boxing.

But what all these fancy new names have in common is none of them are sanctioned by The British Boxing Board of Control (BBBofC). The self-appointed limited company that presides over professional boxing in the UK. Even the more renowned outfits like Ross Minter and Alan Foley's Queensbury league, and Rio de Caro's BIBA, run outside the BBBofC's remit.

The term 'Unlicensed' has become notorious and is firmly embedded in the UK's way of thinking, go into any pub and mention the word *unlicensed*, and people straight away will say boxing!

Now, five decades since it began, this side of boxing is extremely popular, and more unlicensed shows are going on in a month, than professional shows go on in a year.

The popularity has exploded because these shows feature local guys, local tearaways, boys who want to get into the ring and fight! Most of these boys do not possess the talents and skills of professional and top-notch amateurs, but their brutality and courage often replace their lack of expertise.

Unlicensed boxing still has the underground feel about it, and its considerable notoriety has undoubtedly helped gain exposure.

You don't have to look far to find it on TV or the big screen. Guy Ritchie's hit films, Snatch, and Lock, Stock, and Two Smoking Barrels were both deeply influenced by the UK's unlicensed scene.

The unlicensed code has created legends and cemented legacies. Many of the ex-champions have become household names and published bestselling biographies—books that have generated hundreds of thousands of sales. The market is now huge, and YouTube views of these unlicensed fights now go into the hundreds of millions.

Thousands of people up and down the country now earn a living from it, Boxers, trainers, promoters, managers, MC's, referees, card girls, doctors, paramedics, ring suppliers, doormen, stewards, photographers, film producers, and even the people making boxing equipment, shorts, robes boots, etc.

It also gave local gyms the freedom they needed to create additional revenue by staging their 'own' boxing events.

It has created thousands of champions and changed countless lives that may have ended up in prison or even in the graveyard.

Many Fighters I know personally and have promoted have gone on to establish their own gyms, stage shows, and earn a good living from it.

Unlicensed boxing is in itself an industry, and it generates millions of pounds across the country every week.

There are three leading players in the UK professional boxing world, three leading promoters, and two of them come from unlicensed boxing backgrounds.

Many people in the professional code have cut their teeth in the unlicensed world. I can think of dozens of fighters who are now professionals who used to fight on the unlicensed scene.

When I look back over the years and all the shows I have promoted at Caesars (The historic home of unlicensed boxing) it makes me very proud that we started the careers of some boxers who have become champions in the professional ranks

Unlicensed boxing has nowhere near the professional ranks' revenue, but it is a sport of the masses, with thousands of boxers taking part each weekend up and down the country.

All of this started back in the 70s, just because two men wanted to fight each other, and my father and Alex Steene were determined to make that happen.

Ron Stander – Gary Shaw – Nosher Powell – Nat Basso – Roy Shaw – Unknown – Alex Steene – Joe Pyle Jr

I have decided to put pen to paper and write this down as I am sick to death of reading so many lies and twisted facts about unlicensed boxing.

When you think of unlicensed boxing, four names come to your attention, Roy Shaw, Lenny Mclean, Joe Pyle, and Alex Steene.

Four men I knew very well and four men I loved. Joe Pyle was, of course, my father, and Alex Steene was like a second father to me.

Roy Shaw, I've known all my life. And Lenny, who I worked with for almost a year, spending nearly every day with him.

I also attended all three of the fights between Roy and Lenny, I was young, but I remember them well.

I was also at most of the press conferences, weigh-ins, and meetings before the fights, and been privileged to have had countless conversations with all of them about what (really) happened.

Sadly, they have all passed on, and I am quite sure that no one else on the planet can say they had known them (collectively) as well as I did.

Roy, Lenny, and Alex all had sons, and I wouldn't for one moment, suggest I knew their fathers, as well as they, knew them. But as a (collective of men,) I feel I am in a very privileged and unique situation.

Roy's son, Gary, unquestionably knew his father better than me, but I doubt he ever really spoke to Lenny. Let alone be his friend, and the same can be said about Lenny's son, Jamie. (I was very good friends with both of them) Another thing to point out is there is no bias in me about any of them. All four men have made a massive impact on my life, and I would under no circumstance say or do anything to tarnish their reputations.

Nine times out of ten times, if you ask me a question about them, then I will tell you what happened. The other one percent I may hold back because there are few things I know which should remain a secret.

Along with Ricky English, I also resurrected unlicensed boxing in the early 2000s, where we laid the foundations of the (Unlicensed) sport as it is today. Many boxing organisations have flourished because of how we staged our shows at Caesars in Streatham, South London.

You see... I did things backward; I came from a professional boxing background before promoting unlicensed shows, but what I did was a game-changer. I bought that professional expertise to the unlicensed scene.

In the early days, Caesars was like the wild west. We had some crazy times. But we ran the shows just like I ran my professional events. We even began to license boxers and introduced a ranking system with title fights.

No one at the time was doing boxer ratings. It was also the time when the internet was starting to *catch fire.*

Suddenly we had a platform to present all the information we wanted to disclose. MeanMachine Promotions formed a massive website; it had news, events, future shows, past shows, interviews, merchandise, videos, sponsor links, fighter bios.

To be fair, we were innovators. We began marketing shows in ways that had never been used before (social media) we brought glitz to the shows, live singers, comedians, fun, we even had girls stripping in the ring in the intervals. It was crazy times, good times... I hope the information and stories in the following chapters do them justice.

Below is an interview I did in 2008 for our website; it gives an insight into what we were doing at the time.

What was once known as 'Unlicensed' boxing started in the 1970s has been evolving over the years, now often called white-collar boxing, we at MeanMachine Promotions have taken the sport to its next level.

Why Semi-Pro?
We are filling the void created by the two established organisations The BBBofC (British boxing board of control) Professional and what was once known as the ABA (Amateur Boxing Association)

What is the void?
The void is a massive gulf between being an amateur and being a professional.

How does Semi-pro fill this?
Where we come in is, or where we did come in, is we are more flexible in our regulations than the two other ruling bodies. See, some guys who are 28 or 29 and did a bit of boxing as a teenager, might feel that they don't want to go down the road of having to join an amateur club again, and to turn pro is even more daunting, they have to have MRA and MRI brain scans, find a manager, get medicals and eye tests, have interviews with the BBBofC, etc.
All of which is time-consuming and can cost you nearly a grand, then once you're a pro fighter, you still might not even get a fight!
But let's say you're a very fit 34-year-old and boxed as an amateur, then that's where you fall into limbo, see your too old for amateur and the BBBofC will try to convince you you're too old for professional, so what do you do? You're fit, strong, training, and fancy a bout, well, this is where Semi-Pro comes in.

So if you're too old, you should turn Semi-Pro?
Well, yeah! But that's just not what we are; age is only one aspect of our federation, Roberto Duran boxed till he was 54, Bernard Hopkins is still boxing at 44, so we take a different view.
If you're fit enough and you pass the medical, then we will match you accordingly and give you a bout.
I would say that over 50% of the fighters on our shows are under 30, age does play a part in what we offer, but it's not the only reason for semi-pro.

So what else is different?
Okay, let's give you another scenario, say you like playing football, or cricket or even want to ride horses. Let's say that as it's your pastime, well is anyone making you a professional, have you got to be a pro jockey, cause you to wanna ride horses, or be a pro footballer because you want to kick around with your mates on a Sunday afternoon. Well, this is the way we look at boxing; it's a sport, a pastime, so why should you be so regulated if you want to indulge.

Yeah, but you can hardly compare boxing with Horse racing, people get injured in boxing!
Can't you! People get injured being a carpenter or a builder, and most of the injuries in boxing are at the highest level where champions are killing themselves to make weight. And as with horse racing, ask any doctor about horse riding injuries, or rugby, ask a doctor about spinal injuries in rugby. But regardless of all this, it is the man's choice if he feels he is strong enough to want to compete, then why should someone stop him, we have ref's, doctors, we have put on hundreds if not thousands of bouts and we have not had one serious injury.

Okay! What else makes you different from the pro's or amateurs?
Like I said before, we're less stringent than them; we offer an alternative.
We get a lot of amateurs wanting to box on our shows who are fed up with not getting fights. I'm not knocking the amateur scene, it's great for the kids, but I know so many clubs up and down the country who are hardly having any shows. If they fight on our bills, they get a taste of the pro scene, earn some money, and do what they train every night to do.

Some say the quality of fights aren't as good as the pro's or amateurs?
Who says! Look, that's opinions, let's be real here, of course, there are differences, but what you are saying is neither here or there.
If you're asking me if a semi-pro show at Caesars can compete with a Las Vegas, Ricky Hatton Mayweather fight, then it can't but how many times does that happen in boxing, once every few years. It's like saying an Everton football game can't compete with a Man Utd game, some days it can, most days it can't, but they still have the right to play.
Anyway, I have seen some absolute stinkers on Professional TV, it wasn't that long ago Danny Williams boxed Audley Harrison, and the crowd jeered and booed throughout the fight.

I see that Sven Hamer, the ex-pro often fights on your promotions?
Sven's a good fighter, he is unbeaten at the moment, and we are trying to match him with another ex-pro, Mark Potter in the new year, that will be a terrific scrap!

Do you have any other ex-pros on your shows?
We have a few of them Calvin Stonestreet, Steve Yorath, Mark Callaghan, and the list is growing all the time
What's the attraction for ex-pros boxing semi-pro
Simply! They still want to fight! Look, let's say, for example, you have an ex British Champion who is 34, lost his last four pro fights, and retires because no pro promoter can use him anymore. However, he is still fit and wants to pick up a few quid then he can box with us, you see the cost of running a pro show are enormous, Promoters are on a very tight budget, and unless the fighter brings in a high level of interest, then the promoter can't use him.

But surely that goes with you too?
To an extent, but we enforce our own rules. Our budgets are different from the pros. One example is ticket deals which the boxing board frown upon because it makes it difficult for them to calculate the percentage that the boxer's commission is, some of our boys are on 50% ticket sales they sell, that would NEVER happen in the pro's, they would be lucky to get 5 or 10%.

And the Amateurs?

That's an entirely different situation; the boxers get nothing! All the money generated goes to the club. What I would like to happen, is for the Amateur clubs becoming affiliated with us where they could get a percentage of the ticket sales and get their boys boxing more frequent. It's a grey area because they feel that we are taking away their power, but if they only opened their eyes, then they would see that we are offering them a way to earn more money and a means for their boxers to get more experience, it's a win-win situation for them, but some of them are old fashioned and don't want to see change. Still, a change is coming, and there is nothing they can do to stop it, in a few years you'll see there will be good quality professionals leaving the pro ranks and joining us, it's already happening, we just need the word spread that there is an alternative out there for them.

So what's in the future for Semi-Pro and MeanMachine?

We're going to grow, we already put on between 10 to 12 shows a year. Next year we have shows all over the place, Northampton, Cambridge, Kent, Crawley, north and south London, and we are already exploring putting on shows at venues like The Albert Hall, The O2 and Wembley. But mostly we want to expand, pull away from what most people often call 'Unlicensed boxing' as we are not unlicensed, we are sanctioned and licensed by the EBF The English boxing federation. We want to offer the public the chance to take part and watch their pals fighting while improving standards for our champions, the fights are going to get better with big-name fighters joining the organisation, so it's up all the way for us, and as my Dad always told me
"If you're down, GET UP! And keep on boxing."

I will close with that statement and add that if anyone is going to make this happen then I can see it is you and Ricky English that's going to do it, give my regards to Ricky and all the best with MeanMachine.

James Forsyth interviewed Joe Pyle Jnr
October 2008

Unlicensed compared to Professional

No, I haven't gone mad! It's a valid question that I feel needs answering!
First and foremost, the professionals are what boxing is all about. It's the elite boxers fighting the elite, world champion fighting world champion. Muhammed Ali, Mike Tyson, Sugar Ray Leonard, Roberto Duran, Floyd Mayweather, Roy Jones, Rocky Marciano……. I could fill this page with the number of household names.

Unlicensed boxing cannot ever compare to this; it's honestly like a different world.

I like to compare unlicensed to how it was in the old days, the days of John L Sullivan, a time when boxers had just started to put on the gloves, and the rules were often chosen fight by fight.

Some of those fights were crazy! John L Sullivan against Jake Kilrain went into the 76th round. (2 hours and 16 minutes of fighting) and Kilrain's fight against the British fighter Jem Mace went into the 106th round until it was stopped because it was getting too dark to continue, the battle was called a draw.

Those legendary fights were over a century ago, and since then, the sport has evolved dramatically, and now we have universal rules and regulations put in place. Today everything is regulated in the professionals. There are a set number of rounds per fight, 4 – 6 – 8 – 10 – or 12 round fights. All world championships being over 12 x 3-minute rounds, and boxers only fight in 8oz or 10oz gloves.

I'm not knocking that, but what draws me to the unlicensed game is we are flexible. We choose the rounds per fight, choose what weight gloves to wear, and choose a 2 minute or 3-minute round. A governing body does not govern us, so we are free to do what we like.

Most unlicensed shows of today, follow a guideline of having fights over 3 x 2-minute rounds with title fights 5 x 2-minute rounds. That has become the norm. At Caesars, we set this pattern, but it wasn't *'set in stone.'*

We could have a championship fight on one show at 5 x 2-minute rounds and then on the next show, stage the very same championship fight over 3 x 2-minute rounds or even 10 x 2-minute rounds.

See, what we did was arrange the fight around the fighters!
If we thought a title fight would be better over three rounds with 10oz gloves, then that's is precisely what we would do.

We might have matched two fighters and thought to ourselves, "this fight will be boring as fuck over ten rounds! Let's cut this one down to three rounds, so they have to come out swinging straight away.

Most of the fights we promoted were like this - fast and all action, there was no time for a fighter to get a smell at his opponent, all you have is three rounds to win the battle.

Can you imagine Nigel Benn vs Chris Eubank over three rounds? It would be an all-out war from the first bell!

Another difference we had was if we thought you were good enough and challenged one of our champions, there was an excellent chance you would be fighting for a title.

When we started at Caesars, we formed our own governing body called the English Boxing Federation (EBF), and we began to make individual titles. At first, we had the South London title, the London title, the Southern area title, the English title, and the British title. (We even had the kebab title as a joke when two big overweight fellas boxed each other.)

Once we started to get champions in different weight divisions, we began to have eliminators for the titles, or if someone won the London title, then he was on course to challenge for the English title. We did have a rating system in theory, but this was unlicensed! We were flexible. If the public wanted to see a fight, then we would look at making it.

In a way that is the beauty of the unlicensed game, there are no politics involved; it's just about the fighting.

Look at *Dillian Whyte* in the professionals at the moment; it seems like he has been waiting around forever to fight for a title!

In the unlicensed that wouldn't happen, you would get your shot at the title.

A few years ago, when I was doing personal training, I created an 'Unlicensed' training routine. It was training for quick bursts of energy and based on the fight format of 3 x 2-minute rounds. I found it on intensity and speed. It was a training system designed to make you prepared to go full pace from the first bell until the last, like a hundred-metre sprint race.

Maybe that is what makes unlicensed boxing popular? It's a short, fast fight with no time to mess around, it's getting stuck in straight from the first bell!

It's like the old days of battle where heart and guts played as significant a role as skill.

Even back to the gladiator days where it's all or nothing.

One fight at Caesars, we staged was the last man standing fight! It had no limit on rounds, and the two boxers would keep fighting until someone got knocked out, or they said they had had enough. The crowd loved it, and we had a toe to toe war for 12 hard-fought rounds.

Look at the end of the day; it was all about entertaining the crowd and getting a few quid! Some people say what we did was dangerous, but so is bicycle riding or rugby! Most sports have an element of danger; I'm pretty sure I would rather take a left hook and a few uppercuts from someone than come off a motorbike doing 120mph! Or fall off a bloody great horse for that matter.

People do get hurt in boxing, but it's usually just bumps and bruises, I have never seen anyone get a broken neck in boxing. I have seen someone break their leg! (He fell awkwardly after a knockdown) but the vast majority of injuries are

gone in a couple of days. If I think back to all the injuries I have had from fighting, then by far the worst was a bruised rib! I have had a few black eyes, hurt my hands a few times, sore knuckles, even twisted my wrist and few and cut lips, but nothing that (really) hurt me.

Professional boxing is the sport we love! It's where the great fighters preside. But if you gave me a choice of what show I'd rather go to between a small hall professional show at York hall featuring ten journeymen, or an unlicensed show at Caesars, Caesars would win nine times out of ten.

THE SPORT OF BOXING

There has always been fighting, and there has always been fighting for money. Boxing has been around for a very long time. The earliest evidence of boxing goes back to Egypt in 3000 BC. Then the ancient Olympic Games in Greece around the 7th century BC.

Professional boxing as we know it evolved from bare-knuckle fights.

In fact, the first recorded boxing fight in the UK was on Jan. 6th, 1681; the boxing match took place when Christopher Monck, the 2nd Duke of Albemarle, engineered a bout between his butler and his butcher, with the butcher coming out on top. Early fighting had no written rules. There were no weight divisions or round limits, and no referee.

A BRIEF HISTORY OF BOXING

In ancient Greece, boxing was a popular amateur competitive sport and was included in the first Olympic Games.

In ancient Rome, boxers often wore the Cestus, a metal-studded leather hand covering with which they maimed and even killed their opponents, sometimes as part of gladiatorial spectacles. The sport declined in popularity after the fall of the Roman Empire.

In the 18th Century, boxing was revived in London, in the form of bare-knuckle prize-fights which the contestants fought for money and the spectators made wagers on the outcome.

The first boxer to be recognised as a Heavyweight Champion was James Figg in 1719. In 1743 a later Champion, John Broughton, formulated a set of Rules standardising some practices and eliminating others, such as hitting opponents when they are down or seizing opponents by the hair. Broughton

Rules governed boxing until 1838 when the Original London Prize Ring Rules, based on those of Broughton, were devised.

Modifications known as the Revised London Prize Ring Rules were drawn up in 1853, and they controlled the sport until the end of the 19th Century when the Queensberry Rules came into use. These Rules were drafted in 1857 by a boxer, John Graham Chambers, under the auspices of John Sholto Douglas, 8th Marquis of Queensberry.

Emphasising boxing skills rather than wrestling and agility over strength, the Queensberry Rules helped to undo the popular image of boxing as a savage, brutal brawl. The new Rules prohibited bare-fisted fighting, wrestling, hugging, hitting opponents while they are helpless, and fighting to the finish. Under the Broughton Rules - a downed man was allowed 30 seconds to square off at a distance of 1yd (90cm) from the opponent, aided by handlers if necessary. If the boxer failed to square off, the fighter was considered beaten.

Under the London Prize Ring Rules, the boxer had to reach scratch (a mark located in the middle of the ring) unaided within 8 seconds after the 30-second time-lapse; and a round was ended when a boxer went down.

Under the Queensberry Rules, matches were divided into 3-minute rounds with 1-minute intervals of rest between them. A contestant who remained down, either recumbent or on one knee, after 10 seconds, lost the match.

The Rules also stipulated that matches be conducted in a roped-in square, called a ring, measuring 24ft (7.3m) on a side.

The last bare-knuckle Heavyweight Champion was the American John L. Sullivan, who fought and won the last sanctioned bare-knuckle fight in 1889 against Jake Kilrain.

Fighting with gloves under the Queensberry Rules, the popular Sullivan lost the World Heavyweight Boxing Championship to James J. Corbett in New Orleans, Louisiana, on Sept. 7th, 1892. The Queensberry Rules have remained the code governing the conduct of professional boxing.

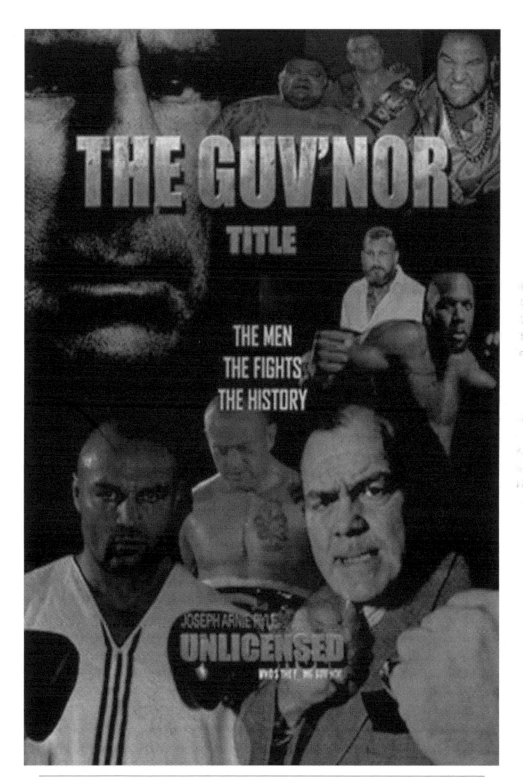

CHAPTER 1
THE HISTORY OF HOW IT ALL BEGAN

In these early days of the 1970s, three men Roy Shaw, Joe Pyle, and Alex Steene. Three men who wanted to box, manage and promote fights, men who were unwilling to be dictated to, by the British Boxing Board of control. (BBBofC.)

1975
Joe Pyle parked his E-Type Jaguar in the underground car park in Panton Street, just off The Haymarket. He grabbed his sports jacket off the back seat and walked up the stairs and over the road to the office of Alex Steene.
Alex Buxton greeted him and told him that Roy Shaw and Alex were waiting for him in Alex's office.
My father walked in, said hello and then sat down and joined in with a conversation. A conversation that would inevitably be the spark that would set about making history!

"Joe, whatever money they want to put on the fight, then that suits me, I'll take his fucking head off," Roy said.
"They say he is unbeaten in over fifty fights," answered Alex Steene to Roy.
"Alex, I don't care, I need some money."
"So they have agreed to it, then?" Joe Pyle asked.
"It's on, Joe … All I want from you is to come with me, so when I knock this mug out, we don't get any problems collecting my winnings."
Joey Pyle took a step back and lit himself a cigarette, Joe always the businessman began to think of a way to maximise their profit.
"So, he has agreed to the fight then, Roy," Joe asked again.
"Yeah … he's agreed to it."
"Right, then this is what we're gonna do, we will promote the event, put up beer tents, serve food, and make a right day out of it … and charge everyone a few quid to get in."

This conversation was how it all started… It was just a small discussion unbeknown to Joe Pyle, Roy Shaw, and Alex Steene, a monumental moment in UK sports history, and the catalyst of unlicensed boxing
It was the flint that ignited the fire!
A new day and generation, the start of something which over the next five decades, would change the lives of thousands.

This meeting took place just a few months before Roy Shaw destroyed Donny' The Bull' Adams on a cold, wet field in Winkfield near Windsor, under the bright lights of Billy Smarts' big top circus tent.

The fight was originally planned to be a bare-knuckle fight in a field in Essex, but due to the enormous interest it generated, that idea was stopped by the Police. Hundreds of people came to see it, and even a news crew from ITN turned up.

The old bill, then warned Joe Pyle that if any fight between these two men were to go ahead, they would arrest everyone involved.

Regardless of what the old bill, said, my father attempted to get the fight on a few times, he wasn't too bothered about their threats, but every time he tried, it was the same story with the law poking their nose in and put an end to it.

But the momentum was too powerful, and there was no way the law was going to stop this fight, so out of panic, they decided to arrest Roy and Donny.

In October 1975 - Roy Shaw and Donny Adams appeared in court to answer the charge of 'disturbing the peace.'

Donny Adams spoke to the magistrate and told him that no matter what he did, he would not be able to stop them fighting, it would happen in an alley, a car park or a gym, but one thing for sure was that a fight would happen!

Roy added that when he was in borstal, he was told that if he had *the needle* with someone, the best way to sort it out would be to get into the ring and *'sort it out'* with gloves on.

The Police then stood up and said that they had to act as it was illegal for men to fight without gloves or any time limit.

The magistrate thought hard for a moment before he announced that as long as Roy and Donny fought each other in a ring with gloves on, with rounds and a referee, they could fight each other and that the fight would be 'unlicensed' but not illegal.

That ruling by the magistrate was just what Joe Pyle wanted; an official blessing from the powers that be, that the fight could go ahead, now nothing could stop them.

The magistrate's words really were a green light for my father. For weeks the boxing board hadn't stopped trying to condemn the fight; they gave interviews in newspapers and TV saying anything to try to have it stopped. They called it illicit and illegal, dangerous, you name it, they called it, but now, my father had the words from a magistrate of the courts that it wasn't illegal, and it *could* go ahead.

The chance of Roy Shaw at 41 years old, getting a license to box from the BBBofC, was totally out of the question. Especially with all the publicity and what had been going on.

So they decided to do it without the BBBofC's involvement, they would stage a boxing show on their own, a fight with gloves on where the old bill couldn't stop it.

It was perfect! And now nothing was going to get in their way.

The original plan for the fight was to get the first round over, and then Roy and Donny were going to rip their gloves off and fight bare-knuckle.

This plan would make all of them some good money and as Joe Pyle said, 'We would get one over the old bill as well,' but Roy came out in round one and destroyed Donny with what some people say is the most brutal assault anyone has ever seen in a boxing ring.

Joe Pyle later said,

"Originally, the gloves were there just so the fight could happen; they were going to tear them off and take whatever punishment the law decided to do after the fight.

We weren't thinking about any other fights other than this one, but when challenges started to come in, we quickly realised that we had the possibility of more shows."

No one thought for a moment just how big that first fight was going to be. The newspapers ran with stories as well as the TV stations like ITN and BBC 1.

Everyone wanted to know more about this new phenomenon called 'Unlicensed Boxing.'

Challenges to Roy were coming in thick and thin, and it began to get very exciting.

My father then had a meeting up the office with Alex and Roy, where they set up some guidelines for challengers.

Fights would be over a specific number of rounds; challengers would have to sell a certain amount of tickets, side bets were discussed, and Winner *Takes All* - fights. The options were endless.

The world was their oyster, and there was no limit as to how far this could go or where they would take it.

They had created something completely different, something for all the blokes in the pubs, the fighting men of the streets, this was raw, gritty, and had an air of menace about it.

Even the people going to watch the fights felt like they were doing something shady.

Imagine for one moment the first fight between Roy Shaw and Donny the bull Adams.

Try to think of the atom bomb that had just exploded in the world of illicit fighting!

A fight planned to take place like all the scraps that had preceded it, in a field on some cold, rainy weekend morning, following a tradition that had been going on for centuries. A tradition steeped in culture, and legend, especially in the traveling world and community.

Now, all of a sudden, this kind of fighting was hijacked by my father. A man labelled a villain with links to the Krays and all the other firms in London. (Joey Pyle had more connections than the national grid - Lew Yates once said)

He took an ancient tradition and turned it on its head; he took it from a muddy field to Billy Smarts circus big top! He made it Big! He made it an event!

All those people who had been going to watch scraps in car parks and fields, shivering their bollocks off in the winter, or sweating like fuck under a hot summer sun were now going to a bloody massive circus tent. There were hot dogs, burgers, music, chairs, booze by the van load.
The buzz and atmosphere was unreal!
It was unbelievable at the time! It was fayre ground fighting on steroids!
Nothing like this had ever been done before!

Once the Donny Adams fight was out the way. Next, they sorted out some ground rules to go forward, and they began talking about the challenges that were starting to come in.
My father and Alex also started looking at different venues to stage the shows and getting good extra fights for the undercards.
It was exciting times where everyone wanted to be a part of it.
One of the things you have to take into consideration is the fact that it was Roy Shaw fighting!
Everyone knew Roy Shaw, faces from all over London came to see him fight, families and firms from all four corners of London, you name them, and they went to the shows.
If it would have been someone unknown, then I don't think unlicensed boxing would have ever taken off.
Even the press was fascinated because it was Roy Shaw fighting … a former armed robber who was pals with the Krays and had served time in Broadmoor mental hospital. It was the perfect storm for headlines in newspapers.

EX ARMED ROBBER…
THE LUNATIC FROM BROADMOOR…
FRIEND OF THE KRAYS!..
UNDERWORLD BOXING…
A MAN WILLING TO FIGHT ANYONE…

The headlines were attractive to the eye, it was romantic, it was powerful, and it got everyone talking about it.

After Donny Adams, they took a challenge from a streetfighter from Kilburn, a fella who no one had heard of. His name was Paddy mad dog Mullins? But he had a few wealthy Irish businessmen who wanted to put up the money.
So a meeting took place just off Notting Hill, in West London, and the Irish boys agreed to the terms, and the fight got made.
My father once told me he couldn't fucking believe it, we didn't have a clue about this Paddy Mullins, but all these Irishmen were offering bundles of money to make the fight. It was bonkers! They even wanted to buy every fucking ticket as well. The first time I saw Mullins, I took just one look at him and thought Roy would kill him with a stare. I suppose the Irish boys had more money than

sense and just wanted a good night out, watch their man fighting and all get on the piss.

Just as my father expected, the Irishman was no challenge for Roy. The fight was so one-sided, with Mullins battered into submission.
Beforehand and on paper, it sounded like a good fight with a man called....
'Mad Dog!' Everyone wanted to see Roy fight again, so they sold the place out.

Roy's record was now, two fights, two wins, and he had hardly broken a sweat.
He had beaten the Bull and destroyed the Mad dog!
who would come forward next.
The wild bear? Or The lion man....
Roy though, couldn't care less!
"Take their money, Joe, and I'll take their fucking heads off!"

My father and Alex once again raised the bar when they brought over a well-known American fighter, **Ron Stander**. A fighter who fought Joe Frazier for the heavyweight title.
It was crazy to think that they went from a makeshift scrap in a field to fighting at the iconic Alexander Palace against a boxer who had boxed the legendary Joe Frazier in the space of a few months.
This fight was monumental! And it brought a whole new light on what they called unlicensed boxing. It also rattled quite a few feathers as it showed the BBBofC and the boxing powers that be, that things were getting very organised. This wasn't just a bunch of crooks staging a glorified pub-fight in a tent, they are here to stay, and they are now booking huge venues. There were real concerns about what and how quickly things were happening.
Behind the scenes, Alex Steene was already in talks with the licensing committees in the USA. (The New York state commission) now picture that! Imagine if you never had to be a so-called *'professional'* fighter in the UK to get into the ratings for the top titles in America.
I know I'm fantasising a bit here, but these were the things that were being discussed at the time. Crazy as it sounds! But other countries have multiple boxing bodies. The British Boxing Board of Control (BBBofC) are not government-appointed.
They are a limited company, and there is nothing illegal to having another limited company creating their very own regulations and getting affiliated with other sanctioning bodies in foreign countries.
Times were changing very quickly.
Times were getting exciting...........

CHAPTER 2
THE FIGHTS

Roy Shaw vs Donny 'The Bull' Adams
Windsor
Dec. 1st,, 1975

It was a cold stormy night in December, a powerful wind was blowing and the rain was pissing down. Despite the weather conditions, people arrived in their droves. They came from every part of the country all eager to see what people were calling (The fight of the Century.)

Two street fighting legends, finally getting to fight each other. A fight everyone wanted to see!

Finally, after months of cancellations, weeks of newspaper and TV interviews, the fight was happening, tonight they **would** meet - and no one was going to stop it this time.

Inside the Circus tent, it was a who's who of London gangland, with plenty of old bill nosing about, seeing who was there and secretly taking pictures of everyone coming in.

The crowd was arriving and cautiously walking inside of this modern-day gladiator arena, old pals were reunited, and the lager was flowing at the bars. The atmosphere was building, danger was in the air, exaggerated by the sound of the torrential rain and the howling wind that shook the tent above their heads.

My father was in a great mood, all the family was there, and now he felt confident that finally, this was going to happen. Everything was going to plan; it was just too good to be true. It was perfect until my Dad's pal Peter Brayham walked over and said to him that the referee hasn't turned up.

My father looked at his watch and saw it was getting late.

"Joe, he's two hours late!" Peter said, looking anxious.

Suddenly, my father had a problem, and it dawned on him that the referee they had planned had bottled it and wasn't going to turn up; maybe he was stuck in traffic, or his car broke down. It didn't really matter now as the fight was getting closer, so my father had to think on his feet and find an alternative.

Out the corner of his eye, he saw one of his pals, Ray Kennet standing at the bar, Ray had bought a ringside seat and was with a few pals. My father bit his lip and walked over to him, a few minutes later, he had convinced Ray to be the new referee.

Together they went to the makeshift changing room where Roy Shaw was relaxing and getting his mind right for the fight.

Ray Kennett was a bit of a face in Kingston, South West London, and he had done a bit boxing when he was younger.

Ray had also not long returned from Sweden accompanying my father for a business trip, where the trip turned sour and poor Ray ended up getting seven bullets put into him.

It was touch and go for a while if Ray would make it, but miraculously, he pulled through and even came home with two bullets still lodged inside him, two bullets which could never be removed.

"Roy, the ref, hasn't shown up, so Ray will be the Ref," My father said, as Ray was laughing and still not believing he had allowed Joe to talk him into being the referee for the fight.

Ray Kennet turned out to be quite a character as the referee.

In the documentary called 'The Guv'nor' you can hear him saying the immortal words as the two men touched gloves before the start of the 1st round, Ray said,

"I want a good clean fight; if I say break, you can please your fucking selves." You can also hear him, saying, "He's dead Roy, he's dead, Roy!" As he was pulling Roy off of Donny Adams.

Poor Ray Kennet, he came to watch a fight and ended up being immortalised in what I think is one of the best boxing documentaries ever produced.

The atmosphere on the night was unbelievable! There was a real feel of testosterone, and there was just something in the air that this was something special, something different, raw, and menacing.
When both fighters entered the ring, Donny walked out smiling and relaxed, greeting members of the crowd with his trainer, former Kray associate Tommy' The Bear' Brown.
On the other hand, Roy was completely different; he ran out like a man possessed, he was on fire with rage, and you could feel the energy coming off him. He was thirsting for the first bell. Roy walked around, pacing the ring, he just wanted the fight to start so he could explode into action. The ring announcer (MC) just started to make the announcements and then some fellow got in the ring and said he wanted to fight the winner.
Everyone started shouting for him to leave, and then Roy told him to fuck off, but he wouldn't leave. Ray Kennet then got involved and was pushing him out,

"Get out the fucking Ring!" Ray was saying, but this idiot who was probably already half pissed just didn't seem to want to listen. All he kept saying was he would fight the winner.
Tempers were now starting to get frayed as this idiots timing was terrible, you challenge someone (after) the fight and not before. (Unless invited)
What happened next was hilarious as everyone had enough of this pest, Donny pushed himself forward and together with Roy, they threw him over the top rope.

The whole crowd cheered, and the idiot has pushed away from ringside, looking a little confused and worse for wear.

Once that was sorted out, the two men gloved up and got back to what everyone was here for – the fight!

The start of round one saw Roy fly out from his corner and knock Adams to the canvas with the first punch he threw. Roy then went crazy, screaming at Adams to get up, Roy even picked poor Donny up and hit him before jumping and stamping on him, the fight was over in the first round, Roy destroyed him with such savagery It was frightening. He was so charged with anger and frustration, he just went crazy, it wasn't a fight for him, this was about battering his opponent to a pulp.

In all the fights I saw him fight, this was where I saw him at his angriest. Donny must have really wound Roy up over the months with all the cancelations, the arrest, and court cases.

Roy was also pissed off with all the publicity Donny was getting. He told my father on more than one occasion that it was fucking annoying him when every time he picked up a paper, there was something in there from Adams saying he was going knock Shaw out.

But in the end, it was a short and a devastating win for Roy. The promotion itself, had been a great success and a complete sell-out. My father had made a bloody fortune and I know for a fact he pocketed more than sixty-five grand in side bets alone. (In 1975, that was a lot of money)

Everyone soon got to hear what happened and what money was being made, so it didn't take long before the phones started ringing with other fighters wanting to make a challenge.

It was funny that after all the publicity, the cancelled field fight, the court cases, the press, and even TV, the fight lasted just one punch and is more famous for Roy picking him up off the canvas to hit him again and stamping on him. Nevertheless, it was a success! At least in the sense that they had created something which they could build on.

Over the next few weeks, my father decided to set out some ground rules for anyone wanting to make a challenge. The fights would be a winner take all, and any fighter would have to guarantee a certain amount of ticket sales.

Roy Shaw was on everyone's lips, he was the talk of the town, and if anyone wanted to fight him or ride on the back of all the publicity, then they would have to bring something to the table.

Evening News Reporter

THE BIG punch-up between Donny "The Bull" Adams and Roy "Pretty Boy" Shaw WILL take place.

But it will be 15 rounds, with gloves, and with the blessing of police.

The last time the two tried to settle their differences they sold tickets at £5 a head for the fight in a field.

Police, fearing a bare-knuckle old-fashioned prizefight, stepped in and stopped them.

Now Billy Smart has offered his big top at Windsor Safari Park and the match will take place on December 1.

SHORT

Co-promoter Mr. Joseph Pyle, said today: "Even with the gloves on, it will be some fight."

Roy Shaw said at his Dagenham home: "We have waited for some time for this. It will be a short fight. Adams won't be able to last more than a couple of rounds."

DONNY ADAMS

ROY SHAW

The press coverage was unbelievable, television and national press couldn't get enough, and they didn't stop running stories on Roy, the new fighting Guvnor, the insane bank-robber and hardened criminal.

The business set-up was working well, Roy was doing the fighting, and my father and Alex were doing the deals.

When the Adams fight unfolded, my father just thought of it as an easy way to earn some 'quick' money by matching Roy and Donny together. But it quickly turned into something much bigger.

Until that fight, there was no such thing as unlicensed boxing or an unaffiliated boxing fight. If you were not a professional boxer with the (British Boxing Board of Control,), then your only option to fight would be at the gypsy horse fairs or car parks or some other gathering. But now an alternative way of fighting had arrived. Former professional boxers soon *'cottoned-on'* that there was easy money to be earned, and it didn't take long before, Joe Pyle had got himself a stable of boxers, all wanting to fight on the undercards of Roy's fights.

Roy Shaw vs Paddy Mad Dog Mullins

Bloomsbury Crest Hotel London
1976

Roy's next challenge came from a street-fighting Irishman who came out of Kilburn town in North West London.

Paddy Mullins was known as 'Mad dog' and had a big reputation on his manor and back in Ireland as being a tough fucker who would fight anyone.

Backed by wealthy Irishmen, Paddy came up with the twenty grand to fight, so the fight was arranged at the Bloomsbury Crest hotel.

The fight itself wasn't much of an event as Roy destroyed him.

The Irishman, strangely enough, had decided to skip for the half-hour before the bout and was dripping so much in sweat, it looked like he just got out the shower!

Mullins entered the ring first and decided to start bouncing off the ropes, he was moving around the ring, and when Roy climbed into ring, he found Mullins in his corner, the blue corner, so Roy got straight through the ropes and pushed Mullins away back towards his corner.

When the fight began, Mullins went immediately into his street fighting mode and grabbed Roy around the legs and wrestled him to the ground. Roy got up and battered him around the ring, Mullins again tried to pull him to the floor, but Roy was too powerful, he punished the Irishman until couldn't continue. His corner and the referee then stopped the fight.

Mullins took a bloody good hiding that night and had no answer for Roy's strength and power.

My father and Alex were not very happy as Mullins and his people had promised so much more, but he was a joke with boxing gloves on.

But a win is a win; they all got a nice few quid, and Roy was still unbeaten. He had now won his 2nd fight... both inside the first round.

However, this show is often remembered for what happened after the Roy fight. The events outside the ring, not inside it.

I'm not going to say too much, but a massive fight broke out between some well-known London firms.

It was actually kicking off in and outside the ring, one of the fighters butted his opponent and then got into an argument with Johnny Simmons, the referee. Johnny Simmons was a local fella out of Carshalton and a moneylender, so he was no mug. But as soon as he started arguing with the fighter, the MC for the evening, Nosher Powell, jumped into the ring to sort things but got straight into a wrestling match with the fighter. The ring was then suddenly swamped as everyone jumped in to calm things down.

Things then escalated as Roy Shaw, who was still not back in his dressing room, jumped inside the ropes to challenge the fighter who had started on Nosher and the referee. Roy shouted at him to a fight him now, but it was very quickly declined. There were a few words said, and the fighter thought it best he fucks off very lively. Joey Carrington saw him say something as he got out of the ring and then run over and hit him a right hand. Then it kicked off again, and then things started to get heated and tense outside the ropes.

In the documentary (The Guv'nor), Freddie Foreman has a heated argument with some Nash family associates. You can clearly see Freddie very animated, and next to him are Jimmy and Johnny Nash.

There was a bit of history attached to the argument where an altercation had previously happened at Ronnie Knights A and R club between Fred's brother in law and the Nashes. Anyway, they all bumped into each other at the show, and a scrap broke out with one of Fred's team getting a pull inside the toilets. Next thing, the whole place went up in the air. A mass brawl erupted with people fighting and throwing chairs. Peter Marshall (an old pal of my fathers and a very respected man) tried to break the fight up and was attacked by Fred and a few other men. You can see him being hit with the chairs in the documentary. Thankfully all the men fighting were big tough fellas, and no one got seriously hurt, which was surprising as it really kicked off.

If you are lucky enough to have seen the footage, you can see Freddie steaming in with chairs. It's funny as over the last few years at the parties and shows where Fred has attended; he comes across as a real, quiet, friendly fella. But believe me, he was a naughty bastard when he had to be. I have seen Fred

Foreman kick off a few times, he could be very fiery, and if you upset him
…then get out the fucking way!

For a few days after the show, London was on a knife-edge, with everyone
worried that some new gang warfare might erupt, but thankfully some sensible
heads got together, and a truce was made. (And strangely enough, some lifelong
friendships were created.)

Once the trouble was put to bed, the gravy train quickly got back on track, and
business got back to normal.

Due to all the newspaper coverage, Roy Shaw was quickly turning into a
celebrity, his notoriety with his links to the Krays and Joe Pyle was making him
one of the most well-known fighters in the UK.

Alex Steene acted quickly to take advantage of this and had posters printed
where Roy challenged Joe Bugner, the British professional champion for a fight.
This fight would never happen.

Still, it all added to Roy's reputation, which ultimately would boost ticket sales.

It was a complete (get-up), the offer to Joe Bugner, (never going to happen) but
the papers grabbed hold and ran with the story, again building more publicity,
which would turn into ticket sales on the night of the shows.

Alex even called out Muhammed Ali, offering a fifty grand (*winner takes all,*)
which was never going to happen, but it once again created more attention from
the British press and public.

Roy Shaw vs Mickey Gluxted

Dagenham
Jul. 7th, 1976

Roy had one more fight in 1976, and that was against Mickey Gluxted;
Gluxted was a well-known bare-knuckle fighter who, in the years after his fight
with Roy, found himself being labelled a child molester.

Mickey Gluxted? I don't really know what to say about him apart from Roy
bashed him up in three rounds.
He is a fantasist and a dreamer and states the following in his autobiography....
Micky beat them all. Roy "Pretty Boy" Shaw, Donny "The Bull" Adams, and
even Lenny McLean, "The Guv'nor" himself, fell before Micky's onslaught.
So he claims to have beaten Roy, Lenny, and Donny Adams?? Well, I haven't
seen any footage. I haven't seen any photographs. I haven't met anyone who
saw it!
Gluxted published his own book on his life story in 2012 called the Devil shook
my hand.'
I haven't read his book, and I'm not sure I want to either.
Gluxted, 41, was found guilty of three charges of buggery, three indecent
assaults, and one offense of gross indecency between 1986 and 1989. It was
revealed that both the boy and his mother have been given new identities and
moved to a secret location 'following,' as one officer put it, very serious threats
to the life of the child and his mother.'
Gluxted, a former bare-fisted knuckle fighter, has a string of convictions
comprising 31 offenses of violence and dishonesty stretching back to 1961. He
has none for sex offenses. Giving evidence he had revealed his own long
criminal record claiming that he was an East End 'hard man' - not a child
molester.
Gluckstead has ardently denied the charge.

Roy Shaw had this to say about Gluxted a few years after...
Then I beat a mongrel named Mickey Gluxted in three rounds. I have been told
this mongrel is now gobbing off about the fight being fixed blah, blah. Well, I
would gladly fight him again right now! He is a scumbag, and scum should keep
their filthy mouths shut! If I knew then what I know now about what he is, I
would have killed him stone dead!

Roy Shaw vs Terry Hollingsworth

Cinatra's Croydon
Mar. 22nd, 1977

Terry Hollingsworth was a tall heavyweight and boxed for the world-famous Repton amateur boxing club; he had an excellent amateur record winning the ABA championship.

For Roy's 4th fight, Joe Pyle had managed to find a local place called Cinatras nightclub to stage the event. The club was off the London Road in Croydon and was one of the biggest clubs in the capital, which could accommodate up to 2000 guests. It was the perfect venue for boxing and had a great atmosphere. The club, however, has a notorious tag to it and was known as a trouble spot by the locals, it was much like Caesars in Streatham, where we promoted the MeanMachine shows in the 2000s

'The sticky carpet, the naff disco lights, the flat beer, the cheap drink-all-you-want entry fee, the even cheaper women, the brawls on the dance floor, grab-a-granny night and the cheap and nasty buffet. Oh, how we lament the loss of Croydon's premier nightclub.'

Comment by a former customer.

The news that Roy would be boxing in Croydon was big news and the tickets sold like hotcakes, this was Joe Pyle's manor, and his pals fell over themselves to grab the best tickets available. My father also got a few local lads to box on the undercard.

A few celebrities had promised to make an appearance like Oliver Reed and Diana Dors, and Charlie Kray had also sold a lot of tickets to his friends.

The actual fight itself between Roy and Terry Hollingsworth was nothing spectacular, Roy dominated the taller opponent working the body and head, it was a demolition job, ending in the first round.

Another 1st round victory that was making Roy look unbeatable, he was smashing these opponents up like they novices.

Speaking as a promoter, what you want is your man to win, but when he keeps winning so quickly, it becomes harder to promote the next fight. People do start talking bollocks like the fight was a fix, and the fella dived.

In the back of my father's mind, he was thinking for the sake of the shows, Roy needed a (toughish) fight, someone who could push him a bit.

Little did he know it would be the unknown young man sitting at ringside... this young man's name was Lenny Boy Mclean.

Lenny climbed in the ring at Cinatras and challenged Roy, everyone looked at each other and wondered who the fuck is this.... It didn't take long for everyone to find out!

ROY SHAW
vs
LENNY MCLEAN

Roy Shaw vs Lenny McLean

Cinatras Croydon
May 23rd, 1977

Around this time, a young man called Lenny McLean, had been travelling around the UK having bare-knuckle fights at horse fairs and fields, suddenly decided to make himself known.

McLean was from the tough streets of the east end of London and was eager to get involved.

He was a strong man, had a fierce reputation, and was very ambitious.

McLean heard all the talk about Roy Shaw being the Guv'nor, and he never liked it. As far as he was concerned, there was only one Guvnor in the fighting world, and that was him. Lenny mentioned that he would - *do Roy and Donny Adams on the same night* - after seeing one of the posters.

Keen to get involved, Lenny and his cousin Bobby Warren travelled down to Croydon for Roy's last fight, where he got into the ring and made a challenge after Roy beat Hollingsworth.

But on the night no one really took any notice, Bobby said to my father that they wanted the fight, but everyone was celebrating, so my father just said something like, *'Okay, if he is serious about it, then get in touch and were talk about it.'*

Lenny was good pals with Roy Nash, who he knew was friends with Joe Pyle, so he asked Roy if he could set up a meeting.

At first, my father laughed it off as he had never heard of McLean, and then thought nothing more of it until one-day, Bobby Warren turned up at Joe and Alex's ticket office on Panton Street.

Bobby Warren explained that he had a lad called Lenny McLean, who he wanted to fight Roy Shaw.

(This was another monumental meeting, a meeting that would create another legend, a man who arguably went on to become even more famous than Roy Shaw.

Lenny would become instantly recognisable to the masses with significant parts in TV dramas like The Knock and playing a leading role in Guy Ritchie's hugely successful film - (Lock Stock and Two Smoking Barrels) plus other leading TV shows.)

"Who is this, Lenny McLean?" asked Joe, smiling. "What's he done then?" he added.

"He challenged Roy at Croydon, Joe, you saw him on the night," Bobby answered.

'Look, I got boxers, bouncers, doormen from here to fucking Scotland wanting to fight Roy, why should we give your boy a go at big money, what's he going to bring to add value?' added my father.

Warren then put his cards on the table, where he promised my father that he would pull the money up and shift a shed load of tickets. And that Lenny would make a real fight of it.

At first, my father wasn't too bothered about the fight as he had a couple of fights already being lined up. One match was against a well-known gypsy man from Kent, and the side bets were enormous!

Joe Pyle agreed that the fight could go ahead, but he insisted on the usual terms that it was a winner take all fight, Bobby Warren agreed, and the fight was on. But in the back of my father's mind, the Lenny fight was just a standby as he was still hopeful that the other fight with the gypsy was going to happen.

My Dad was hedging his bets, "Let's put Lenny on standby, and if the gypsy fight falls through then we still have a nice earner lined up,"

Anyway, a week or so passed, and the gypsy fight did fall through. Alex called him one morning and told him the bad news, "Joe, I've just had Jasper on the phone and its Off!"

"What's the matter?"

"He's been nicked Joe, something about an old assault and threatening someone's life."

So that was that! He was arrested and charged and remanded, so the fight with him wasn't happening. But my Dad did have a backup, Lenny McLean! He called Bobby Warren and told him he would have to '**up**' the side bets, and if he agreed, then the posters and tickets can go to print next week.

The fight was arranged and took place at Cinatra's nightclub, Croydon, South London, and the build-up for the fight to my father's delight was far better than expected.

Lenny McLean came from Hoxton in London, a very rough part of town, and it was also where my father originally came from.

My father would often go over there to see some of his old pals, and he was delighted when he heard the news, 'all of the manor is talking about it.

Everyone wanted to see this fight between Lenny and Roy'. The tickets were flying out.

As expected on the night of the show, it was sold-out!

Bobby Warren had made good on his promise, and a big crowd had travelled down from the east end and north London to support their man. Lenny played his part well and over the last few weeks hadn't stopped trying to promote the fight and was telling every newspaper he could get himself into, that he would be ripping Roy Shaw's head off!

The atmosphere on the evening was absolutely electric. It was like a football match with two opposing sets of fans urging their man to win.

The tale of the tape made it look like McLean was the favourite; Lenny was twenty years younger, and six inches taller. Yet in heavyweight boxing, this could sometimes happen, Roy didn't seem that bothered,

"As long as I can hit his chin, then it doesn't matter how fucking tall or heavy he is," Roy said to Joe.

Out of the three fights they had together, you could say it was this first fight that holds the most controversy. Firstly, the filming of it has disappeared and secondly the stories about the mysterious, 'Doctored Gloves'

If you read Lenny McLean's book, The Guv'nor, he says that Joe Pyle stitched him up by giving him doctored gloves ... This accusation isn't true!

I can honestly say hand on heart that there were no special gloves that sprung open; in fact, in all my years in the boxing world, I have never seen a glove that *springs open'* when you make a fist.

However, there **was** a dispute over the gloves as Lenny's hands were so big that the 8oz gloves were too tight when he put them on over his bandages.

Heavyweights fight in 10-ounce gloves, but Roy, if given the option, would box in the smallest gloves possible, even 6-ounce gloves. When Lenny tried to put his hands in the 8oz gloves, they naturally felt tight.

Lenny and his corner had a good moan about it, but nothing else was (really) said about it, until after the fight.

I have always thought it was a bizarre statement by Lenny regarding the gloves as I discovered later that someone from Lenny's corner ran back to the dressing room and fetched a pair of gloves that actually belonged to Lenny. (Which he boxed in)

They were his training gloves, not fighting gloves, they were enormous - 16 or 18oz gloves.

Alex's son Greg Steene was the timekeeper for the fight, and he can confirm that Lenny boxed in different gloves than Roy. Greg even mentioned to me that his gloves looked huge compared to Roy's gloves.

When the bell sounded for round one, both men rushed at each other where Lenny threw the first big shot, a big right hand which hit Roy square on the chin, Roy didn't even blink, he just pushed McLean up against the ropes and began to pound away at his belly.

McLean then started playing up to the crowd, and started calling Roy names and laughing at his punches; he shouted out, things like...

'You can't hurt me!' and "You punch like a woman!"

Roy took no notice and just continued to push him back and throw punch after punch. Lenny was holding on and continued to talk, but the first round was a big round for Roy Shaw.

When the bell rang to end the round, McLean walked back to his corner, feeling the pace of the fight and was puffing heavily.

It was a bizarre first round! It was all action, but Lenny did look confused, he started reasonably well and then just covered up on the ropes taking punches and doing antics for the crowd.

The second round was another landslide for Roy; he managed to wedge Lenny into a corner and then landed punch after punch on his chin and belly. During this round, Lenny did not even land a shot on Roy. He just stood with his back against the ropes soaking up the punishment, Roy was all over him, but the onslaught was also now beginning to wear Roy out.

In round three Roy came out seething because Lenny had called him a little c**t at the end of the second round,

"I'm gonna kill him!' Roy told his cornermen.

Roy was over McLean like a rash, connecting with substantial rights and lefts, McLean's face opened up, and blood was all over the place. Roy then hit him with a haymaker right hand, which had Lenny fall back into the ropes, Roy followed up with a right and some left hooks forcing McLean to cover up and clear his head, the ropes were the only thing keeping him up. One more good shot from Roy could knock him out. Roy kept asking him if he had had enough, and Lenny was replying that Roy couldn't knock him out! Over and over again, Lenny kept repeating, " You can't fucking knock me out!"

Lenny looked demoralised and *fucked*, he was a big strong man, yet he had no stamina for this fight.

As the round came to an end, he waved his hands and turned away, and then he mouthed to Roy and the referee that he had had enough.

The fight was stopped in the third round, and Roy's hand got raised in victory. Despite all the moaning about the gloves from the McLean camp, Lenny finally admitted to me years later that Roy was on the night the (better man,) and in his own words he said,

"I don't want to make any excuses, and I don't want to take anything away from Roy, I have to hold my hands up and say he beat me, alright the gloves didn't help, but I let myself down by not being ready for the fight."

If you want my opinion, I think Roy was indeed the better man on the night. I like Lenny, but It was a big fight for both men, and there was a lot of money on the table for the winner. Both men trained hard for the match, but Roy was better in the first fight.

Maybe it was Roy's experience that shocked Lenny? Or power. Lenny McLean took a proper beating that night, but he never hit the canvas. Lenny also hurt Roy with a few punches.

Like I said at the start of this book, I will tell the truth, and in this fight, my opinion is that Lenny, for some reason in his head, decided he had had enough, and he quit!.... Maybe he was worried about getting knocked out? Perhaps he was just so frustrated with being so tired that he thought, bollocks to it!

It's one of those questions only Lenny himself truly knew. I have heard people try to make excuses for this loss, saying he wasn't ready and stuff like that, but the one fact that cannot be changed is that Roy won the first fight!

Lenny wasn't fit enough, and that is the truth of the matter.

In boxing you have a winner and a loser, people always try to make excuses for the loser, but that's life, some people make excuses for Roy's defeats to Lenny, but in the history books, it says Roy beat Lenny in the first and then lost the next two fights! That fact, no matter what people say, those facts will never change. I'm not interested in hearing opinions from people who weren't there. I was there, and so were a lot of people I know. It was a tough fight for both of them, but there was a winner and a loser.

Maybe Lenny just didn't expect the fight to be so draining? Roy came out for the first round at a blistering pace and possibly took Lenny by surprise. For the time it lasted it was all action, and Lenny did hit Roy with some hard hurtful punches

I did ask Lenny years later about it, and in his own words, he told me, 'I was just fucked!' meaning he was exhausted. It's such a shame the footage for this fight has been lost over time. Some people even doubt it ever happened; it did, I was there.

Maybe one day, the footage will turn up, but until it does, all we have is the words of those who saw it, to go by.

Even to this day, I see groups on things like Facebook where people say shit like,

"The gloves were fiddled with!"

Told by people who weren't fucking there. It pisses me off when I read these so-called experts. Some of them are so naïve and biased, it's laughable.

But then again, it's like the old saying; opinions are like arseholes - everyone has one!

Roy Shaw vs Ron Stander

Alexander Palace Muswell Hill, London

After winning against his latest challenger (Lenny McLean,) Roy Shaw was now on the crest of a wave. He had already beaten most of the hard men in the UK, so it was around this time Joe Pyle thought it was a good idea to branch out and get a fighter from the USA.

Jack O'Halloran was an American six-foot six-inch former professional boxer who was currently in the UK starring in the new Superman movie at Pinewood Studios, and he was a good pal of my fathers.

Jack was at ringside with fellow actor Gene Hackman, when Roy had beat Lenny and mentioned to Joe that Roy fights like a friend and former opponent of his in the states, a fighter named Ron Stander, 'Hell, he even looks like Stander" Jack added.

"Ron Stander, who boxed Joe Frazier for the World title," my father replied, talking about the world heavyweight title.

"That's him."

"What's he doing now, Jack?"

"Same as every other motherfucker, just trying to get a buck."

The next day at the request of Joe Pyle, Jack O'Halloran was on the phone to the states talking to his pal Ron Stander.

The conversation went something like this...

"Ron, I got a fight for you in London, England."

"In London? You for real!"

"If you want to fight, we can set it up."

"Set the fucking thing up, Jack! What the fuck do those limeys know about fighting!" Stander said, thinking about a chance for some very easy money as all heavyweight fighters in the UK were laughed at by the yanks.

If you looked at this fight on paper, it was a complete mismatch. Roy was in his forties, spent the most of the last decade in a cell, had only had a handful of professional bouts, and now fighting against a fighter who had challenged Joe Frazier for the heavyweight championship of the world.

Ron Stander was a seasoned professional whose boxing record included fighters like Earnie Shavers (who he beat) when Shavers was regarded as the biggest punching heavyweight in history. Plus, he also shared the ring with the legendary Ken Norton (who had three fights with Muhammed Ali and won one of them) and the up and coming unbeaten Gerry Coetzee.

Ron Stander fought Joe Frazier in Omaha on 5-25-1972. He also fought former Heavyweight Champions Ken Norton and Gerrie Coetzee.

RON STANDER

Some people said this was madness, but Joe Pyle knew the fight game like the back of his hand and had done his homework where he knew that Stander would think this was such an easy payday, he would turn up without hardly stepping foot in a gym in preparation. My father also had a few other tricks up his sleeve.

Ron Stander arrived in London three days before the fight and came by himself because he was so confident of winning he didn't want to bring over a trainer who would eat into his profit.

Ron was taken to his room at a west end hotel and told someone would come and see him for dinner and speak about the fight, Joe Pyle arrived at around eight o'clock with two pretty blondes on his arm. My father welcomed him, and then the four of them went downstairs to the restaurant and sat down for dinner. My father ordered the first round of drinks before a waiter came over and said there was a phone call for Joe Pyle, my father quickly went away and then returned with a troubled look on his face.

"Ron, I've gotta go, mate, one of my pals, is in some bother, and I need to go and get it sorted, it shouldn't take too long, so I'll leave the girls here with you and come back later."

"Okay, Joe!" Ron replied.

Joe Pyle, still with a confused look on his face, nodded and turned away until he reached a corner where he burst into a smile.

"That's him fucked," he said silently to himself.

My father never returned that night, his good friend and former middleweight champion of the world, Terry Downes collected Stander and his pal and together with the two girls he took them all out for a drink to show them London town.

The girls my father left with Stander, were two hookers from Ladbroke Grove, and they had strict orders to get him to drink as much alcohol as they could get him to consume and draw as much strength out of the big American.

The girls stayed with Stander every day until the fight; they even went with him to the Thomas a Becket gym, where Stander had a workout.

On the morning of the fight, my father was delighted to hear that the girls were still with Stander.

"How'd it go?" Joe whispered to one of the girls as Stander got into the shower.

"He is an animal Joe, if he has any energy left then he is not human!" the girl sighed.

"What about the grub and booze, have you fed him up," asked Joe, after previously telling the girls not to worry about the expenses and get him as much booze and food as he could handle.

The girl laughed.

"He hasn't stopped eating Joe; He has had a pound of bacon this morning. He has drunk three bottles of whiskey in two days and eaten the hotel out of steak and chips."

The plan had worked beautifully, the day of the fight, and Stander had been awake until 5 in the morning, banging the life out of the two hookers.

It wasn't that my father thought he was a complete fool, but my father knew what his mindset would be for this fight.

The fight itself, wouldn't be on his fighting record, and hardly anyone back in the states would know about it. It was just a payday for him, and he probably didn't care if he won or lost. Just a short holiday, see the famous London town, get some pictures and pick up a nice little earner (tax-free) so if he got his leg over in the process, got drunk, smoke a few joints and had some coke, then it was just the icing on the cake for him.

Ron stander didn't for one moment believe Roy Shaw could do him any real damage. Remember, this fighter had shared the ring with men like Joe Frazier

and Earnie Shavers (two men who could put you in the hospital) Roy Shaw was a small English heavyweight who no one in America had heard of!
Easy money, for what Stander thought was nothing more than a hard sparring session.

Alexander Palace was a majestic venue built by the Lucus brothers on the top of a hill in Alexander Park in North London.
Joe Pyle, with his son Joe Jr and brother Ted, drove up the hill to the venue. Posters of the fight lined the street as they pulled the car to a halt and then entered the doors to walk inside.

The ring was already set up, and there were dozens of workers busy laying out the chairs, Joe Pyle Jr remembers,
"I was just a kid at the time, but I can remember getting to the venue, and there were these massive shiny wooden floors, I had my skateboard with me so spent most of the afternoon skating all over the place. I was getting more excited about the fight as my dad wanted me to carry the Union Jack flag in front of Roy during his ring entrance.
I remember being in the dressing room just before the fight and then someone called out -.
'It's time.'

Roy, my dad, and around ten other people started to make their way to the ring, as we entered the hall I could hear Gary Glitters 'Do you wanna be in my gang' starting to play, and we all began to walk towards the ring. I was in front of Roy carrying the flag with Greg Steene, son of Alex when Roy told us to speed up; moments later, we were all running to the ring.

I stood next to my dad and Roy as the national anthems were played and then someone took me to my uncle at ringside, I can also remember the ring card girls walking around with the cards topless, the place was completely packed. Ron Stander looked heavy around the belly, but the way he moved even before the fight showed everyone he was an experienced and seasoned fighter. When the first round began, Roy in usual fashion, flew out the corner and tore into him, Roy hit him with every punch but didn't even make a dent. Later Roy said.

"I hit Stander harder than I have ever hit anyone harder in my life, but no matter what I did, I couldn't hurt him."

It was not until the second round when Roy turned to the body, that his punches started to make any impact.

In the third round, Roy just concentrated on body shots, and then Stander went down on one knee, he slowly got up, and Roy continued his onslaught of Stander's body, again he went down for an eight-count, casually he got to his feet and Roy flew back at him. Roy put everything he had into the shots and a big right hand just below the heart sent Stander falling against the ropes, the referee began to count, but this time Stander stayed down, holding his body and wincing in pain.

Roy Shaw had done it; he had beaten a World heavyweight contender in three rounds.

The crowd went wild, and my father and friends jumped in to congratulate the winner.

But as soon as the fight finished, Lenny McLean got into the ring and challenged Roy, Lenny had boxed a couple of times since his defeat and was looking good, plus it was a fight the whole country wanted to see. Roy and a few others half fucked him off, telling him to fuck off out of the ring and said he could have some next. Lenny smiled and waved to the crowd to a mixture of boos and cheers.

Roy Shaw was now on everyone's lips, his fight and victory against someone like Ron stander at a sell-out Alexander Palace, looked very impressive.

My father's plan to fight a big name American had worked out!

*In the years that followed, there have been loads of rumours about Stander fighting with a broken rib. It wasn't broken. He did have some soreness from a fall, but it never stopped him shagging the arses off two brasses for a couple of days. In my opinion, he just turned up to get paid and didn't care about the fight. Win or lose didn't matter to him.

Ron Stander was no fool, and he had connections (like a lot of fighters in the states) to guys in the mob.

Jack O'Halloran, who introduced him to my father, was related to the Meyer Lansky family by marriage, and I know (for a fact) he told Ron Stander all about my father and the people in London he was going to meet.

Jack personally told me years later that Ron underestimated Roy Shaw, but he wasn't stupid; he knew full well he was brought over to lose.

Now I am not saying the fight was a fix! That was never discussed.

I'm just saying that Ron was a fighter who knew the game, he knew full well he was walking into the lion's den… coming to meet, what he thought was the London mafia, did he decide not to upset the apple cart?

We will never really know……

Joe Pyle Sr – Ron Stander – Gary Shaw – Nat basso – Nosher Powell – Alex Steene – Joe Pyle jr

Roy Shaw vs Lenny Mclean 2

Cinatras Croydon
Apr. 10th, 1978

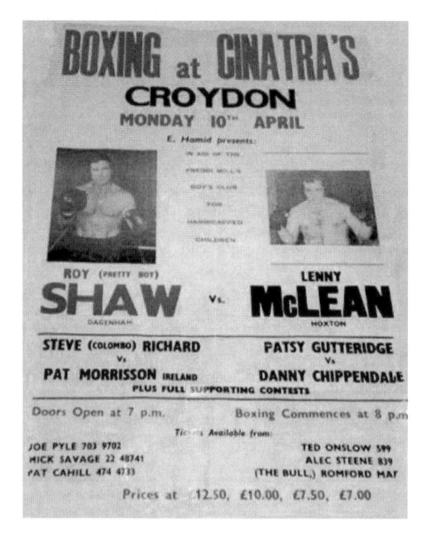

Since losing to Roy, Lenny had been making a right nuisance of himself, calling out Roy at every opportunity, and it was starting to get under Roy Shaw's skin. Roy had already beaten him once, and to be honest, Joe Pyle wasn't interested in the return, but Lenny wouldn't go away.

Years later, my father told me that he thought Lenny was all wrong for Roy; he was too big, too cocky, and too powerful.

Despite losing the first time, Lenny did hurt Roy a few times in their first fight. My dad was a good fighter, a professional boxer, and he knew the game inside out! And he knew watching that first fight, even though Roy had won, that Lenny was dangerous.

Lenny had already jumped in the ring to challenge Roy at Alexander Palace, and Frank and Bobby Warren pestered the life out of my father and Alex with their constant calls for Lenny to fight Roy again.

Joe Pyle told them time and again that there would be no rematch, but the Warrens kept coming back and each time making the offer more attractive. Finally, and only after Roy said he wanted the fight, the rematch was agreed. Roy was confident of the same outcome, he thought it was easy money, but Lenny, seething after the first fight had gone away and started training with Freddie Hill and Kevin Finnegan.

Freddie Hill was a very well respected trainer who had worked with fighters such as Alan Rudkin, both the Finnegan brothers, Billy Walker and Bobby Neil; he had a gym in Lavender Hill, South London.

Full time training under his tutelage, McLean became a different fighter; Hill got him working off the jab. Plus, he developed a game plan to beat Roy.

Freddie Hill got Lenny, the taller man to grab Roy behind the head and pull his head down with his left hand while punching with his right, it is an old trick used by Muhammed Ali, it was illegal in boxing terms, but some refs let it go. Watch Ali's fights, and you can see he did it all the time.

Believe me, if you're the opponent on the receiving end of this trick, it's horrible! It saps your strength and also blinds you to the next punch coming.

It didn't take long for Joe Pyle to hear about Lenny training with Freddie Hill, and the second fight against McLean was a match Joe Pyle was not too keen on making.

As a former professional boxer, he knew too well just how disadvantaged Roy was against Lenny, Roy won the first fight, but it highlighted the difference in size and weight. Joe secretly thought that Lenny was always going to be a handful for Roy. Still, Roy didn't seem too concerned. In his mind, he had beaten him once, and he would do it again.

There would be a lot of money to be earned, and the fight was a certainty to be a sell-out, but still, Joe Pyle felt reluctant, there was just something about McLean. My father was also friendly with Lenny's new trainer, and he called Freddie to ask how McLean was shaping up. Freddie joked at the phone call as he knew Roy was with my dad, but he did say that McLean was looking fit and very strong.

"We don't need him, Roy." My father said, shaking his head to Roy at the Thomas a Becket gym.

"Joe, he got up in the ring and called it on, I'm fucking sick to death of him, how the fuck can I back down, mate?"

Regardless of any doubts, it was too late to back out now, and My father had more concerns when he heard that Roy had not been training as hard as he usually did. Rumours had started to come back about him skipping training sessions and staying out having late nights.

I'm not making excuses here, but if you look at the shape, Roy was in when he beat Donny Adams he was solid with hardly an ounce of fat on him, and then compare his shape and physique in his last two fights with Lenny, you can clearly see the difference.

Roy had also been on holiday after the Stander fight and got a bollocking from my father when he returned looking two stone heavier than when he left. Roy was away sunbathing, eating, and drinking. While at the same time, McLean was with Freddie Hill training like a Spartan warrior.

Another unknown fact is Roy had a car accident three weeks before the 2nd fight. This fact has never been made public as Roy didn't want to come across making excuses, even though he did say the ginseng thing after the 2nd fight.
 If you knew Roy, then you knew what a terrible driver he was! Roy hurt his forearm and elbow; at first, they thought it was a broken forearm, and the fight would have to be postponed, but after looking at the x-ray, it was found not to be broken, only severely bruised.

Whether this injury had an impact on the result, I don't know? It must have interrupted Roy's training camp?

Years later, when I asked my father more about this fight, he told me he had doubts going into it. There was something about Lenny, which concerned him. He saw the danger of the first fight where Lenny did hurt Roy a few times. Around this time, my father and Alex were also talking to some of their contacts in New York. There were plans to take Roy over there and get him licensed, and then a possible big fight. So Lenny was a potential big fucking banana skin. There was big money being discussed overseas, "Why the fuck are we giving McLean another chance?" was the view taken by my father.

Once again, at Cinatra's nightclub in Croydon, South London on Apr. 10th, 1978, Roy Shaw got into the ring with Lenny McLean.

The show was a complete sell-out with VIP tickets selling for three times their face value, and the audience was filled with celebrities. Footballers from Chelsea and West Ham, world-famous actors like Gene Hackman and Jack O Halloran, and even a superstar footballer, Georgie Best, sat in the VIP seats.

As soon as my father arrived at the venue, he immediately sensed that something wasn't right. He immediately saw that Roy was in a joking mood, laughing and smiling with people. At the same time, Lenny McLean, along with Frank Warren and Johnny Wall, had locked themselves in their dressing room and were looking and acting deadly serious.

"There was a strange atmosphere in the venue when Roy fought Lenny ... at the first fight we all felt confident, but this time it just didn't feel the same, I don't know how to describe it, but something was in the air," Joe Pyle later said.

As the two men got into the ring, everyone could see the difference in size, and it was also plain to see the difference in the two men's physiques and conditions. Lenny looked cut to pieces and fit as a fiddle while Roy was carrying a few pounds around his waist and looked nowhere as fit and strong as he had looked in the past.

Nosher Powell was the Mc, and he introduced the fighters to the crowd, I was only a young kid, but I was in the ring during the announcements. I can still see Lenny's face looking at Roy as they both gloved up. Lenny never took his eyes off him.

When the bell rang to start the first round, Lenny flew across the ring towards Roy. He was like a man possessed, intent on revenge after carrying the shame of his defeat for over a year.

Roy tried to fight back and cover-up, but the onslaught from Lenny was devastating, Lenny used his weight advantage and threw Roy into the ropes, he threw punch after punch, Roy tried his best, but the disadvantages of age, weight, and size caught up with him.

Fighting to stay on his feet, Roy crashed heavily to the ground as Lenny continued to hit him while he was down; suddenly, everyone jumped into the ring and began pulling Lenny off as he tried to stamp on Roy, Lenny was screaming at Roy to get up. Alex Steene was one of the first to jump in the ring as was Roy's friend Joe Carrington, who confronted Lenny and it looked like the place was going to go up in the air,

I was sitting with Roy's son, Gary, and I remember he picked up a glass from someone's table and went to throw it at Lenny, only for someone to grab him and stop him before he could throw it.

During all the commotion, Roy had got to his feet and was standing in a neutral corner, but was completely out of it, he had no idea where he was; (I am sure that he would have torn into Lenny for stamping on him if he did.)

Everyone calmed things down, and then the fight continued, but Roy was gone! Lenny flew at Roy again, and after a barrage of punches Roy went down again, the referee started the count, but Roy jumped up still out of it.

As they started trading blows again, somehow, Roy began to fight back, but Lenny was grabbing Roy behind the neck with his left glove and then hitting him with right hands. Lenny then caught Roy with a hell of a right hand that nearly took his head off, and then my father ran over to the timekeeper and screamed at him.

"Ring the fucking bell!" he shouted, which ended the round fifteen seconds early.

With the help of the bell, Roy had survived the round and staggered back to his corner. But he didn't have a clue where he was. The break could have been two minutes long as it wouldn't have mattered.

In round two, Roy came out swinging, but Lenny was just too big. His plan to tie Roy up when he came inside was working perfectly. Lenny then again began to grab Roy behind the neck with his left glove as he smashed away with his right hand, moments later, Roy was walloped, and he ended up going through the ropes, tired, and out of it, Roy tried to get up, but Alex Steene called off the fight.

Lenny McLean had won the fight and got his revenge, there was a new era beginning, and there was a new Guv'nor on the scene.

After this fight, Roy said he took a bottle of ginseng on the way to fight, and it spaced him out of it. I have no reason to doubt what Roy was saying is valid, but I will add that I have seen Lenny fight a few times, and his two wins against Roy were the best I saw him. He seemed to be a completely different fighter against Roy.

Lenny was a monster, so very strong and powerful, and you could sense the menace coming from him.

He was now The Guv'nor! And the odds for Roy getting it back did not look good.

Roy Shaw vs Lenny McLean 3

Rainbow Theatre - Finsbury park.
Sept. 11th, 1978
The third fight of the trilogy.

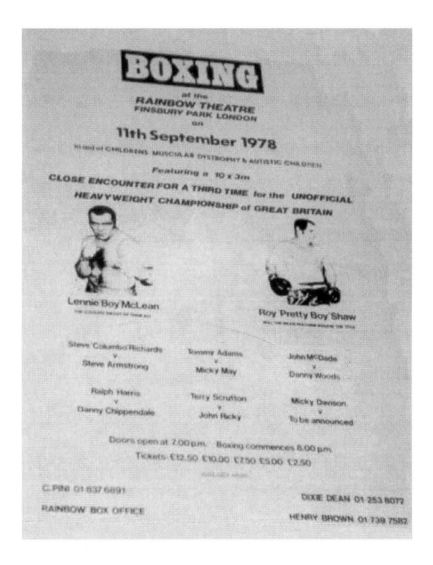

Roy's unbeaten record was now gone, and wheels had well and truly fell off the gravy train. Roy hadn't just lost the last fight; he was well and truly beaten up! Lenny McLean was now on top of the world and calling himself the new Guv'nor of London. The name Lenny McLean was on everyone's lips.

Any talk of taking Roy to America was now finished; he had only one option, fight McLean again and win the decider. There was no other fight for him; he had to reverse the loss.

Frank Warren, who was handling Lenny, was now holding all the cards, he had the Guv'nor of London, so he took the plunge into promoting and staged his own show with Lenny topping the bill against a doorman called Solli Francis. It was a one-sided fight with Lenny destroying Francis and something of a mismatch from what I've been told.

Frank Warren, though, was no fool, and he heard the whispers going around that the **only** fight out for any real money was a decider against Roy Shaw. The extra money that could be earned on side bets utterly dwarfed any other fight he had lined up for McLean.

In Roy's new book written after his death, 'Mean Machine – Roy Shaw,' fledgling author Jamie Boyle states that it was Frank Warren and not Joe Pyle who made the fight....... That is incorrect!

The fight was **made** when Frank and Bobby Warren met with Joe Pyle and Alex Steene. After a long good meeting, where many other boxing matters were discussed, it was decided that the show would earn more money at the Rainbow Theatre in Finsbury Park. At this venue, Lenny had just boxed and could accommodate up to 4000 people.

** See, when you are in the boxing game, you know how boxing promoters work. One thing you do as a promoter is secure an (exclusive) at the venue so no other promoter can promote there. I had an exclusive deal at Caesars in Streatham, and loads of other promoters went there wanting to promote shows. But, they couldn't because it was my venue.

Frank had the same exclusive deal at the Rainbow, just like my father did at Cinatras, but the Rainbow had better facilities. It could hold more spectators, so it was common sense to stage the third fight in the bigger venue, where the most money could, of course, be generated. **

(In the same book (Roy Shaw - Mean Machine), it also says that in the second fight between Shaw / McLean, Roy was beaten in one round, which again is incorrect as the fight went into the 2nd round.)

It is also worth noting that the fight was billed as 'For the unofficial heavyweight championship of Great Britain.'

Not for, (The Guv'nor title) as some people today like to call it, the Guvnor title was a belt made by myself and Ricky English in the 2000s at Caesars.......

Never once did Roy or Lenny box for a so-called - Guvnor title.

With terms agreed and Both men now boasting one victory apiece. The stage was set for a massive third fight. (The decider)

I was a young kid, but I can still remember the excitement with everyone talking about it and seeing loads of my dad's mates coming to our house to pick up fight tickets.

The fight was huge, and the national press and TV couldn't get enough of it. Everyone wanted to be there, the venue could house 4000 people, but it could have sold that, twice over.

Local bookmakers like Ivor Thomas was offering odds in his betting shops in Tooting and Colliers Wood, and numerous pubs were running 'books' on the fight. Everyone had an opinion, and everyone wanted to be there. This was a fight you had to see, and there was no TV link for it; if you wanted to see it, you had to be there. Tickets were sold out in days and were being touted at three times over the asking price.

The weeks before the fight, I spent a lot of time with my father dropping off tickets and going to meetings with him; I have great memories of my father taking me to the Thomas a Becket pub to watch Roy training.

My father had a car showroom in Peckham just around the corner, and we would see Roy and Alex Steene almost every day at the gym.

The famous gym was a mecca for professional boxing champions, anyone who was anyone in those days trained in 'The Becket.'

It was Henry Cooper's favourite gym, and when the Sugar Ray Leonard came over to the UK, he chose to do a work out there, it had a fantastic atmosphere, and there was always great world-class fighters training. (It was an autograph hunters treasure box!)

Johnny Cheshire from Ayr in Scotland was always training there. John was a good fighter, a former Olympian and could have been a champion, he fought Jim watt for the British title, but he loved a drink and a party, he would train upstairs in the gym and when he finished, go straight downstairs to the bar and start on the whiskey.

I liked John or 'Chesh' as everyone called him; he was always at the car site and staying around our house. I went to Scotland with him once to stay with his parents when my father was spending time with her majesty.

I had a great time in the Ayrshire countryside, going fishing and stuff. John also used to train me years later as an amateur boxer when I boxed for Epsom and Ewell.

On the night of the big fight, I went up to Roy's changing room with my uncle Ted, the changing room was packed, I remember seeing my father, Alex, H, Johnny Simmons, and Stevie Elwood. Roy looked fidgety, and he kept pacing the room, clenching his fists and trying to psyche himself up for the fight. I stayed with my father a few minutes before my uncle Ted took us down to our ringside seats.

Roy came to the ring with his usual music, 'Do you wanna be in my gang' and then Lenny came into sight to his tune 'Daddy cool.'

Both fighters ran to the ring. I remember thinking Lenny looked like a giant as he ran with his hand in the air to the ringside.

I also recollect a strange atmosphere that night; it was like everything was in slow motion. I was there to support Roy, and it felt like he was the underdog. Roy was not his usual self. He looked tired, while Lenny looked confident, Lenny looked huge as he got into the ring.

The MC announced both boxers, and Lenny got the biggest cheer, and then both men were called to the centre of the ring. Roy then went back to his corner and looked very flat, Lenny, however, looked like a coiled spring, ready to explode into action.

Round one started, both men came to the centre of the ring and started to trade punches. Lenny landed the first punch a left jab come hook, and then Roy pushed forward, trying to land only for Lenny to do the old trick that worked in the last fight, holding Roy behind the head with his left glove while hitting him with his right. Roy tried to push Lenny back and punch his body, but Lenny was pulling Roy's head down.

If it had been a professional fight, then the referee would have stopped it and warned Lenny of what he was doing.

Roy was getting frustrated and pushed Lenny into a corner where the referee broke them up. When they started fighting again, Lenny caught Roy with a big right hand, followed by a swinging left. Roy was hurt and tried to fight back, but Lenny was now throwing bombs. Roy got backed up into a corner, where Lenny unleashed over twenty unanswered shots all connecting; it was a miracle that Roy stayed on his feet so long, but he finally hit the canvas.

He got up quickly, but his senses were gone, after a short count the action started again, and Lenny continued to throw bombs. Roy was once more backed up into the corner completely out of it until he hit the canvas and banged his head hard. It was over! Lenny had won devastatingly.

Roy's cornermen jumped into the ring to help Roy as Lenny screamed in celebration, Lenny addressed the crowd

'IM THE GUVNOR!" he shouted

"WHO'S THE GUVNOR!" he shouted out to the crowd, who shouted back, "You are!"

Roy was pulled to his feet and was still dazed; he didn't know where he was and said: "WHO'S DONE ME."

Joe Carrington then pushed Roy back, "It's finished, you done it!" he said to him as Roy, who was still confused and wanted to fight on.

Lenny was still celebrating, walking around the ring flexing his muscles and punching the air while Joe Pyle and Joe Carrington continued to tell Roy it was over, he had lost.

(A few years later, I found out that Roy had asked for his gloves to be removed so he could attack Lenny bare-fisted, but my father refused to let that happen.)

That was the third fight! It was over, and Lenny had won the decider.

Looking back at it all now and the three big fights, it was a trilogy of epic battles that cemented the legacies of **'Both'** men and three contests that immortalised unlicensed boxing.

There have been some good fights over the years since, but nothing can compare to Roy Shaw fighting Lenny McLean.

Both men were as tough as they come, and both were 'huge characters.'

It was a fight for the man on the street, the fellas down the pub who knew all the chaps and loved a tear up, the only thing I could compare it with is if there would have been three fights with Ronnie Kray vs. Charlie Richardson! It was huge in those days, and for weeks it was the talk of almost every pub in London. They created history and created legacies; little did they know that they also created a way of life for thousands of people in the years to follow.

The years that followed, I spent a lot of time with both Lenny and Roy. I don't think they hated each other, but one hundred percent disliked each other. They were both powerful and proud men, and I have heard both of them sling the odd insult regarding the other. They both knew I was friends with them both, so whatever they said to me, I took with a pinch of salt.

Sometimes I would even wind them both up about each other, id joke about, and say to Lenny, 'I saw Roy the other night Len, he sent his regards and said say hello to the big poof McLean!'

Lenny would most of the time, pull a face, and we would laugh it off.

One night me and Roy were at a boxing show, and I joked about saying I have just seen Lenny at the bar, and I've told him to come over to our table for a drink.

"Tell him he can drink my fucking piss!" Roy said, snarling, but not in a nasty way.

There was always friction when they were both in the same room, but nothing ever got out of hand. You could feel the energy coming off both of them as they cautiously stood on guard against each other.

Another time I remember we was at a party at a time when my father was in Belmarsh prison; I was standing next to Lenny and Charlie Kray at the bar when Roy walked in with his pal Alfie Hutchinson. Roy stopped and said hello to Charlie and me, but ignored Lenny.

It was a bit embarrassing, and we could all feel the awkward atmosphere, so I said to Roy,

"Me and Lenny went to visit the old man a couple of days ago, he was in good spirits and sent his regards, Roy."

With that comment, the atmosphere relaxed, and once again, my father was the icebreaker, Roy even asked Lenny how he was.

"Was Joe, alright?" Roy asked him

Lenny nodded, "he looked well!" he replied sharply, giving his usual scowl.

There was a short silence, and then Charlie spoke, asking everyone if they wanted a drink, Roy said he was okay, and he was going over to his table before saying - *see you later,* to everyone and walking off.

I remember smiling to myself when Roy walked off, I was happy they spoke to each other, and then Charlie leaned closer to me, "I thought it was going to kick off then," he whispered in my ear as he grabbed my arm in a gesture to say well done for smoothing it over.

I Had some great times with both men and fond memories.

There is an old saying that says ….. They don't make them like that anymore!

Ain't that the truth about Roy Shaw and Lenny McLean!

CHAPTER 3
AFTER THE TRILOGY

After the third fight there was a massive dip in the unlicensed scene, Roy retired and then came back in a year to fight Harry Starbuck in Dartford, winning in one round and Lenny went off to lose three fights on the spin, two against Cliff Fields and then against Kevin Paddock.

The three fights between Roy and Lenny set London on fire!
They were epic encounters. The boxing and fights themselves may not have been epic battles, but for the excitement they generated, nothing got close to it, and even now, after forty-odd years, there is still nothing like it.
Both men had different lives and successes; however, it is difficult to mention one of them without thinking of the other.
It's ironic how much they disliked each other, yet their names will always be linked together.

Once the third fight was done and dusted, it was inevitable that there would be a substantial dip on the excitement level.
Frank Warren played on the publicity of Lenny's success in the third fight, but any excitement or buzz surrounding Lenny was quickly quashed in his very next fight when Cliff Fields destroyed the new Guv'nor of London in two rounds.
Warren's golden egg was smashed, and all the invincibility that Lenny had been credited with for his destruction of Roy, had just flown out the window.
If you ask me, then I would say that around this time, unlicensed boxing began to lose its attraction.
Frank Warren was still running shows, and people like Bert McCarthy started to get involved, and Frank, with his eye on bigger things, started to clean up the image. The raw, gritty underground feel disappeared as he began to run his events like the professional shows.
The way Frank Warren was promoting shows, he must have thought to himself, "If I'm running shows like the professionals, then I may as well be one."
So he took out his professional license. The rest is history. He went on to become the most successful UK boxing promoter in history and even got inducted into the boxing hall of fame in Canastota USA.

After Roy lost to Lenny, my father and Alex Steene still had a few fighters on their books. But shortly after Roy's defeat, my father was arrested and placed on remand at wormwood scrubs for aiding and abating the fugitive (Johnny Bindon), who was accused of murdering Johnny Darke. The law said it was my father who arranged and got him out of the country to Ireland when Bindon was wanted and on the run.

My father spent months on remand, but was released when Bindon was found not guilty of murder. (The law had no option but to release my father and Brian Emmett because once Bindon was acquitted, they could not be put on trial for helping an innocent man.')

When my father got out, he 'Lost-the-flavour' for the promotion game and went back into doing other things. He was still working with Alex Steene, but Alex and his son, just like Frank Warren, had their eye on the professional boxing scene.

My father knew he would never get a license with the boxing board in a million years, so he stayed in the background. Just keeping his eyes on things and seeing if anything popped up that might interest him.

However, two years later, Roy came back again to fight Lou' Wild Thing' Yates, where he beat him in 3 rounds. A few weeks later, he beat the man who had beaten Lenny McLean, Kevin Paddock, on points over eight rounds.

Roy Shaw retired with a record of nine wins and two losses with eight knockouts.

Roy then dabbled with promoting and did a couple of shows with his good pal Joey Carrington over in Essex.

In particular, one show springs to mind where Roy even decided to be the referee as well as the promoter.

Alex Steene's son Greg was the timekeeper, and he told me about this fight where one of the fighters came back to the corner after the 3rd round and said he had had enough. Roy walked over to the corner and asked what was going on,

"I've had enough Roy. I'm finished," said the fighter.

"What do you mean you're fucking finished?" Roy shouted back at him

"I'm done mate, finished, had enough!"

Roy grabbed the fighter round the head and shouted at him,

"I'll show you when you're fucking finished!" he said before punching him in the face and dragging him up like a rag doll.

"Now go and fucking fight!" Roy shouted as he told Greg to ring the bell to start the 4th round.

The poor fighter got up and fought until the 5th round, where he was ultimately stopped.

Lenny McLean, however, carried on boxing up to 1986 against mediocre opponents, but never reached the stellar heights that his fights against Roy Shaw brought him.

After his three losses on the spin, he boxed Steve 'Columbo' Richards, who was a bit of a crazy match up, to be honest.

Columbo, as we called him, was an undercard fighter on most of my father's promotions. Steve was a real character and got the name Columbo as he would enter the ring wearing a long tan mac. He would joke about during fights and really get the crowd going. I remember him once coming back to the corner and seeing someone drinking a bottle of beer, Steve called the man at ringside and asked for a sip, the crowd burst into laughter as he took a large swig in the corner.

I was at this fight against Lenny, and I remember Columbo being stopped, which was hardly surprising as he was really a middleweight and must have been well into his mid-forties when this fight happened.

Columbo though, could fight! He was an ex-professional, and for most of his fights he played around with his opponents.

His fight against Lenny was supposed to be an exhibition after Lenny's original opponent dropped out. (I think it was Physco Dave Spelling?)

It was supposed to be just a move around, but Colombo didn't read the script. Ever the showman he couldn't help himself playing about, he came out in the 1st round and started sticking his chin out to Lenny and putting his hands behind his back, Lenny was getting more and more frustrated as Steve was taking the piss and the crowd was laughing and joking.

Eventually, Lenny caught up with him, and the weight and size difference was just too much for Colombo. He was utterly knackered, just trying to hold and clinch the larger man.

Lenny then had two more wins, one against former light heavyweight professional boxer Ron Redrup. In his day, Ron was a very decent amateur and a capable professional, but only won half of his fifty-odd fights. When Lenny beat him, he was 45 years old, skint and just trying to pick up the odd pound here and there.

Lenny then had two fights against former light heavyweight professional boxer Johnny Waldron, the first fight losing by KO in the third round.

After this defeat, Lenny started working with my father and Alex Steene, where a return against Waldron was arranged and took place at the Cat's Whiskers in Streatham (later to be called Caesars)

Again, I was in this fight, and I can remember that Lenny started to take the piss out of Waldron in the first round, Lenny was sticking his chin out, goading Waldron to hit it, Waldron dipped his shoulder, feinted with a left and then hit Lenny with a big right hand, that was Goodnight! Lenny was knocked out.

Lenny then boxed Johnny Clark in Tottenham, winning in the 2nd round before disappearing off the scene for four years.

He returned to the ring in 1986 about four stone heavier and had two fights against two cobble fighters, Brian' mad gypsy' Bradshaw, and Man Mountain York, Lenny won both fights, both ending in the 1st round.

He then retired from the ring with a record of nine wins and six losses.

George Pappy Langley also claims to have beaten Lenny in one round, but to be honest, I wasn't there or didn't know much about it. I have heard he beat Lenny easily and heard it ended in both boxers being disqualified, and I have also heard it never even happened.

I have never seen a poster or a picture or even a photograph of George pappy Langley.

So I will not include it in Lenny Mclean's record.

If I am honest here and it's not biased, I think Roy had a better unlicensed fighting record. In the chapter on Lenny McLean, you will see what he meant to me as a friend, so there is absolutely no favouritism in my view.

However, apart from his two wins against Roy, Lenny's career was not that spectacular. Two losses against Cliff fields, two against Johnny Waldron and a loss against Paddock, who Roy Shaw beat.

You can also say Roy's record isn't too stellar either, but he beat a boxer like Ron Stander, who fought Joe Frazier for the World heavyweight title. Roy also beat Paddock, who beat Lenny and two other fighters who had massive fighting reputations, Lew Yates and Donny 'the bull' Adams.

Roy Shaw vs Lenny McLean 4.

The fight that never was.

There has always been the rumour that a 4th fight almost happened. Some have said it was rubbish, and some have said it's just a myth, but in later years, my father and Alex attempted to get the fourth fight between Roy and Lenny.

Both men had gained more notoriety over the years, and any fight between these two would have been a massive spectacle. There was still no love lost between them, and it was a very icy atmosphere when the two men were in the same room or at the same event.

My father spoke to both men over the phone, and in theory, got them to agree to fight. Next, my father set up a meeting to discuss the fight, take some pictures, and start building momentum and interest.

The meeting was arranged at a gymnasium in Mitcham Lane, Streatham called The Park Tavern.

Roy and Lenny both turned up to a packed gym and as soon as they arrived and were both in the same room, the atmosphere changed, people were saying hello to them, but you could see they were eyeing each other up, it felt like the slightest silly thing said or heard would start them off.

My father made sure they were both separated, and then Roy took off his shirt and got into the ring to have some pictures done, he put his hands up and posed for a few pictures as Lenny watched on.

Roy then got out the ring, and Lenny took off his shirt, and someone commented on the scars on Lenny's back, Lenny then started explaining them saying one was a stabbing and one was from being shot, then Roy who had been listening and looking like he was getting the hump decided to shout out to Lenny,

"It's funny how all your scars are on your back! ….. What do you keep running away?!"

Lenny grimaced at Roy and looked like he was turning back to walk towards him, only to be held back by Alex Steene, who said to both of them, 'Act like men.'

A few tense moments passed before Lenny then got in the ring and had a few pictures taken. The photographer suggested that both men have some pictures done together, but my father said, smiling, 'No way, we're not getting those two together in the ring again until fight night.'

Later on, that evening, when I spoke to my dad, I could see he was relieved that there wasn't any trouble; he did tell them both to turn it in a couple of times, and he was pleased nothing silly happened.

I know my father was then looking for a venue to stage the event, and It had to be a big place as there would be so many people wanting to go. Alexander Palace was mentioned, and even Albert Hall.

Unfortunately, my father was then arrested on a charge and remanded in Wormwood Scrubs, and with that arrest ended any chance of a 4th fight.

I think Alex Steene was willing to go ahead and try to stage it, but with things so uncertain with my father, they all agreed not to go ahead with it.

It was a shame it never happened, and we will never know how a fourth fight might have panned out.

Speaking hypothetically, I think the fourth fight might have been very difficult for Roy. The age difference would have been much more a factor with him in his fifties, and also, the size difference had increased as Lenny was now walking around over 20 stone.

My father spent about nine months on remand before being acquitted at trial, but when he came home, everyone had moved on to other things in their life.

Alex and my father did stage a couple of more shows in the '80s at the Dog and Fox pub in Wimbledon village. One was a dinner show and one an open show. A few local fighters fought, but the excitement of Roy or Lenny had gone.

I remember one show which was bloody comical. Steve Columbo Richards boxed in the main event and got up to all his usual tricks. He was karate chopping his opponent, dancing around and slapping him with a backhand and generally winding his opponent right up, a local fella with a big support.

At first, the crowd took it well, but after a couple of rounds, they began to get more angered at Columbo, for taking the piss out their man.

Sitting at ringside was Oliver Reed and ex-middleweight world champion, Terry Downes.

If anyone went to a boxing show in the 70s or 80s at venues like the Albert Hall or Wembley or some of the bath shows, they would fondly remember the antics of Terry Downes at ringside.

In those days, the crowd tended to behave themselves more than the crowds today. Some fights it was silent during the rounds, especially in the Albert Hall.

All except Terry Downes, who you could see at ringside chain-smoking cigars and dressed up to the nines, looking like The Great Gatsby.

But then you would hear him! Terry had this deep cockney voice, like someone talking through their nose, and he was notorious at the shows.

"HIT THAT FUCKING WANKER!" he would shout or "YOU'RE BOTH A PAIR OF FUCKING MUGS!". I have seen him absolutely crucify boxers in the ring before, one time even the referee was struggling not to burst into laughter. Trust me, seeing Terry in action was one of the highlights of the night.

Imagine sitting there during a round at the Albert Hall, all the boxing board inspectors are there, and it's dead quiet. All you can hear is the sound of the fighter's feet on the canvas and the sound of their punches. Then all of a sudden, you hear this deep nasal cockney voice yell out from ringside, "WHAAAT A PAIR OF FUUUUCKING MUGS!"

It was bloody hilarious; I've even seen the referee in a fight tell him to SHOOSH, which Terry replied, "BOLLOCKS YOU BLIND C..T!" Adding "IF YOU DID YOUR FUCKING JOB WE WOULDN'T BE SHOUTING OUT!"

Anyway, getting back to the Columbo fight, Terry Downes was sitting ringside, shouting out his usual antics, and opposite him was sitting Oliver Reed, who was worse for wear for drink and was really enjoying listening to Terry's insulting commentary.

So Oliver decides it's a great laugh to start mimicking Terry Downes, so Terry starts shouting out, "HIT THE FUCKING MUG!" Then, a moment later, Oliver, on the other side of the ring, would put on his cockney accent and copy what Terry had said.

Now Terry was just as pissed as Oliver Reed, so they both start really going to town. It was so hilarious that everyone stopped watching the fight and just watched Terry and Oliver.

In the end, Alex Steene (Ever the gentleman) went over and asked them both to quieten down.

The fight itself fizzled out, and the local boy was given the win on points (a hooky decision.)

The boxing finished, and the lights went up, but some of the locals were still mooching about and being a bit boisterous. Oliver Reed was still playing up, shouting and taking the piss, but all harmless and just being merry.

My father, together with Oliver Reed, thought it would be a good idea to send Toby von Judge into the middle of the ring and sing an opera song.

The same little Toby, who some ludicrously call (your grace) the self-proclaimed Underboss or tutu fruity, nutty of the cornetto or Dolmio family!

To us who knew him, he was 'pub-hound Toby,' he could sing though, and we always got him up singing, when we all had a drink.

He can't speak Italian, but he would sing Nessan Dorma and Solo Mio and then just make up the words that sound Italian.

He would give it all the face twitches and arm movements.

After a few suggestions, Toby gets in the ring and goes into Solo Mio, and the crowd fucking loved it!

Everyone was laughing and cheering.

Is was the perfect ending to a bloody good night, and it got rid of the drunks at the end of the night!

Another funny story on the same night as I gave Charlie Kray a lift home. I never drunk in those days as I was boxing, so when the night ended, Charlie asked for a cab, and I said, don't be silly, mate ill drive you.

I had just bought a brand new Ford RS turbo in red, and I loved driving it, especially at night, with the empty roads.

So me and Charlie and his pal get in the car, and just as we drive into Wimbledon high street, an old bill car pulls out right behind us. Charlie sees them and asks if they are still following, and I'm driving thirty miles an hour and clocking them in the mirror. We all had that feeling you get when the old bill is behind you and think you're going to get pulled over.

"Fuck it! I think they're going to pull us over, mate." I said, sounding pissed off.

"You're taxed and Insured ain't you?" Charlie asked, sounding concerned.

I paused for a moment before answering, "Yeah...... that's okay, but that's not what I'm bothered about." I said, sounding worried.

"What's the matter then?" Charlie asked.

"The cars taxed, but I'm worried about the kilo of puff and the sawn-off shotgun I have in the boot," I replied seriously.

Suddenly the look on Charlie's face was an absolute picture, and he was once completely lost for words, I looked across at him and then started laughing.

"I'm fucking winding you up!" I said joking

"Ah,.. Joe, you bastard!" he said, now smiling and sighing in relief.

CHAPTER 4
OTHER FIGHTING MEN FROM THE GOLDEN ERA

Paul Sykes

Paul Sykes was a tough professional boxer who boxed John L Gardner in 1979 for the British heavyweight title, losing by TKO in round 6.

Paul was very good friends with his fellow Yorkshire man Alex Steene and had a big reputation as a street fighter who was feared and tremendously well respected when he was behind the door in prison.

There was talk about him meeting Lenny in the ring and speak of the fight being made and even tickets and posters being printed.

The fight never happened in the end.

As far as I know, it was going to be on a newly formed NBC show (the National Boxing Council), the rival boxing board set up by Frank Warren, Alex Steene, and my father.

A few stories are floating around as to why it never happened, one story was - One week before he was supposed to box, he had a fight in a pub and cut his eye. Another story I heard was that Frank Warren pulled the plug on the show as he had agreed to get his professional promoter's license with the British Boxing Board of Control (BBBofC)

One of the restrictions put on Warren for having his license granted was that he must not promote or be involved in any more unlicensed shows.

There are a couple of other rumours, but I won't comment on them so I will leave it there, but I will say that I think Sykes would have won relatively easy if it would have happened. He was a seasoned top-notch professional boxer.

Bartley Gorman

Mr. Gorman is another name that seems to pop up in forums and social media, but from my recollection, at the time, none of us had heard of him.

Below is a short article about Bartley Gorman on the Birmingham Live web page by reporter Mike Lockley in 2017 and is... COMPLETE COBBLERS!!

"Bartley Gorman's blood-and-bruises story is a gripping tale of a world light-years from the controlled, regulated violence that has made Tyson Fury a fortune.

But the new world champ is acutely aware of Bartley's legacy and can be seen on YouTube paying tribute to the undisputed bare-knuckle boss.

Bartley's life is crammed with larger-than-life tales that have become embedded in gypsy folklore.

In the shadowy world of illegal fighting, sifting the fact from the fiction can prove problematic.

He certainly couldn't match 18-stone Fury's vital statistics.

Gorman stood 6ft 1in tall and weighed 15 stone, but regularly sparked out much bigger men.

Among his **many victims** were London stars of the underground fight scene, **Lenny McLean and Roy "Pretty Boy" Shaw.**

The first time I ever met Bartley Gorman was at Ronnie Kray's funeral. I was standing talking to Roy Shaw and Vic Dark and this strong looking very smart fella came over and said hello to Roy, it was a brief encounter where Bartley just shook Roy's hand. Roy then turned to me and asked me, 'who's that?" I said I don't know, and so did Vic.

Later that day, someone told me it was Bartley Gorman but said I'd never heard of him or what he was.

There was talk he challenged Lenny McLean, but I don't know anything about that, but I can honestly say hand on heart there was never a challenge to Roy from Bartley, at least what I know of.

From what people who knew Bartley Gorman had told me is he was a very decent man, and from a couple of times I met him, he always looked astute and had impeccable manners.

So I don't know where the rumours came from, but you can take it from me as an absolute certainty that Bartley Gorman was never in the frame to fight Roy, nor even mentioned.

In September 1976, in a local Coventry newspaper, Gorman stated that he challenged Roy Shaw to a bare-fisted winner takes all fight. It was in the paper, but he never actually made a phone call to my father or Alex. No one ever reached out and made the challenge legit.

Maybe this over the years was why people say he challenged Roy? But how on earth would you expect my father and Roy to discover a challenge in some local paper from Coventry?

David Bomber Pearce

There were also rumours of another fighter who Alex Steene, had an interest in, Dave Pearce from Newport, Wales,

Pearce was an excellent fighter, nicknamed 'the bomber,' and was the former British and Welsh Heavyweight champion and drew against Lucian Rodriguez when he challenged for the European heavyweight title.

To be honest, any match made for Lenny or Roy against Pearce would have been a complete mismatch. Pearce was quality and one of the best fighters to have come out of Wales. Pearce lost his professional license due to medical issues and then tried to get a pro license in some foreign country, but the board stopped it. Pearce then toyed with the idea of going on the unlicensed scene. He was in his prime when this happened, and if he had boxed unlicensed, he would have been head and shoulders above any of the fighters on the scene.

Cliff Field

Whenever you mention the *Guvnor Title*, people always say the name, Cliff Field. Roy wrote a great forward for his book, but to be honest; it was very complimenting as Cliff was in poor health. Roy says he would have never fought Cliff, but again that was Roy being kind to his pal who was sick.
Cliff was an ex-professional and had a mediocre pro record. (Certainly not as good as Ron stander – who Roy fought)
Cliff was knocked out a few times as a pro, twice by Billy Aird, then stopped by Richard Dunn and stopped by Brian Jewit, who was a *journeyman.*
Cliff, did however have two well-documented fights with Lenny McLean and won both of them.
Unlicensed boxing is different from professional boxing.
It differs because you can sometimes have an ex-professional boxer fighting someone who has **never been** a professional boxer.
Being a professional boxer gives you an enormous advantage, you have probably been training inside the ropes for most of your life.
Cliff was an ex-pro, and he knew how to fight in the ring, he knew how to slip punches, move in and out of range and had the balance and skills he had spent a lifetime developing.
Sven Hamer was also an ex-professional, and a fight with him against Cliff Field would have been a decent fight.
But in the early days of Roy and Lenny, where they were fighting mostly street fighters, Cliff had an enormous advantage in a boxing ring.
Nine times out of ten, if you put an ex-professional boxer in the ring against a street fighter, then the professional boxer will win the fight.
Cliff was a decent fighter, but his professional career was nothing spectacular! The boxers who beat him were good fighters, but not world-class.
When we started things back up in the early 2000s, I think there would have been quite a few fighters who would have beaten Cliff - Sven Hamer, Joe Kacz, and Mark Potter, (who was boxing for the Mortlocks.) All of these boys, in my opinion, would have been too much for Cliff.
But regardless of the above, Cliff Field was a decent fighter, he could fight and scrap and he definitely deserves a place amongst the unlicensed royalty

Johnny Waldron

Johnny, just like Cliff Fields, was another fighter to come out of the professional ranks. He was unbeaten as a pro, winning eight on the spin and picking up the Southern Area Light Heavyweight Championship.
His last fight and first loss was against Dennis Andries (managed by Alex Steene) losing to Andries is no disgrace as Andries went on to become a world champion.
Johnny beat Lenny McLean, twice and won a load more fights with different promoters.
Jackie Bowers used to train him, and he knew the game inside out!
Jackie was an old boxing booth lad, so he learned the boxing game the hard way.
I saw John box a couple of times and I remember his fight with Lenny at the Cats whiskers.
I think one of the reasons why Johnny, Cliff field and Sven hamer to that matter don't get as much publicity as the other fighters is because they were ex professionals and they came from the environment of having to have discipline.
The streetfighters of the unlicensed game, the Lennys' and the Roys', Welsh Phill and even Buckland, they don't put the gloves on and think they have to behave themselves! They stick the fucking nut in, or even bite you.
The ex-professionals have the edge in the boxing ring but they are usually the nice guys! The behaved guys! It's a shame really … but the public like the wild men, the baddies.
John could also have a good fight on the cobbles. He was a very tough man, he was a better boxer in the ring that Roy or Lenny, but he didn't have the charisma of them two.

Johnny Bindon

A few people have asked me about Johnny' Biffo' Bindon, and rightly so as he was a very tough fella back in the day.
He was an infamous character and very well known around South West London.
John mixed with a host of celebrities around the Kings road, and it is also said he had a relationship or fling with the queen's sister, Princess Margaret.
In late 1978, John found himself on the run with the old bill searching for him for the murder of Johnny Darke.
Johnny Darke was also well known around the manors of Fulham and Battersea, and it is well documented that he and Bindon got themselves into a fight where Darke ended up murdered.
With the old bill looking for Bindon, he sneaked out of England and hid in Ireland, and shortly after that, my father and his pal Brian Emmett were arrested for what the old bill said was helping to get John out of the country.

My father spent a few months on remand, but the old bill had to drop the charges when Bindon was acquitted of the murder at the Old Bailey.

The coppers hated having to order an immediate release for my father and Brian, but they had no choice as you cannot be guilty of helping an innocent man.

John and my father remained good friends, and they mixed in the same drinking circles from time to time.

One night my father and a few pals were having a drink with Bindon in the Dog and Fox pub in Wimbledon, and they got talking about John putting the boxing gloves on. He loved a fight, and there was still a lot of publicity around him at this time, so he would undoubtedly sell loads of tickets.

They discussed fighting Roy or Lenny, and Bindon at first seemed to fancy it. Lenny McLean was now working with my father and Alex Steene after leaving Frank Warren, and he was going to be the first choice. So after a few weeks, the discussions grew in seriousness, and they planned to have John Bindon get into the ring and challenge Lenny at the Cat's Whiskers club where he was having a return fight against Johnny Waldron.

The plan was for Lenny to beat Waldron, and then, Bindon would climb through the ropes, call him out, have a bit of a scuffle, and light the fuse for a big fight between them sometime in the future.

That was the plan! However, plans don't always go as you wish.

Bindon was sitting at ringside ready to jump in and make some noise, but Lenny's second fight against Waldron *'didn't go to plan,'* He lost the bloody fight. Everyone except Waldron and his cornermen was sick. Bindon didn't get in the ring as he felt like he couldn't get in there and challenge a beaten man. (Lenny McLean)

In the real world, he would have gotten in the ring and challenged the winner (Waldron,) but the money fight was against Lenny.

John just sat there, not knowing what to do, and my dad was furious. I was at the fight, and I remember my father cursing under his breath as he just watched a bloody good earner fly out the window.

It's a shame it didn't materialise, as who knows what would have happened if it had come off.

Who would have won? …Would there have been another trilogy of fights like there was with Roy Shaw? … It will always be a mystery and a *what-if* question. After Lenny was beaten a second time by Waldron, I think that was it for my father. He lost interest.

I remember my dad telling me, they were all looking forward to making a big thing out of the fight with … Biffo Bindon.

Mark Potter

Mark was a very decent professional boxer who then turned to the unlicensed game where he started boxing for the Mortlocks.

As a professional, he fought for the heavyweight British and Commonwealth titles and was the Southern Area Champion.

Mark was a bloody good fighter and, without a doubt, was one of the best ex-professionals to fight unlicensed.

One of the things I regret is not having the pleasure of working with Mark, he was loyal to the Mortlocks, and they promoted (good shows0 on the other side of the Thames.

I think Mark Potter vs Sven Hamer would have been one hell of a fight! Both were powerful, had solid chins, and had the experience of being a professional.

I did speak to Alan Mortlock a few times in the early 2000s where we discussed merging our organisations and creating something like the British Boxing Board of Control. We discussed various things and Sven vs Potter was one of the things talked about.

We had some good ideas, but it's very hard to merge promotions. It's like asking Frank Warren to merge his fighters with Eddie Hearn, it sounds good, but the practicality usually stops things like this from happening.

Dominic Negus

Dom' was another fighter attached to the Mortlocks, boxing mainly over in Essex at the circus Tavern. Dom was and is a good pal of mine, and he is another I regret not working with/

Like Potter, he was a former heavyweight pro. He started as a Cruiserweight, won the Southern Area title, moved up to heavyweight, and famously lost to Audley Harrison in controversy.

Harrison hit Dominic while down on one knee, which caused chaos as Dom, spat out his gumshield and then tried to butt Harrison, the fight was live on BBC 1.

Dominic against Sven or Joe Kacz would have whetted the appetite. It's a shame it never happened, but what a competition that would have been, Sven Hamer – Mark Potter – Dominic Negus and Joe Kacz!

Dominic is now a successful professional boxing coach and I usually bump into him behind the scenes at the Frank warren shows or York hall and Brentwood shows.

I wish Dominic, all the best, he's a tough but lovely fella.

Pat McCann

Pat was another professional boxer floating around and toying with the idea of going on the unlicensed scene. Pat was my cousin on my mother's side, and he could fight.

As a professional, he boxed Kevin Finnegan and twice beat Johnny Frankham to win the southern area light heavyweight title. He retired in 1981 with a record of 23 wins and 6 losses.

It's a shame Pat never boxed on the circuit; he would have definitely been a handful.

Steve Columbo Richards

Steve or Columbo, as we called him, was a tough fucker. He grew up in Hungary just after world war two and moved to England in the 50s. When he arrived in the UK, he settled in Bermondsey and made quite a name for himself. Steve had his professional debut in 1959 and had over forty fights as a professional.

He was a decent fighter, but he boxed to earn money rather than fight to be a world champion. Steve was also a black belt in karate.

I saw Steve box a lot of times, and he always messed around. He just couldn't help himself.

Steve is definitely an unlicensed legend, he was always at the shows and always floating around with a few bags of things to sell.

He used to make me laugh when I bumped into him in the pubs and bars around the Old Kent Road. He would pull me to one side and reach into a bag and pull out this horrible fucking shirt and ask if I wanted to buy it! I used to shake my head, "Steve, mate... If you're going to nick something, try to nick something someone would fucking like!" I'd joke with him.

CHAPTER 5
THE GUV'NORS

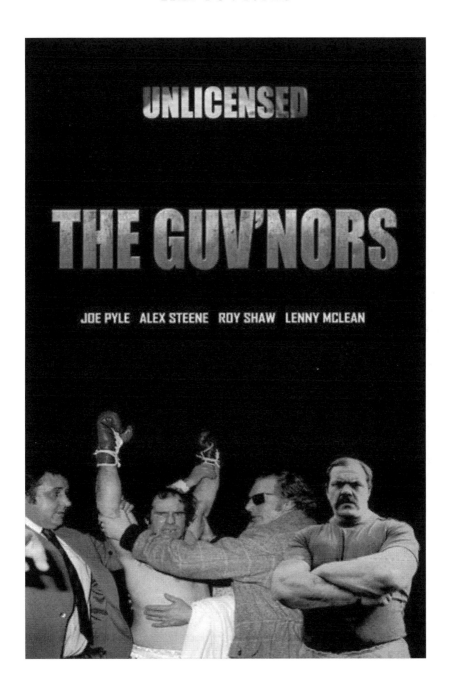

Roy 'Pretty Boy' Shaw (Mean Machine)
The original Guvnor

Roy Shaw is a former unlicensed boxer, convicted armed robber, and category 'A' prisoner. A well-respected member of London's underworld.

Shaw did an armed robbery in Dartford, which, for the exception of the great train robbery, was the biggest in Britain at the time. Roy was grassed up by a so-called friend and did 15 years for it.

He turned his hand to unlicensed boxing after the boxing board of control (BBBofC) refused him a license to fight. The trilogy of fights he had against Lenny McLean are considered the bloodiest of the 20th century.

Without a doubt, Roy Shaw was the **original** Guvnor and, in my opinion, the Godfather of the Guv'nors.

Roy wasn't just respected for what he could do inside the ring; he was respected by what kind of man he was outside the ropes.

Staunch, loyal and the best friend you could wish to have. He was pals with all the faces, my father, the Nashes, the Krays, Richardsons, Freddie Foreman, Frankie Fraser, Ronnie Biggs, Vic Dark, they all respected Roy.

To me, Roy was part of the family because, as far back as I can remember, he has always been a part of my life. One of my earliest memories of him was at a time in the seventies when my father was arrested and remanded, and Roy with my uncle Ted came round my dad's house to move a Rolls Royce car.

The car was being driven by my dad when he was arrested, and the old bill had the keys and was not releasing them, so the car was blocking the drive where no other car could get past it. I can remember Roy and Teddy lifting the back of the car and bunny hopping it to one side so the drive could be used. It was mad, seeing this great big car being dragged to one side by Roy.

Roy and my father's friendship go back before I was born, meeting each other in prison in the early sixties.

When Roy was released, he came down to Tooting, where my dad had an interest in a drinking club. My dad said to his brother Ted that a fella he met inside is coming down for a drink and to make sure all the locals behaved themselves because if they wind Roy up and he kicks off, then no one would be able to stop him if he went into one.

Roy came down, they had a great drink and night, and he and my father became best friends.

Roy always said that my father was his best pal, and I'm not talking out of turn here, but my father was the only one who could control Roy when he lost it, or my father was the only one who Roy would take advice from.

Another early experience I had of Roy was in the early eighties, and my father owned a big restaurant with Peter Tilley in Stockwell, South London. Roy walked into the restaurant with marks on his face and a swollen eye. My father asked him what the fuck had happened to his face.

Roy said he had a row with a bunch of Irish builders in a pub over the East End, there was about ten of them, and he done four of them, but it was proper tear up. My dad sighed and said, why the fuck didn't he call him, as he would have gone with Roy to the pub.

Roy replied it was alright, and he preferred to be on his own when having a row, that way, he didn't have to worry about looking out for who he was with. That was Roy in-a-nutshell. He just wanted to go into the pub on his own and not worry about anyone else, walk in the doors, and go completely into one, punching everyone near him until he won.

When people ask me what Roy was really like, I tell them a short story of when my father passed away in 2007 and how Roy stood beside me in what became a power struggle of finances between myself and a few of my father's (false) mates.

When my father passed away, he left a few weekly pensions that needed collecting every week, and a couple of his mates decided they would take it upon themselves to collect them.

I called them up and arranged a meeting where I told them the pensions were mine and asked them straight (If we were on a collision course,) then let's get it out in the open right here and now.

My father's mates backed down and said they would respect my wishes and some cobblers about me now being the head of the family. (Honestly, it was like some cobblers out of the Godfather film)

But behind my back, I was still hearing the rumours of them trying to get their hands on the pensions or slip into the people giving them.

I must have warned them half a dozen times to stop, but it carried on regardless. I tried to sort things amicably, and believe me, I didn't want any shenanigans; they were my dad's mates, men I had known for years, but no matter how diplomatic I tried to be, they wouldn't listen.

Things escalated, a few people got slapped, some properties got visited and damaged, and it turned into a proper gangland feud. I was still grieving, so this was very personal to me, and I wasn't bothered how far it went. One day after a meeting with my brothers Alan and Warren, we decided to up the stakes and gave them a message to show just how serious we were, a message letting them know this wasn't a game anymore, and there was no way we were backing down.

They got the message loud and clear, and they ran to a very respected and notorious London villain who called me and said we need a sit down to resolve this.

A meeting was called or a 'Kangaroo court,' and believe me; some serious faces were attending; it was probably the most significant *sit-down* for a few decades. There were a lot of people who could get *middled* up if this escalated any further. The meeting was for 3; 00 pm at a working man's club, but I decided not to turn up until 4; 00 pm to make everyone wait.

We were in a pub down the road with my brothers, Alan, Warren, Dave Thursting, Roy Shaw, and Brian Emmett Snr and Jr.

When we finally arrived, me and Roy walked in first to find the two mates of my father with the respected villain and Wilf Pine, with about a dozen others waiting for us. Dave Courtney was also there.

I could see they were annoyed at me being late, but I couldn't care less, I was late on purpose, I wanted them to know that I was not going to be intimidated by anyone. I would arrive when I felt like it.

I walked inside and said straight away that I was not here to discuss anything, I was here to tell these two c***s that if they didn't fuck off, then they were getting it again!

Wilf calmly asked me to relax and asked me to sit down, but then Roy interrupted him and looked at everyone at the table where he said the following. "I don't care if Joe is in the right or wrong! He is my best mate's son, and if any c**t wants to have a row with him, then they will have to come through me first!"

That statement pretty much ended the meeting! It was direct, and it was firm and straight to the point.

That, to me, sums Roy up!

There were no agendas with Roy, no middle ground; if he loved you, he was with you, through thick or thin.

Everyone on that table was or had been my father's pals. They should have taken the same stance as Roy, maybe Wilf and the villain would have come down on my side, I don't know, I probably think they would have, but Roy wasn't having any sit down to discuss it, he just told it straight, as soon as he walked into the room.

I fucking loved Roy even more for what he did that day; it wasn't because I needed help, but I loved what he did out of the loyalty for my father. He stayed true to his pal even when he wasn't here anymore.

Another tale of Roy that sticks in my head was when my father fell ill, just before passing away in February 2007.

I got a phone call to say my father had collapsed and had been taken to St Anthony's hospice in Cheam, Surrey. So I quickly jumped in my car and drove there to find him very ill, but still able to talk a little, he had been suffering from Motor Neuron Disease for over a year now, and I knew this day would come when his body couldn't fight anymore. I spoke to the doctors, and they said he wouldn't last the day, so I called the priest to come and administer 'Last Rights,' and then I got on the phone to tell the immediate family to come up to the hospice.

By the evening, there must have been a hundred people outside the hospice, most of which I took to my father's side to say their final farewells. It was a sad, sad day, and almost everyone was in tears.

It was really flattering that So many people turned up to say goodbye.

In the space of two days, I would say over 300 people turned up.

Roy was living over in Essex, and as soon as he got word from me, he came straight over and arrived just after seven in the evening. Roy just parked his Bentley right outside the building, two wheels on the kerb, on double red lines, but he didn't care about the car, he just had to see his friend. When he walked into the hospice, there were loads of people trying to say hello to him, Roy didn't see any of them, he was in tears and just barged past everyone to get to his old pal.

As he came into my father's room, he broke down in tears seeing my father barely conscience; he grabbed my dad's hand and was oblivious to anyone else in the room, Charlie Richardson, myself, and my uncle Ted.

Roy leaned down and cried out to my father…

"FIGHT IT JOE ….FUCKING FIGHT IT!" he said completely losing it.

Roy backed away and just leaned his back on a wall; he was lost in his emotions, just looking blankly at my father. I walked over and hugged Roy, and he just burst into tears on my shoulder.

"He can't die, Joe; he can't leave us!" Roy said.

Writing this now still chokes me up, I was emotional myself, but with all my heart, I can say I have never seen such love for a friend as Roy showed that day for my father.

I chose Roy to be a pallbearer at my father's funeral where me and Roy were at the front of the coffin, Ronnie Nash and Freddie Foreman were behind us. Roy was still in pieces, but he stayed composed for his great friend, and we somehow got through a very hard and emotional day.

After the funeral we went back to a pub in Wimbledon, it was the only pub in the area which would allow us to go back after the funeral. (The old bill had been busy the day before, ordering all the pubs in the area to close – Fuck knows why?) Anyway, back at the pub, I remember seeing Roy on his own in the car park just sitting on a wall. I went over and grabbed his arm,

"You okay, mate?" I asked him

"He's gone, Joe...... he's fucking gone," Roy said with a blank look on his face. I honestly believe that from the day he came to say goodbye to my father, right up to the funeral day, Roy was actually in shock!

Their friendship was on a different level! It was... 'Unbreakable'

After my father died in 2007 and right up to Roy's passing in 2012, me and Roy grew very close, where we would speak almost every week to each other.

In a small way I became what my father was Roy, he would often call me for advice, and we discussed various problems, I think he missed my father so much that in some way I became what my father was to him. There was still a Joe Pyle in his life, still a Joe Pyle in his phone contacts and a Joe Pyle he could call and someone he could trust and love.

I loved Roy very much, he is a massive part of my life, part of my past, and he will always be in my heart until the day I die.

Rest in peace, Roy

Me and Roy on a night out.

Below is one of the many interviews that Roy gave.
Terry Currie conducted an interview with Roy Shaw back in 2003 and gives you
an insight into Roy's life.

Terry Currie – When did you first realise you had a gift for fighting?
Roy Shaw – At school. Like a lot of kids, I was bullied. I was bullied for five
years, I was small for my age and didn't mix too well so that may have been the
reason why, I don't really know. When I was very young my father who I
adored was killed on a motorbike, that really did me in and I struggle even now
to talk about him ..
I actually threw myself on top of the coffin at the funeral! Three days later I was
back at school and being bullied again. Eight boys circled me, by this time fear
had turned to anger, anger at losing my dad and there was nothing they could

do to me that was worse than I had already been through. I felt a type of electric charge overtake my body, I felt superhuman, I threw a punch and down went one, then two, then three... CRASH!! That was when I first realized I had the gift of punch power.

Unlicensed Boxing

Terry Currie – And then you found a love of boxing?

Roy Shaw – Yes, I had found my purpose. I had ten professional fights and won them all, six by knock out and Mickey Duff was the manager. But then I started to get into trouble… Mickey Duff has apparently denied managing me in some interviews. That's understandable in some respects as Joe Pyle and I started the first boxing organization not controlled by the BBBC. Duff of course, is a British boxing board promoter so being the first manager of the man who would give his employers so many major headaches must have been a nightmare!!

My pro record has been scrapped as well. Of course, there will be idiots who think I am making the whole thing up but you really have to understand the tense relationship between unlicensed and the BBBC before you can have an informed opinion of that one. The thing that makes me laugh is why the hell would I make up being managed by Mickey Duff? He's not exactly the most reputation enhancing bloke in the world is he? It's not like I'm claiming I knocked out Ali or floored Marciano in sparring is it!! Mickey Duff managed me, so what? I didn't need to mention a promoter at all. If it was a lie I wouldn't give details I didn't need to. If I was going to lie it would have been better than 'I was managed by Mickey Duff' (LAUGHS)

Armed Robbery

TC – On the naughty side of things, you were involved in a big robbery in Dartford weren't you?

Roy Shaw – Yes, the Dartford one was a big one! Before the great train robbery, it was the biggest ever robbery in Britain. Things happened though and I got a 15 stretch for that one. I was grassed up by a so called friend.

TC – Did the violence carried on in prison?

RS – Yes. You have no choice in prison, it's the only way to survive. If you don't get yourself established one way or another they will destroy you. The early days are the toughest inside, but after you have done a few of them you get a reputation. Then, people know you can have a row and think twice, because they know there is no way they are not going to get hurt in the process. Most of my rows after that were with screws and the prison bullies. I broke the jaws of a lot of bullies and I am not ashamed of that in the slightest! I wasn't really fighting individuals but the whole system, I despised authority. I smashed my way out of 2 locked cell doors from the inside! That's never been done before or since and is still talked about in prison.

I had so much energy, anger, hate and adrenaline in me it gave me the power of ten men. I tell the story of my prison time as it was without beefing it up. I'm not one of those who exaggerates what they did beyond all proportion just to build a reputation. What I tell you is no frills facts. I'm not proud of everything I done but I'm not ashamed either, at least I know I am not fooling myself by claiming things that never happened.

You don't end up in the dungeons of Broadmoor by telling porkies about what you did. Of course, I can't recall or tell you about all the rows I had inside. There are literally too many to recount although, I did have the pleasure of switching off a few nonces. Jack the hat would join me on these occasions he was a tough, solid man. The thought of scum that abuse children still gets my blood up.

Broadmoor

TC – *Then you were moved to Broadmoor?*

Roy Shaw – That's right. Broadmoor is thought of as a place for nutters, but they also send you there when the normal prison system can't handle you. A lot of people who are sent there do not have a mental illness, but are top class rascals! They couldn't handle me in there either and I ended up in the hellhole of hellholes… the Broadmoor dungeons. That is the ends of the earth, you can't get sent to anywhere worse than that. All around are the haunting cries of lunatics twenty-four hours of every day.

This is where you are pumped up with drugs and experimented on. If you have no real good friends, you could easily be forgotten down there and rot away!! Luckily I did have and have still got good, solid, loyal friends so I came out the other end. It's well documented now but I was beaten, experimented on and even given electric shocks to the brain. But they never broke me, never had me where they wanted me. In the dungeons it was pitch black and the only sound was of lunatics. It was like 'one flew over the cuckoo's nest' I had an instinct of charging head first into the screws that unlocked the door.

Even in the bowels of the earth, my hatred for authority hadn't faded. I behaved when I wanted to not when I was told too. Most people including Broadmoor staff were certain I would die and rot in the dungeons, they really saw that as my only future. And the way they saw it, what with all the drugs I was being pumped up with I wouldn't be alive much longer. It really was that bad for me. Luckily my friend Joey Pyle didn't give up on me and if it wasn't for Joe I would still be in there if I was alive at all, which I doubt I would be. Joe saved my life.

TC – *Any memorable rows in Broadmoor?*

Roy Shaw – Yeah a fair few, one is mentioned in Ronnie Kray's book 'My Story' although Ron got that one a bit wrong. I had a fight with a guy called Freddie Mills, who was no relative of the famous boxer by the way. Mills was a big, flash bully and I hate bullies with a passion. Anyway, I knocked this bloke spark out with about two punches…. CRACK!! All over!!! Ron says it went on for an hour and a half and it makes a good story, but in truth it was over in seconds. But again there are too many to recount.

Meeting The Krays

TC – *Did you and the Kray Twins meet in prison?*

Roy Shaw – Oh yeah, well, before they were nicked Ronnie came to see me in Broadmoor and asked if there was anything he could do for me. My wife was having an affair and I wanted this guy hurt…. Bad! Ronnie said "Consider it done, don't worry about anything, I'll take care of it. A few days later Ronnie came back to tell me "It's done. The slag's been shot" Anyone who knew Ronnie will tell you he was a real man a man of his word. We had a lot of mutual respect Ron and I. The twins came to see me again just after they done Jack Mcvitie who I knew well and was a sound man at the time I knew him. Jack the hat was always with us in rows with the screws, you could count on him being there with you he was game, solid and totally fearless. He was nothing like the way they portrayed him in the Kray film. Anyway, I wanted Ronnie and Reggie to come and see me as I didn't like what they were putting around about my pal Ray Mills. After I had a word with them we got on fine. Reggie and I were together in Parkhurst. We had a three-man weight lifting team… me, Reg and another guy. We beat all the other prisons in the U.K., I still have the certificate for it. I have nothing but respect for Ron, Reg and Charlie, I know they respected me as well. I attended all three funerals.Make no mistake, they were a formidable firm but so were Joey Pyle and the Nashes and also the Richardson's. The twins certainly weren't any more powerful than them. In prison Frankie Fraser was very, very respected. In them days everyone feared Frank don't worry about that, he was the man. Joey Pyle though has worked with the lot. Right back to Jack Spot, Billy Hill and Albert Dimes through the twins, Nashes and Richardsons, Bindon right through to today's faces. Even the American mafia! Joe has seen the lot.

Weightlifting Regime

TC – *Talking of weightlifting, did you do a lot of this in prison?*

RS – Absolutely… it was my lifeline, it kept me sane and strong in mind and body. Having a focus, a goal, is crucial in there, it kept me going.

TC – *Can you give an example of your regime?*

RS – It would be low reps and heavy weights. We would do 3 sets and then add some more weight and squeeze out another 2, finishing by stripping the weight a bit for 1 more set. I would train most days. I still train 4 times a week now but with less weight & more reps performed faster with less rest between sets. I am still in good shape for a 38-year-old!!

TC – *What were your best lifts?*

RS – Bench press- 365 lbs Squat- 500 lbs and deadlift 600lbs All on prison food!!!!! I pumped up to about 16 stone.

Joey Pyle

TC – *And then upon release you and Joey Pyle started unlicensed boxing.*

Roy Shaw – Yes, Joe was the promoter I was the fighter. The British boxing board refused to give me my license back, so we just thought…. well, we don't need you, we will start our own boxing body, so that's what we did. It is called unlicensed because it doesn't have approval from the British Boxing Board. People tend to think it's illegal but it's not, it's just a separate controlling body. Anyway, before this I went to Barnet Fair, won a few bare knuckle fights and a nice few quid. Someone there said, "well, there is only one opponent for you…. Donny Adams…"

I had been inside with Adams and believe me he was no mug, unbeaten on the cobbles! The idea was to have a bare knuckle 'fight to the death'. We ran into all sorts of legal troubles and had to wear gloves, but we certainly didn't want to. There was also talk of ripping the gloves off when the bell went and steaming into each other, while the chaps linked arms around the ring to stop old bill breaking it up. This never happened in the end though. Joey Pyle took over the promotion and we staged it at Billy Smarts 'Big Top' in Windsor.

On the night, I was ready to explode, I was like a volcano. As the bell went, I threw a right hander and over Adams went, I kept punching, picking him up again, knocked him back down and stamped on his head!! Someone shouted "He's dead Roy, he's dead" he wasn't, but he was spark out, it was over in seconds and I was the Guv'nor!

'Mad Dog' Mullins

TC – *Who was next?*

Roy Shaw – Next was an Irishman called 'Mad Dog' Mullins, I finished him in the first round. Then I beat a mongrel named Mickey Gluxted in three rounds. I have been told this mongrel is now gobbing off about the fight being fixed blah, blah. Well I would gladly fight him again right now!

He is a scumbag and scum should keep their filthy mouths shut! If I knew then what I know now about what he is I would have killed him stone dead! and then Terry Hollingsworth, the A.B.A. champion was taken care of in round one.

Lenny Mclean

TC – *Next of course……… Lenny Mclean! …*

Roy Shaw – Yep, he was next. At this point neither Joey Pyle nor I had heard of him, but if you could put enough money up, you got a fight. Mclean, I have to say, was not my cup of tea. He was loud and growled at people a lot. He was a very big man, a lot bigger than me, but that never bothered me in the past and it certainly didn't bother me at this fight either. It was all set for Cinatra's in Croyden, a contest over ten rounds.

Lenny Mclean wrote in his book, that when he tried the gloves in the dressing room, they kept springing open and blamed Joey Pyle for giving him doctored gloves. It's complete rubbish as the gloves Joe gave him were too small for him. His camp then got him some of their own… they were his own gloves he was wearing!!!

Also, if you are about to fight and your gloves keep springing open in the dressing room, it doesn't matter if you are fighting Donald Duck, you don't go to the ring with them! Remember at this point, nobody had heard of Lenny Mclean so why would I insist on dodgy gloves? Surely, I would have pulled this trick against men I considered real threats like Ron Stander. Ron was a full-blooded heavyweight contender. He had fought Joe Frazier and knocked out Ernie Shavers in five rounds… now, there WAS a threat!

Lenny Mclean was just another fight with just another fighter. The night came and after a delay for the gloves change over, we were at each other. I was working his body when he started looking at the crowd and pretending he couldn't be hurt shouting "He can't hurt me" It was a con act because everyone could see he was in trouble. I moved upstairs and smashed him in the face… WALLOP, that shut him up!

It really was a very one-sided fight and everyone who was there will tell you that. I hammered away until the third round when the referee dived in to save him from further damage. He says in his book he challenged me to fight him for the first time after I had beaten Lou Yates. Again rubbish! When I fought Yates I had already fought Mclean 3 times.

Yates was my second to last fight. He also says I Kevin Paddock challenged me after the same fight and I knocked him spark out. Well, I fought Paddock next in my last ever fight and couldn't knock him out then so I don't see how I done it that time (laughs) Mclean couldn't knock Paddock out either & lost a very one sided fight with Kevin.

Ron Stander

TC – *Next Ron Stander?*

Roy Shaw – That's right. As I said he was the business a real natural big heavyweight. Unbeknown to me he had injured his ribs in training. At first I was smashing him with almighty head shots, that would of put other fighters to sleep, but Ron Standerr was saying "That's it keep it up" I couldn't believe it! In the third round I switched to his body as the head hunting was a waste of effort. I threw a hook into his ribs and heard him groan in pain, I thought "At last, a weakness!" A few more shots and over he went, I had never been so pleased to finish a fight. I don't think I could have beaten him without the rib injury he picked up.

TC – *Then didn't you have two further bouts with Lenny Mclean?*
Roy Shaw – That's right. I documented the reasons for losing these fights to some extent in my autobiography 'Pretty Boy' and don't really want to go through the whole thing again, not because I have anything to hide, it's all in the book. The reason is, I will get stick for for it as Lenny Mclean is no longer with us, but anyone who knows me will know, there was nothing left unsaid to him, I said everything I had to say to his face on more than one occasion, I also challenged him to fight me bare knuckle, his reply was "I am too old now Roy" a bit rich as he was only the same age as me when I beat him and of course he was still younger than me.
So it is very irritating when idiots who don't know their facts take his book as gospel and start spouting off like they are experts!! There are valid reasons why I lost to Mclean in the second and third fight and I swear they are true. Not much more can be said. I am not speaking ill of the dead merely stating facts, if Mclean had not told so many untruths, I would not be forced to correct them would I?

I swigged half a bottle of ginseng before the fight and I was totally out of it, not right at all. Anyone who was there will tell you that. Again, it's only the idiots who weren't there, no nothing of the sport and never knew either myself or Mclean that shout about me lying….. why is that? Again, it's only ever on a computer. Like the Mickey Duff scenario, I really could of made up a better excuse than that if I was lying. Fact is, I didn't need an excuse with the size and age difference it was like Lennox v Nigel Benn !! in regular boxing it would never have been allowed to happen.
I didn't need excuses for those losses, I defied all logic by stopping him in the first fight. His punches never hurt me then, I just walked through them, so how did I just fall over with the first dig in the other fights? Surely, even people who don't like me can work that one out. And give my imagination some credit, I could of used an injury or any of a million things as more believable excuses but they would be lies. That's the honest truth. But there you go, I can't force people to believe me can I.

TC – *Did you carry on fighting?*

Roy Shaw – Yes, because I knew those two Mclean fights were freaks and not the real me, I carried on. I knocked out the unbeaten Harry Starbuck in the first, Lou 'wild thing' Yates in three. My final fight was against Kevin Paddock who I beat on points. Kevin had beaten Lenny Mclean on points and was a good defensive fighter.

TC – *Were any of those fight fixed?*

Roy Shaw – Well whoever says that is not going to believe me anyway. Like the Mickey Duff thing a lot of this is simple logic. Take the Adams fight. Adams was the favourite and got most of the media attention, that's why a nick name was invented for me 'Pretty Boy' because he had one (The Bull) It was the first unlicensed fight ever and whoever had won would have been the main man and packed places out. So why fix that fight? It wouldn't have mattered who had of won to a promoter he would of just built them up.

Joe was the promoter and my friend but business is business and if you can't beat who is front of you without them being fixed, you are not a good investment. You will just get found out further along the road. Both Adams and I both agreed to fight to the death and that's why I kicked and stamped on him. I certainly would not have done that if I knew the man was going to fall over anyway, that would have been out of order a real liberty. What would have been the point?

I beat Stander but that wasn't fixed. He was injured and I have said before it was only that injury that allowed me to win. He would have mullered me otherwise. If a fight was going to be fixed in my favour wouldn't it be obvious it would be the third Mclean fight, the decider? But look what happened. So can the fights be fixed? If they were, we fixed the wrong ones! (laughs) In the first Mclean fight he was unheard of. He was less known than Adams and Hollingsworth so why fix that one? Mclean became known later on.

Harry Starbuck, who is a great bloke was knocked spark out and Lou Yates had his eye hanging out! I think that claim is another one banded about by idiots who don't understand the game and just want to upset things, get a bit of attention. Mind you, nobody has ever walked up to me and said it, the internet seems to make mugs into very brave heroes. Ha ha. I suppose it was fixed when Cliff Field and Johnny Waldren knocked Mclean out twice apiece as well… (laughs)

Financially fixing fights doesn't make sense. Why pay someone handsomely to dive when you can just do your matchmaking right? Don't forget the backers of these fighters have to match a large amount of money and promise a certain amount of ticket sales before they are even considered as an opponent. Do people really think the money men would let them just fall over when a victory would put them in control of the whole scene?

That also means these idiots are calling honorable men like Adams, Starbuck, Stander etc divers. Now that's out of order! By the way, Terry Hollingsworth didn't do too well out of me. I beat him in one round, so he thought he would get his revenge. He put all his money into backing another fighter against me who he was sure could do the job. It was all Hollingsworth's stake money that got Lou Yates his fight with me. Oh dear, two bad nights for Terry Hollingsworth. Needless to say, Terry never sends me a Christmas card!

Bartley Gorman

TC – *AND BARTLEY GORMAN?*

Roy Shaw – Well, you told me about him & showed me his book, I had never heard of him. If he was the King of the gypsies, why didn't he cop the hump with Donny Adams using his title without asking? (laughs) It seems the fashion to make a name for yourself on other peoples hard earned reputations these days. You showed me a photo with him at Reg's funeral before, well I spoke to hundreds of people that day and thousands of photos were taken. I can't know them all. Didn't you say he claimed Mclean & the Frankhams bottled it from him as well? yeah right!!!!!!!! (laughs)

I just want to make it clear that I am not into slagging people in public but when they write complete crap about you very, very publicly what can you do? So I answer back without being abusive and then get the I'm being disrespectful to the dead bit!! I tell you this much. There is nothing I have said here, in my book or anywhere else about Lenny Mclean that I wouldn't say to his face, and the first person who would have agreed with that would be Mclean himself. I didn't like him and he knew it. I can't speak for the Bartley Gorman fella as I don't know who he was. That's not disrespect just truth..... Who did he fight then?

TC – *So who was really the Guv'nor ?*

RS – Well as he knocked Lenny Mclean spark out twice, it has to be Cliffy Fields. It was nice seeing him after all those years the other day wasn't it? Good old Cliff, now that man was a real handful.

TC – *And what did you do after you retired?*

RS – I went into property and have done very well for myself. I have a nice home, nice car and am doing well in business. The film of my life is about to be made, I have my own website royprettyboyshaw.com and as well as 'Pretty Boy', 'Roy Shaw- Unleashed' is also on the book shelves. Most importantly I have very good, very loyal family and friends. I can't complain.... Roll on the film.

From Tina Shaw (Roy's daughter)

My dad was very different from the run of the mill average man; he was definitely a one off! Unique, he was well known for his fighting ability, he's abnormal strength ect, he could be cold and merciless, all of those things are common knowledge! He had a terrific sense of humour and loved to party, in fact the best nights out I've ever had were with my dad. But he did have another side that only very saw, he could be very loving, caring and kind, he once told me that every man has a weakness and that I was his, he hated me having boyfriends, a man thing I suppose, once he bought me a Ford fiesta, when he gave it to me he said don't let your boyfriend drive it, well I did let him drive it and my dad had seen him, dad didn't mention it when I next see him but a couple of weeks after he came over n took me to a car showroom that he used to rent out, in the middle of the forecourt was a very shiny PINK Suzuki vicarage soft top jeep, he said ta'da, I said wow what a lovely car, who's is it? He replied its yours darling, thought I'd treat ya! Well I'm not your pink jeep kinda girl, I put a smile on n tried to look grateful as it must have cost a bob or 2, he then put his arm around me n whispered in my ear bet your knob boyfriend won't wanna drive this one! Lol. He had like a sixth sense, if I was up to something he would always catch me bang to rights or if I was having a bad time or some kind of dilemma he would instinctively know, he would turn up out the blue n say you've been on my mind a lot today, you alright darling, 9 times out of 10 I would just burst into tears, I used to think how did he know?! He would always try to make things better, he gave the best daddy cuddles ever! When he put his strong arms around me I instantly felt safe and loved, his advice was always spot on and his words of wisdom put me in good stead! I find myself saying his pearls of wisdom to my own girls today. Life is not the same without him, he was my hero! And in my eyes there will only ever be one guvnor n that's my dad.

Roy Shaw had an unlicensed fight record of 11 fights, 9 wins (8 KO's), and 2 loses.

Donny The Bull Adams	Won	KO 1	Windsor
Paddy mad dog Mullins	Won	KO 1	Bloomsbury
Mickey Gluxted	Won	TKO 3	Dagenham
Terry Hollingsworth	Won	KO 1	Croydon
Lenny Mclean	Won	TKO 2	Croydon
Ron Stander	won	KO 3	Muswell Hill
Lenny Mclean	Lost	KO 1	Croydon
Lenny Mclean	Lost	KO 1	Finsbury
Harry Starbuck	Won	KO 1	Dartford
Lou wild thing Yates	Won	KO 3	Ilford
Kevin Paddock	Won	PTS 8	Ilford

Lenny Mclean (Daddy Cool)

Lenny McLean ...... what can you say about Lenny McLean? ... Some say the hardest man ever to walk the streets of London, he was a man-mountain, that's for sure, a giant of a man both in stature and character, bare-knuckle champion, unlicensed champion, bestselling author, actor and a good friend to many a notorious face.
Lenny even has a movie about his life, called 'My name is Lenny,'
If you search online, there are hundreds of things written about the life of Lenny McLean and countless interviews, so I won't go over what everyone already knows, but I will give you an insight into the man I knew personally.

Me and Lenny go back a very long way, I first saw him when I was just a boy at the first Roy Shaw fight. If I'm honest, even as a young boy, he scared the life out of me. Lenny was larger than life, he was one of those who dominated a room, and when he spoke, he had a voice that made you listen.

I saw Lenny fight at all three shows against Roy, and then I saw him again when he started working with my father and Alex and boxed at the Cat's Whiskers in Streatham.

The next time I heard anything about Lenny was when my father was on remand in the Wormwood Scrubs, he visited my father and afterward got someone to drop some money off to my mother. I respected Lenny for that. (My opinion of him started to change because of this)

In the old days that was a thing to do when your pal was in prison, you helped out his wife and kids the best you could, it still happens today, but it is not so commonplace as it used to be.

When I was in my twenties and thirties, and would drink with my father and uncles in the Red Lion pub in Sutton.

Every Friday night, we would have a whip around for those currently in prison. The money collected would be divided by how many of our mates were away, so the next day, the money would be dropped off to their wives.

The next time I saw Lenny, I was in my twenties, and I went up to the Camden Palais night club, where he was the head doorman. We were queuing up when I saw him, so I called out to him, and we had a chat where I introduced myself, it was a funny conversation as I remember I was half pissed and my mates shit themselves when I started talking.

"Lenny, you are pals with my father, Joe Pyle."

"Yeah, your Joe's son, come in," Lenny answered as he invited my pals and me in, jumping the queue.

We walked inside, then I asked Len for a quick chat.

"You know Lenny; I never liked you! I was obviously in Roy's corner, but what you did for my father and mother when he was banged up meant a lot to me, that got my respect mate. I fucking respect you for that and your good stuff in my book," I said to him as I patted him on the arm.

"Okay, good." Lenny replied half grimacing and smiling in that way he did when he nodded his head before adding, "Look, have a good time lad, and if anyone bothers you, then give me a shout."

It's funny now when I look back at it as Lenny was probably thinking who is this young kid talking like that, but that was me, I say what's on my mind, always have and likely always will.

The next time I used to see Lenny was when he and Johnny Wall were doing the door at the Hippodrome nightclub, I think it was the late 80s or early 90s.

At that time, I was earning a good living out of the hostess clubs in the west end.

It was a result of me working for Alex Steene a few years earlier, I had a host of contacts in the hotels of the west end, what I did was tell my contacts (Concierges) that if guests at the hotel wanted a bit of excitement like a strip club then send them to these clubs and say that 'Fritz' sent them.

You would be surprised at how many married businessmen who were over in London for a couple of days would look for the company of a woman; this was before the internet so they couldn't just go online and find an escort.

They would approach the concierge, or if the concierge were good at his job, he would *suss* out who were more likely candidates, and would approach them. They would be sent down the club where basically a woman would sit next to them and ask for a drink, then another drink or as many as she could get, and then the bill would come, and it would be a bloody joke! Something like a glass of champagne costing £50 a glass or something.

The people who ran these hostess clubs were very good at what they were doing. After an argument about the bill, they would threaten the customer that they would call the police, now if a customer is married and he is away on business, then the last thing he wants, is to get arrested for being in a strip club. It was a bloody good living for me as I was 30% of the bill!

Every Friday night in used to drive up to the clubs and collect my share, some weeks I collected over £500 a week and that in the late eighties for a lad in his twenties was bloody good money. I'd give the concierges their share and sometimes some of the cabbies if they took someone there.

I never used to drink in those days, and I drove a brand new red Ford RS Turbo. So I would be flying about from club to club doing the rounds.

One of the clubs I used to collect from was around the corner from the hippodrome, so I would usually pop in to see Lenny, where we often ended up downstairs in a small kitchen having a cuppa and a chat.

I was always suited and booted on collection night, and Lenny enjoyed my company; I wasn't flashy or loud spoken, which Lenny hated, and we often chat about things that had been happening in the west end and about the fights between him and Roy. The west end was a good place to be in those days, some of the clubs I collected from; I would often see faces in there like Terry or Tommy Adams, the Arifs, Roy Nash was a regular I would see. Sometimes I would pop across the road to The Tin Pan Alley, where I'd see Jimmy and Frankie Fraser, Gary Dennis, and the others who used to get in there for a drink.

I remember one night when I called into Chatterley's in Albemarle Street, Mayfair and saw a couple of pals of mine in there, anyway a big argument broke out, and one of my pals (I won't say his name) stuck a glass into Bill the Bomb's Williams face. Billy was an ex-fighter and very notorious around the east end. They were the good old days, and I used to really enjoy talking to Lenny at the hippodrome, he would make me laugh, he could be a funny fucker at times, he used to grimace when he spoke about some of the punters at the club, 'Sovereign Jacks' he used to call them.

"You can spot the c***s a mile away, Joe, hands full of fucking sovereign rings… the fucking mugs," he would say.

I also saw Lenny and Johnny in action a few times, and believe me, he would sometimes give people a fair warning, but I've also seen him pick people up and throw them out the door like a rag doll. One time I remember Lenny grabbing some idiot by the throat and lifting him off the ground, the poor fella turned white as he was pushed against the wall.

I can also remember one night when it kicked off, and me and Lenny were in the office when he got the call over the walkie talkie, I ran with him upstairs, and there were about twenty fellas all fighting, one of the men fighting pulled out a tool, it was a small knife on one of the doormen, Lenny saw it, so quickly jumped over and almost punched the blokes head off, Bosch! It was over as he then squared up to the rest. Lenny had now lost his temper, and when that happens, it's like seeing a mad gorilla thrown into the middle of the crowd.

I also remember seeing Lenny on the film set of 'The Krays,' the film by the Kemp brothers. There was a boxing booth scene being filmed, and Alex had invited all his mates there to get in the movie. I was talking to John H Stracey, Jack kid berg, and Davey Lane when Lenny arrived, everyone had a good laugh that day, but I wouldn't be in the film as I didn't want to be filmed. Jack Kid Berg was funny doing his tricks, one trick he would do was shake your hand, and while he was doing it, he would remove your watch! Then ask you the time, and you would look at your empty wrist, thinking where's my fucking watch gone? Then Jack smiling would hold it out in front of you, and you would be like, how the fuck did he do that. Jack was a real character and was an ex-world champion. He moved to New York as a boy and became friends with Legs Diamond and Al Capone.

When the nineties come me, and my father was put in prison for a complete load of bollocks, the old bill fitted my father up and stitched me up.

My father's first trial ended because of jury tampering, and just before his second trial, the old bill managed to get me sentenced to nine months. During my case, where the prosecution had to give me loads of paperwork, I discovered that the old bill suspected I was something to do with the jury tampering of the first trial. They wanted me behind bars for my father's second trial.

While I was away, my father was found guilty and originally received 27 years. I was released from Belmarsh in late 1991.

My father was a double category A prisoner, so if you wanted to visit him you had to apply to the home office to be accepted on his list, Lenny applied and had to have the old bill come to his home and give them loads of ID. I always respected Lenny for going through all that so he could go and visit my father.

When Lenny was nicked for that murder charge, he was in Brixton for a while at the same time as my pal Teddy Bam Bam.

I remember being told Lenny was inside, so we got a message to some of the chaps in there to look after Len, not that he needed, looking after physically, but Teddy was pretty much running the wing, so I got a message to get Lenny some canteen stuff, tobacco and chocolates, etc.

Thankfully Len was found not guilty of murder and ended up serving nine months of an eighteen-month sentence.

After his release, we kept in touch, and the next time I saw Lenny was at my engagement party in Morden in November 1994. Lenny and Roy were both there, and I was pleased to say they both stayed apart and even shook hands. It was a great evening, and everyone enjoyed themselves, it was great seeing Lenny and Roy, both on form and both looking fit and well.

At the party, Lenny told me he had just taken over a pub called 'Guvners' with Charlie Kray, it was just off of Cambridge Heath Road, a stone's throw away from The Blind Beggar pub. He told me he had loads of business going on, so would I be interested in getting involved.

I told him I would think about it, and a week later, he called me, and I drove over the east end so have a meeting with him.

The pub was done up nice, and I met with fast Eddie Jeffries and the twins George and Andrew Wadham out of Bermondsey, we had a good meeting, and I decided to get involved.

Next to the pub was a small off-license so I put my brother in law Anthony to work and he lived in the flat above the pub.

Every day I would travel from Morden, but the business was slow; we tried to make the most of it but couldn't get the trade there. The pub was slap bang in the middle of a council estate full of Bangladeshi Muslims (who most don't drink!"

Lenny, though, used to pop in every day to see how things were going, and we would have a chat. Lenny was doing a few debt collection jobs for me at the time, so we were getting a few quid from that.

In March 1995, Ronnie Kray passed away, all of the sudden Bethnal Green went crazy, Ronnie was lying in state in the undertakers on the Bethnal Green Road where Dave Courtney had some security looking after him. We were just around the corner, so loads of people were coming onto the pub for meetings before and after visiting Ronnie.

It was sad times as Ronnie had died, but the pub became an unofficial meeting point, the place was packed out every day. It was mad around the area, and the old bill even put a few traffic coppers outside English funeral parlour as so many people were driving past and stopping just to see if they could catch a glimpse of someone.

Charlie Kray was having loads of meetings and was doing the best he could with the arrangements, the poor soul there was so much for him to do, everyone wanted to see him, and then he had the press, the tv. You name it; everyone was turning up! Like I said before, we were just around the corner, so Charlie would make his meetings at the pub, and it kind of turned into his office during this time.

With Charlie being at the pub every day, it was a natural progression that the pub was chosen to hold the wake there after the funeral.

The funeral was beyond belief; it was estimated that over a hundred thousand people had lined the streets to pay their respects to Ronnie Kray.

The whole east end of London came to a standstill.

I was in limo No.4 or 5, with Lenny McLean, Ray Winstone, Vic Dark, big Rob Davis, and Barry Fox.

The traffic was horrendous; we drove around a few streets in the east end (Vallance Road), where the coffin stopped outside a block of flats, which used to be the house the Krays grew up in. Then we drove to the church.

After the service, we got back into the limos and drove to Chingford mount cemetery for the burial. It was a good ten-mile drive to the cemetery, and I'm not kidding you; people were standing on the roadsides for the whole ten miles. It was a hot day so we had the windows down and I can remember when the traffic had to slow because of the crowds. People were looking inside the limo and recognising Lenny; they were saying "Hello Len," or you could see them saying to one another, "That's Lenny McLean."

It was a strange feeling crawling through thousands of people, and they're all looking into the limo at you, it made you feel like a film star just sitting inside it.

Lenny, however, took it all in his stride and nodded at people and said hello to the old ladies who had been waiting all day to see the procession.

Vic made me laugh when we got outside the limo as loads of people walked past saying hello to us. Vic said to me, "fucking hell, where's all the east end boys? It's all fucking south London here!"

Once all the funeral was out of the way, everyone went back to the pub, and it was so packed you couldn't move in there.

We had a bloody good drink that night, and every face you could imagine was there (apart from my father who was still in prison) the night ended with me Ray Winstone, Jamie foreman and my brother-in-law Tony upstairs in his flat drinking Jack Daniels until 7;00 AM.

Ex-model Flanagan with CharlieKray, and me and Ray Winstone in the background at the wake.

Having the wake at the pub seemed like a good idea at first, we thought it might help boost future business, but actually, it backfired on us. The weeks after the wake, the pub was like a ghost house, and people avoided it like the plague. We were wondering what the fucking hell was going on until a customer who drank at a pub across the road, The Carpenter's Arms told us that people around the area were saying stay away from there as it's a gangsters pub.

It's a shame as the pub inside was absolutely stunning! I stayed around a few more weeks, but the business just ebbed away, so reluctantly, I had to pull away.

We did have some fun times there and created some great memories. Because of the funeral, the pub became so notorious, we even had Kray autograph hunters travelling from different parts of the country, making their way, just to come to see us.

I remember one day I had just finished dropping off some stock to the off-license next door when I walked into the pub, and there was this girl she was about thirty years old and completely bloody naked, standing there playing pool! She had got the train up from Southampton and was in love with the Krays, and a few lads in the pub had got her going and told her to play pool with them nude.

I just laughed and said, what the fuck is going on here then, only for the twins to smile and say... Do I want a game next?

Anyway, I will leave it up to your imagination what happened next.

When I told Lenny I would be leaving, he was sweet with the decision and understood. We were still working on the odd debt together, so we were still in touch.

Debt collection is a funny old game; you never really know how the day will turn out! It's not like having a normal job where you go to work and get paid at the end of the week. Sometimes you go to work and you get Fuck All! As you can't get blood out of a stone.

One time made me laugh when I took Lenny on a bit of work, we had to go to a gypsy site to see someone who owed someone a few grand, I banged on the trailer and the fella inside shouted out for us to fuck off! Lenny grabbed the handle and shouted out, but got the same reply, so he punched a great hole in the caravan side. Next thing this weasel came out shouting, so we grabbed hold of him.

There was a little green outside the trailer and it had one of those grass, water sprinklers watering the grass, so I told Lenny to grab the fella and I pulled the hose out of the sprinkler and stuck it down the bloke's throat. He started coughing and his belly started to swell up, I was shouting at him, telling him we wanted our money when Lenny suddenly let him go.

"Your fucking killing him." Lenny said to me.

I was initially pissed off that Lenny let him go, but we got most of our money that day, so it ended up a good day, we got a few grand off him and on the ride home Lenny made me laugh, he said: "for fucks sake joe, I don't mind giving some mug a right-hander, but I'm not fucking drowning them!"

Another time we had a good laugh was when my good pal from Mitcham, Rod Doll asked me to set up a meeting with Lenny as he had a pal who had a big debt that needed to be collected, and they wanted to talk to him.

I went to see Rod in the morning at his pal's house and his pal decided to do a big line of cocaine before we left. It was 11 in the morning and we had arranged a meeting in a café opposite the Hippodrome nightclub in Leicester Square for one o clock.

By the time we had got there, Rod's pal had snorted about another five lines and was off his head.

We met Lenny in the café and I introduced Rod's pal, we sat down and then started to talk about the debt. Rod's pal started the conversation, but was talking a hundred miles an hour, I could see Lenny was getting the hump with this as he was grimacing and huffing and puffing and occasionally looking at me with a look like, "What the fuck have you bought me here, joe?"

Lenny asked the fella to calm down a few times, which I found the funny side off, but he was so fidgety and high he just kept rabbiting on, Lenny finally gave a long sigh and looked at me,

"What the fuck is he on?" Lenny said which made me laugh.

The fella with us just kept on and on until finally, Lenny snapped,

"ENOUGH!" He shouted out,

"Look, I'll talk to Joe about it; you're doing my fucking head in, now just go and sit over there while we talk about it." he added, raising his big arm and pointing.

Me and Rod couldn't stop laughing as Rod's mate was sent to sit in the corner.

Another fond memory I had was the time when Lenny let me stay in his caravan in St O'syphs, near Clacton on sea. I was going through a bit of a rough patch, so Lenny suggested I take the keys and go and have a few days by the coast to relax.

I accepted, and a few days later, I packed a bag and set off for Clacton.

It was a beautiful summer day and I had a convertible Escort XR3i, and drove all the way there from Tooting with the roof down and got burnt driving.

I got to the caravan park, found the caravan, put my bags inside, and then searched for something to eat. When I was out, I grabbed myself some bits and bobs, bread, milk, butter, and cheese so I could have a few snacks in the caravan.

Anyway, I parked the car close by, and as I was walking back to the caravan, one of the bags split, and two glass bottles of milk smashed on the ground.

A few people were sitting around, and I dropped the bag about ten feet from someone's door.

Bollocks! I said out loud. I gathered up what food I could save. It was a right mess, so I tried to pick some of the glass up, and then I said to the girl I was with to go to the caravan and find a brush or something to clean up the mess.

She ran off and after a few moments shouted back, she couldn't find anything, so I thought I would go and look for myself. But just as I started to walk off, someone came out of the door closest to the mess and shouted out to me

"Oi! You're not just fucking leaving that there are you?!" he shouted.

I turned and was just about to explain I was going to get a brush or something when I heard him talk again, only this time it was slightly under his breath.

"c**t! I got fucking kids in here!" he said, walking towards the mess.

"Calm your fucking self down!" I snapped back at him, now angry at being called a c**t.

We looked at each other and it was getting heated, we both started to walk towards each other when the girl I was with shouted out from Lenny's caravan that she had found something to clean it up. The rude prick suddenly stopped in his tracks.

"You with Lenny?" he said, now looking and sounding like a completely different man.

"Nah, Lenny's not here." I said

"Sorry mate, I thought you were pissed or something and throwing glass about, fuck me, sorry mate." he sighed as he started picking up the glass.

To cut a long story short, we both ended up clearing the mess up together, and later that night, we had a few lagers in the small bar nearby.

I remember telling Len about it when I came home and he laughed, "Cheeky bastard, I'll fucking tell him next time I see him." Len said with his usual sneer.

Over the years and all the times, me and Lenny spent together, we did have a few conversations about Roy, Lenny knew I loved Roy, and from our conversations, I know Lenny did respect Roy, I remember him telling me once that in another life we would probably be good mates.

I had seen the pair of them shake hands a few times and been there when they bumped into each other at various functions and parties. Once at a charity event, I even said to the pair of them,

"Why don't you two just fucking turn it in, you're both good pals of my fathers and both good men."

Roy smiled and shook Lenny's hand, and they did have a quiet word together, I never heard what was said, but it looked like they were both acknowledging one another.

If I'm honest, I think it was more Roy than Lenny holding the grudge. I know Roy calmed down quite a bit because of Lenny's friendship with my father. And over the years, I have heard my father a few times, usually on the telephone telling Roy or Lenny to turn all this cobblers in.

Personally, I have spent a lot of time with them both and I respected and loved both men, to me, both of them were family.

Lenny getting ill and the funeral.

When we first heard that Lenny was very ill, we were all in shock. He was doing so well with his book and acting. And also all the talk of his film about his life. At first, we were all asking how bad is Lenny and can he get better? When we found out it was terminal, we just couldn't believe it! This big strong giant of a man, still relatively young. (It can't be true)

Sadly, it was, and the shock I felt was shared all over London.

I saw Lenny a few months before, and he put on a brave face, but he wasn't well, it was sickening to see him fading so quick.

I kept in contact with Lenny until around two weeks of his death, but the calls became harder and harder to cope with as he was deteriorating so fast. Sometimes I would call and he was too sick to take the call. Val would ask me to call later or the next day. But even when I did speak to him, it was so hard. What the fuck do you talk about, to someone who has only weeks to live. Sometimes we would have a laugh and a joke about the old days and I would mention I saw Roy and he sends his best and Lenny would say tell him to fuck off! Then start laughing.

Other times Lenny would be in a more emotional mood and he would say he couldn't believe he got ill just when he had finally gotten out of all the shit and started to do something positive with his life. Lenny didn't like the doors, he may have found it fun when he was younger, but the conversations I had with him, he used to say things like, I can't wait to do my movie and get away from the mugs I have to deal with on the doors.

It was heart-wrenching having to listen to Lenny in so much pain, he was also scared of leaving his family behind, and he said to me on a few occasions to please keep an eye on Jamie and Kelly for him.

As I said, the calls got harder and harder, and I could hear Lenny's voice going at times.

When he did pass away, everyone who knew him because of the time he was ill had prepared themselves for the news. It doesn't make the blow any softer, but there isn't the surprise element attached to it.

Once the funeral details were available, I made sure all my crowd would be going to show their respects. There were me and Warren and Rob Davis, Barry Fox, big Lee, and Patrick. Loads more of my pals met us up at the funeral.

I was in one of the funeral cars with George and Andrew Wadham, the twins who we all worked together at the Guvners pub. The car drove through Lenny's old manor, Hoxton. I can remember looking at some of the street names, which I remembered from my childhood as my father used to live in Hoxton when he was a boy.

The funeral itself was a very respectful ceremony, it was a sad day, and I remember feeling upset for Kelly, who was the apple of her father's eye.

When he heard about the funeral, Roy Shaw didn't really know what to do. He was torn between showing his respects and possibly upsetting the family. One part of him said he should show his respects, but the other side said, could it be seen as inappropriate, could it cause a scene?

Roy spoke to my father a few times about it and in the end, my father said it would be best if Roy just sends some flowers.

Him and Lenny weren't friends, but at least Roy is showing some respect by sending a wreath.

There were many old faces at the funeral, I saw Johnny Nash there and a few of the old East End faces. Tony Lambrianou was there with Jimmy and Chris. It was a good turnout.

I can recall Tony and me having a cigarette by a shop doorway and we were saying hello to loads of people walking by, and Tony turns to me and says, "Joe, who the fuck are we going to send to collect debts now?"

Rest in Peace my friend.

Fight record of Lenny McLean

Roy Shaw	Lost	TKO 1	Croydon
Roy Shaw	Won	KO 2	Croydon
Solli Francis	Won		Finsbury
Roy Shaw	Won	KO 1	Finsbury
Cliff Field	Lost	TKO 2	Finsbury
Cliff Field	Lost	TKO 3	Finsbury
Kevin Paddock	Lost	PTS 8	Finsbury
Steve Columbo Riichards	Won		London
Ishaq Hussein	Won		London
Ron Redrup	Won		Tottenham
Johnny Waldron	Lost	KO3	Ilford
Johnny Waldron	Lost	KO 1	Streatham
Johnny Clark	Won	KO 2	Tottenham
Brian mad gypsy Bradshaw	Won	KO 1	
Man Mountain York	Won	KO 1	Essex

** I have not included the fight with George Pappy Langley where it is said Lenny was
knocked out in one round, **
I wasn't at that fight so the legitimacy is questionable.

Alex Steene

Charlie Richardson – Joe Pyle – Alex Steene

No doubt about it, Alex Steene was one of a kind! And one of the sincerest men I ever met. He was a true friend and loyal to the core.

Alex didn't come from a criminal background, but he admired a man's man, he loved the fight game and idolised my father. Apart from my father, Alex Steene would be the man I strive to live up to.

There was no pettiness with Alex. He never had time for small talk. I have spent hours, days (in his company,) and I cannot ever remember making talk for the sake of talking.

Alex Steene was very close to my father, to Alex my father was his best mate, and no one could get between them, he had friends all over London, but his best friend was Joe Pyle.

Yet everyone loved Alex. I have never heard a bad word spoken about him. He was a deep man and very generous, and he always respected people who were less fortunate than himself. It's a rare quality in a man who can show empathy without thinking about it, but that was Alex Steene. He saw the best in people, and he always gave you a chance.

He was a second father to me. He took me on holidays away with his family and took me away to boxing shows and business meetings. One day when I was at school, I got called to the headmaster's office around 1;30, where my mum was waiting for me. The headmaster wasn't happy as she had come to take me out of school early because Alex had called her and said he had a couple of spare tickets to go watch the football at Wembley that evening, but I had to get to the office by 4;30 latest. After a heated discussion I was allowed to leave early and off I went to Wembley to watch an England football game. England vs. Italy in 1979, England won 2-0 with Kevin Keegan and Trevor Booking both scoring.

When my father was in prison in the nineties, every single Sunday morning, Alex came round to drop my mother off some money. Some weeks it was £40, sometimes £200 but without fail every week for six long years, he would make sure something was given to her.

That is so unheard of in today's world. I have seen people drop off a few quid to people's families, but only Alex have I ever seen, do it every week without fail right up until the day his friend walked out the gate.

Alex was a different class! He really was a special gift to this world.

Alex Steene had been around the faces for years. Ever since he came down to London in the late forties and set up shop in the capital, he was great friends with Bert Battles Rossi, Albert Dimes, and Billy Hill. He had known my father from the early sixties and was good friends with the twins and Charlie.

People often say they visited the Kray twins in prison, but no one looked after the twins like Alex did, he would visit Ronnie in Broadmoor at least once a week, and he did that for years and was always helping them out financially. Ronnie Kray was another who loved Alex, and he told me on numerous occasions what a wonderful man he was.

Alex would also look after Violet Kray if and when he had the opportunity. Every year because of his ticket business, he always managed to secure himself a box at the annual Royal Command Performance, which was held at places like the Palladium or Drury lane and was always attended by her majesty, the queen or one of the senior royals.

On this specific night in 1980, it was held at the London Palladium. Alex had someone collect Violet Kray and brought her to the event. We were in a box directly above the Queen Mother and Prince Charles.

I was seated next to Violet, and there were Alex and his wife Anna, and boxers John Conteh and Tommy Farr with us. It was a fantastic event with some stellar performances by Lionel Blair, Una subs, Arthur Askey, Chesnie Allen, Arthur English, Bruce Forsyth, Sheena Easton, Rowan Atkinson, Peggy Lee, Sammy Davis Junior, Danny Kaye, Aretha Franklin, Larry Hagman (JR) and then right at the end a very special guest was presented, I remember the crowd went absolutely crazy as James Cagney walked onto the stage and bowed to the royal family.

Alex Steene's ticket company was called 'Obtainables,' and he had contacts all over the country who would sell him tickets which he sold on again with a mark-up on top. His office was on Panton street, just off the Haymarket and a stone's throw away from Trafalgar and Leicester square.

It was a good business in those days, and Alex was a pioneer in the ticket game industry, long before the internet came into fruition and companies like Stubhub and Via Gogo.

1981 Royal Command performance at Drury Lane, Joe Pyle Jnr, Billy Wells, Alex & Anna Steene, Jackie & Greg Steene.

His office was always full of old faces, it was more like a social club than an actual office, I can remember going there as a young boy, and people like the old spiv Mikey Connors (who got cut to pieces by Ronnie Kray) was always there doing little errands for Alex.

Alex liked having people around him, and he always looked after them financially, he had Davey Lane, old boxer Alec Buxton and amateur star Billy Wells working for him, but to be honest, they were more like tea makers and his pals than employees, but never the less, Alex had them around him and made sure they always had a wage at the end of the week.

He truly had a heart of gold did Alex and a moral compass I have never seen matched.

Once someone was helping Alex out with the office expenses (incomes and outgoings etc.), this fella pulled Alex to one side and said his outgoings were far too high, and he had to think about letting some of the staff go or he could be looking at going bust! Alex hit the roof! "I will not do that!" he said, rising to his feet. "This is their job. It is all that they have; I can't fire a man for doing nothing wrong!" he added sternly.

"But Mr Steen, if you don't cut some of your overheads, then you could end up losing the business."

"Then I'll lose the business! I'll lose everything before taking a man's job from him!"

That was Alex! Always thinking of others before himself. We all need money to live, but money was never his master.

Former world champion Jack Kid berg was another, who was always there at the office, Alex would often take Jack with him to boxing shows and concerts. I remember another old face: 'Jewish Woofy'; he was a proper old ducker and diver, originally out the east end but now a familiar face in the coffee shops in Greek and Dean street in Soho.

Woofy would sit for hours telling me about the old days and all the old Jewish villains that used to frequent Soho. He also used to be a minder for Jack Spot, and he told me loads of old stories of some of the things they would get up to. Woofy would always make me laugh, he always had a trick up his sleeve and used to grab my arm and say 'Joeboy …. East End boys and South London boys … fuck all the rest!"

When I turned sixteen, I started my first job with Alex; I ran around London to pick up tickets and drop them off to places.

It was an easy job really; the office would get a call from someone, usually a foreigner at a hotel in London, or one of the many concierges he had straightened up.

My job would be to jump on the tube or bus, go somewhere like the Palladium or another ticket office, purchase the tickets at cost price, and then drop them off to the customer at an inflated price.

I enjoyed the job and working with me at the time was a young actor called Ray Winstone, a few years earlier Ray been the main actor in the film - Scum, and had found himself out of work so through my father he ended up working with

Alex doing the same job as me. Me and Ray would have a right laugh; we would do our jobs and then go for a few pints in Covent Garden or Mayfair.
They were really good days, and I made some fantastic contacts with all the hotel concierges. These contacts earned me good money years later when I would get commissions for sending punters to the hostess clubs in the west end.

There was a funny story from those days when I had to go away for a bit, and I had this old Citroen Pallas car when I came home, my car was missing off the drive, so I walked in and asked my mum where my car was.
"Your dad gave it away," she replied.
"What you mean? Who did he give it away to? That was my bloody car!"
"He gave it away to that bloody actor, Ray!" answered my mum.
"Ray Winstone."
"Yeah, that's him."
"Bloody cheek, he gave Ray, my car."
"I told him not to, Joey, but you know what he is like, he said Ray didn't have a car, so he gave him yours."
"Mum, dad owns a bloody car showroom! He has over a hundred motors on his site."
"I don't know; you sort it out with him."
So Ray Winstone had my old Citroen, and I had a right argument with my father, but it worked out well as a few days later, I was sent down to Charlie Richardson's car site in New Cross where I picked up a Ford Cortina MK4.

Alex Steene was always involved in boxing in some shape or another; he would always be ringside at all the London shows and would take me along with him where we would sit down next some of the old characters like former middleweight champion Terry Downes. Terry was mad as a hatter; he would sit ringside smoking big cigars endlessly and take the constant piss out of the boxers, he would shout out all the time calling them wankers or mugs.
Alex had contacts all over the world in boxing.
One of his great pals was Angelo Dundee, and his brother Chris, Angelo was Muhammed Ali's trainer and manager. He was also great friends with Floyd Patterson.
Boxing was his big love, and his love for the boxing world also influenced his generosity, he funded the Leeds Ex-Boxers association and became their president, and he also held regular charity events for the London ex-Boxers Association (LEBA) and always helped them out money-wise.
Alex was such a regular at all the meetings, and boxing shows in London that they painted his face in the famous Muriel at the Thomas a Becket Gym in the Old Kent Road.
When Alex suddenly passed away, it really hit my father hard. I had never seen him so choked up as when he heard about Alex. I remember him taking a telephone call and just going silent. He said a few words and then hung up and

walked over to my mother. He told her that Alex had died and she burst into tears, and then my father just walked off by himself into the back garden.

That day I truly believe my father lost a piece of himself, he was not his usual self for days on end. On the day of the funeral, he was asked by Alex's family if he could give a eulogy and say a few words about his special friend.

The church was packed, and my father rose slowly to the front where he paused for a moment, he cleared his throat and started to speak, but he barely said three words until his voice broke. He raised his hand to his face and looked at Alex's wife, Anna, and his son Greg and apologised to them.

"I'm sorry, I just can't do this." he said barely managing to get his words out before walking back to his seat, looking disappointed with himself, I remember noticing some people tap his arm as he walked back to me.

"it's alright, Joe," someone said to him.

My dad sat down and bit his lip hard trying to compose himself. I had never ever seen my father so emotional or broken up.

That was the love my father had for Alex, he loved the man, and it was likewise with Alex to my father.

There are not too many times in life where you meet or even be friends with a truly exceptional man, if you were lucky enough to have Alex Steene in your life, then you were truly blessed.

I just cannot compliment him enough; he was the pinnacle of a man's man! There was no pettiness in him, and he only ever cared about his family and friends, everything he did in his life was for them.

I have never heard him swear or talk ill once about women, children or elders, he was a champion for the man who tries, and he would always go out of his way to help someone not so fortunate as himself.

Rest in peace Alex, you really were - the best of the best.

Below is from Alex's son, Greg

Alex was born in Leeds Yorkshire and came to London in the late 1940s after serving in the Royal Marines and Royal Navy during the war. In 1943 in the Royal Marines he took part in the mini invasion of Dieppe and was one of the lucky ones to get back to England when so many of his mates were killed or captured.

In 1944 he was part of the special services, a forerunner of the SAS when he took part in the D Day landings. A month later he was wounded at the battle of Caen and had to be brought back to England to recover.

When he was deemed recovered after several months he was told that he was not fit enough again for front line duty so rather than be medically discharged he begged to be transferred to the Royal Navy which was accepted and where he saw out the rest of the war manning Guns on a free Dutch armed merchant ship.

Some merchant vessels had Lewis guns attached to them and small compliments of royal naval crews to Mann them which Alex was doing.

Early in 1945 During a German aircraft attack on his convoy he helped bring down an enemy aircraft and was later awarded the Queen Willamina medal by Holland for bravery.

After the war he made a name for himself in fairgrounds in Skegness and was made deputy manager by the fairgrounds boss. He could have been very successful and was promised that he would eventually be the boss if he had stayed in Skegness However the lure for him of coming to London was too great.

When he arrived he was one of the first people to recognise the money making potential of the secondary ticket market and he recruited about 20 ex wartime servicemen to work for him. He and his men was buying up and reselling tickets for hit shows in London.

He wanted tough men who he could rely on and who would not be afraid of police and would be resourceful.

He cemented his reputation during the mid-1950s when he was working outside the theatre royal Drury lane when the mega hit show My Fair Lady was selling out every night. Three plainclothes police officers tried to jump him but Alex who was a good amateur boxer before he joined the Royal Marines took all three on. He knocked all three unconscious one after the other as they grappled with him right outside the Theatre Royal in front of hundreds of witnesses. He was quickly arrested after more police arrived from the nearby Bow Street police station.

Upon being arrested he faced many charges. Including GBH, resisting arrest, assaulting police officers etc.

While on remand he asked his Solicitor how he saw the case and the brief told him that he would be lucky if he only got 7 years. My dad was furious and sacked him on the spot and told the authorities that he was now going to defend himself. This he did after researching many law books.

At his trial he was able to prove that the 3 coppers had not identified themselves properly as police officers, their argument was that Alex knew each of them after arresting him several times before. He said he did not know them or who they were and thought they were three muggers trying rob and attack him.

Also the police notes were added after the event and all police officers were shown to be lying one way or another in court. Add to that the judge took into account my Alex good war record he was found not guilty and allowed to go home immediately.

Of course he was a marked man after that but he did not resist arrest again. Shortly after this Alex met up with the Kray twins and they liked him because he was strong and fearless. Alex had killed many Germans during the war. They liked Alex a lot and respected him and Alex worked with them on many things and Alex brought his own people in too

One time when I was a kid my dad took me shopping for new clothes in Brixton. He parked the car in a Brixton backstreet but then two young fit looking mixed race men came out and said he could not park in front of their house and when a few of their friends came over they were abusive to Alex and said they would smash our car up if we left it there.

Alex kept cool and told them it's parked and staying there. When we went into Brixton my dad was fuming. He bought me the pair of trousers I wanted but he also went to Woolworths and bought a small short handle club hammer.

I knew what he was planning as I was only a kid I asked him to call the twins for support but he refused saying he did not need any help and would sort it himself.

When we got back to the car it was undamaged and I expected my dad to get into the car and just drive off instead he knocked on the door. When one of the abusive young men opened the door Alex smashed him in the face with the hammer knocking him out cold and my dad charged in over the man's body. I could see the other man who was the brother of the unconscious one at the door running up the passage way to try to fight my dad. Alex battered him with his fists first then gave him a blow of the hammer on the man's head knocking him cold as well.

As we left I was a little surprised that Alex did not appear to be in any hurry though he made me promise not to say anything to my Mum. It turned out later that these two were enforcers connected with a well-known south London crime gang but after enquires with their boss no one wanted to take the matter further and it was dropped.

Greg Steene.

Joe Pyle

"When you're talking about hard men, I'm talking about Lenny McLean, Roy Shaw, Joey Pyle, they could be wicked bastards."
(Nosher Powell – Interview)

Joe Pyle – Roy Shaw – Roberto Duran – Freddie Foreman

The ultimate hard bastards (The truth about the toughest men in the world)_
by Kate Kray

Joey Pyle is the archetypal gangster, like the godfather, Don Corleone. He wouldn't look out of place in movies like the long good Friday or Goodfellas, Joey has ruled the roost in the underworld for more than four decades. He is the original 'Teflon don'- nothing sticks.

Each and every man I interviewed for this book had either known or heard of Joey Pyle. He is the most respected of them all. I've never heard anyone say a bad word about him, whether that's fear or admiration, I'm really not sure, either way, he's held in the highest esteem by everyone.

The beauty of Joey Pyle is that he has the capability of mixing in any circles, whether it be royalty, celebrities' MP's or murderers. He's at ease with them all. Maybe it's this quality that has given him the longevity in the underworld. He is a man of few words, a shrewd businessman, someone you'd be reluctant to approach without an introduction. His very size and presence is enough to make you stand back.

His hair is black, slicked back with grey around the sides, making him appear distinguished. Remove his dark sunglasses and they reveal twinkling blue eyes that are soft around women and cold as ice to men.

He has the ability to hold everyone at arm's length and you're only in Joe's company if you're invited. No problem is too big for joe and he can minimalise any problem with just a word or a wave of his hand. Wherever he goes he is well respected, but only a fool would take his kindness as a weakness.

Above was written by Kate Kray

'Unlicensed' was a cheeky term created by the press and the British Boxing Board of Control. It basically means not affiliated to them.

The term unlicensed makes it sound illegal, but it's not illegal to stage a boxing fight as long as there are rounds and a referee.'

Joe Pyle

That statement above completely changed the industry of boxing in the UK. Joe Pyle had always been a rebel if you tell him something cannot be done then that was like showing a red flag to a bull.

He was born in 1935, just before the second world war, and by the time he was supposed to be in school, he was living Kings Cross, a part of London which was being bombed every night by the German air force.

For weeks on end, areas like Kings Cross in London was bombarded by hundreds of bombs. The whole area was decimated.

In today's day and age when it starts to get dark, kids go up to their rooms and turn the tv on or Xbox, in my father's time they waited for the sound of the siren and then legged it to the nearest underground train station and hid from the carnage that was about to happen above their heads.

Every night for weeks on end, they huddled together, not knowing if their home would still be in one piece when they came out.

What kind of men did this meld? What did it do to a young boys' mind? These boys of war-torn London grew into men who have become notorious, the Krays, the Richardson's, The Nash family, Freddie Foreman, Frasers, the Great Train Robbers.

All of the above had the same things in common, rebellious, loyal, courageous, and old school manners.

From a very early age, my father always had a passion for boxing. His father's twin brother Joe was a boxer, and my father took up boxing at Tiverton and Preedy athletics and boxing club in Penton Street, North London.

When my father moved to Carshalton after the war, he joined the local amateur boxing club, Rosehill. One of the club's founders was Billy English, the father of my friend and business partner Ricky English.

While boxing for Rosehill, my father got to the quarter-finals of the All England championships and also got himself awarded 'the most stylish boxer in Surrey.'

When he turned eighteen, everything stopped to make way for national service. He signed up to do a physical training instructor course, thinking it would help keep his fitness going but soon found out the class had a lot of negative stuff attached to it and he found himself becoming uninterested,

Then one day, the corps wanted to know if they had any boxers, so my father put his hand up, which resulted in him being transferred to Sandhurst as an instructor, training officer cadets.

This was much more like it as he never had much of the army duties to do; it was just training all day long, boxing and teaching boxing. He was part of the southern command team, fighting at middleweight. The main man on the team was a certain heavyweight called Henry Cooper, his twin brother George was also on the team.

They were one of the best boxing teams in the army. My father loved it, fought many times, and became the middleweight army champion.

But typical for my father, he then got himself into a bit of bother when he and a kid called Harris used to take girls out on the town. They didn't have cars, so they used to (borrow) the ones belonging to the officers. They'd take a different car each week and then bring it back at the end of the night, and no one ever seemed to notice. But then one day they borrowed a car which belonged to a Brigadier, they were on their way back when they were spotted, so they dumped the car and legged it, but was caught in hiding in an alleyway.

The army decided to prosecute my father in the criminal courts, rather than give him a court-martial. He ended up being sent to borstal.

When he was released, he carried on with his boxing career and ended up going off to fight on the boxing booths. My father loved the booths, and life was a bit crazy traveling around the country. Still, he was getting fitter and stronger by the day until he thought he was ready to turn professional, which was his dream as a kid.

He lost his first professional fight, which was a big shock, but it did little to put him off his chosen career. It only made him more determined. He stepped up his training routine, dedicated himself entirely to the game, and over the next couple of years, he won his next 23 professional fights on the row.

My father was an outstanding professional boxer.

In today's times, you would be a champion if you went 23 fights unbeaten. Kids today are fighting for British titles after 12 to 15 fights.

It's funny thinking of my father promoting the shows; he had a much better boxing background than Roy or Lenny combined.

It is well documented that my father's life took a different route from the one intended, boxing. But the love for the sport never left him.

My father and Roy Shaw were friends for a long time before the infamous Donny the Bull Adams fight. They went back years, and Roy always had respect for my father, he told me on more than one occasion that my father was without a doubt his best friend. When Roy was once interviewed and asked about the Kray twins, this is what he said about my father,

Joey Pyle and the Nashes and also the Richardson's. The twins certainly weren't any more powerful than them. In prison, Frankie Fraser was very, very respected. In those days everyone feared Frank don't worry about that, he was the man. Joey Pyle, though has worked with the lot. Right back to Jack Spot, Billy Hill, and Albert Dimes through to the twins, Nashes and Richardsons, Bindon right through to today's faces. Even the American mafia! Joe has seen the lot.

When I think back into my past and my life, I remember Roy always being a part of it, he was like my father's brother, always with him, and with Johnny Nash, the three of them were a potent combination.

All three of them had a presence, and all of them knew how to look after themselves. Back in the 60s, my father and Johnny were almost joined at the hip. They would often pop into the Grave Maurice pub to see the Krays because they had shared business interests. Sometimes Roy would be with them, and when those three walked in, into the Krays and all the hangers-on, you would be a fool not to notice the real strength had just walked into the pub. It's no secret that Johnny Nash never had any time for the twins, he worked with them, but he didn't like all the flash stuff. Johnny was quiet, he did what he had to do and stayed out of the limelight, and all the glitz and arseholes surrounding the twins would drive him mad. Johnny once told me, "Everywhere they went, the twins were always ten-fifteen mob-handed! They surrounded themselves with these idiots who would jump if asked. me and your dad used to laugh at it. It was like something out of a Cagney film!"

Roy was always just a phone call away from us, sometimes my father and Roy might not see each other for a few months, but when they were together, you could feel and sense the bond they shared. No one could get between them. When Roy and my dad walked into a room, the whole fucking room took notice!

A couple of months ago, I saw a documentary about Albert Reading, saying my father sent Roy Shaw down to his two bob pub in Canning Town to put the arm on him. (Protection rackets)

What a complete load of bollocks!

Firstly, that's not how may father acted and secondly there must be thousands of pubs and clubs in London so why the fuck would he choose to go all the way to Canning Town to collect a pension from a small pisshole of a pub.

Reading then says he done Roy and told Pyle to fuck off!

Again, cobblers! He is living in fantasy land, and it's not a coincidence he says this happened when my father and Roy both passed away. He had enough opportunity to say it when they were both alive, he didn't! I wonder why??

When Roy came out of prison in the seventies, it was my father who was there for him, together with Alex they put a few quid in his pocket and got him a car to run about in. Roy was in good physical shape, and I've heard he would have liked to go back into the professional boxing game, but because of his age, and criminal record, he wouldn't have got a license. The British Boxing Board of Control (BBBofC) governs boxing in the UK and has held say over the sport in this country for decades.

License restrictions have become a lot more relaxed in recent years, but in the seventies, you had almost no chance of getting a BBBofC license if you had any criminal record or were over 30 years of age.

I was only a young kid back then, but I used to often go with my father to his car site in Peckham, I loved it there, it was just around the corner from the Thomas a Becket pub and my uncles Den and Ted were always there, and Roy would always be about.

When Roy started doing a bit of fighting at the fairgrounds and country fayres, I can remember my father asking him one day what the fuck he was doing. Why was he fighting for a few hundred quid in these backstreet alleys? Mugging himself off, as my dad put it.

But Roy had been getting quite a name for himself on the bare-knuckle circuit, and he had got himself into a proposed fight with Donny The Bull Adams, who went by the name the 'King of Gypsies.'

We have all read what happened next, where that fight initially to be fought in a field ended up being staged under a packed circus tent in a field in Windsor. This fight started a generation and created what we know as unlicensed boxing.

It was second nature for my father to spot an opportunity to earn money and common sense to market the fight, sell tickets, and get in on the side betting action. He came from a professional boxing background where fights were promoted at venues, not car parks, and you had to pay to see them.

When he saw the interest that the fight was generating, it was natural for him to monetise it, and turn it into an event.

Alex Steene had the office and ticket connections, so they had the perfect platform between the three of them.

Alex and my father also used their media connections to pump up as much publicity as possible. Roy was getting more paper space than British professional champions. Putting shows on isn't as easy as people think, and over the years, there have plenty of people who got burned thinking it would all just fall into place. It doesn't! You have to have a few quid behind you, a good business brain, plus a fair bit of bottle. Shit happens, and it WILL happen, you have to be able to adapt and adapt quickly, or you will fall flat on your face.

Getting the media exposure was a very clever move by my father and Alex. Believe it or not, it was the British Boxing Board of Control who started all the publicity by releasing a statement saying the fight was nothing to do with them. They made it sound sinister, calling it an 'unlicensed event,' the media lapped it up, they had never heard of unlicensed boxing, now they were intrigued and wanted to know more.

It ignited the public's appetite with the names Roy Pretty Shaw against the King of the Gypsies - Donny The Bull Adams. Indirectly, the board had started an avalanche that made everyone want to know more; even the TV came knocking! It was only a few years since the Krays were put away for life. The leading voice of boxing in this country said there is an underground, unlicensed boxing event, led by gangs associated with the Krays. (It couldn't if you tried, be more attractive to the press!)

The BBBoC helped create it! And not being slow off the mark, my father and Alex Steene took full advantage of the can of worms they had opened.
The boxing board only have themselves to blame; the term they used 'Unlicensed' made everything sound illegal. Under the table stuff!
If they had used the word -Unsanctioned, things might have turned out very different, but when they said - Unlicensed, the press stood up and asked, WHAT? What is that?

Take this book, for example ..... If I named it **'UNSANCTIONED'** would it have the same effect as **'UNLICENSED!'**

With all the publicity created, it became a bloody good business! If you act quickly, publicity means pound notes. Challenges were coming in thick and fast, and the side money was getting bigger with every new challenge.
The boxing board just didn't learn from their mistakes, they dropped the ball when they called it unlicensed, but they wouldn't let it rest, they carried on condemning it. They couldn't help themselves adding fuel to the fire!
Once the business model was working, there was a lot of money being made. Roy Shaw became a millionaire from his winnings after he invested wisely in land and property.

Frank Warren went onto become the most successful professional boxing promoter the UK has ever known. He has promoted hundreds of champions and worked with every known boxing celebrity/personality in the business.

Alex Steene's son Greg also took out his professional boxing promoters' license and steered numerous champions' careers.

My father always kept in touch with the boxing, but after Roy, not in a business way, he helped me when I needed it and made a few good introductions, but he went off doing his own thing. My father was never one to let the moss grow under his feet.
They were good times and made a lot of lives for lots of people ..... books, films, money, all happened because of the actions of these men.

Ronnie Kray – Alex Steene and my father who was best man at Ron's first wedding to Elaine in Broadmoor.

(There was a funny story to this as Ron wouldn't smile at first, until my dad started winding him up and singing – Ding Dong the bells are ringing! Then Ronnie began laughing and getting all excited."

I will end this chapter on my father with a few words from Roy Shaw

As boxing promoters go, Joey Pyle is the best, he is a silver-tongued, charismatic, dangerous fucker. He has the ability to hold everyone at arm's length, and you're only in Joey's company if invited. He's a good friend but a bad enemy. No problem is too big for Joey and he has the ability to minimise and problem with just a word or a wave of his hand. In fact, I've never heard anyone say a bad word about Joey Pyle, wherever he goes he is well respected, but only a fool would take his kindness as weakness.
Roy Shaw.

Other men around at the time

Many other people were helping out at the shows, some well-known and some lesser well-known faces, but My father and Alex had an excellent team around them, some of whom deserve mention in the book.

Nosher Powell

Nosher Powell was very well known face around London in the 60s and 70s. He had done a bit of everything, doorman, actor, stuntman, boxer, publican.

He knew everyone from his days on the doors around the West end, the Krays, Nashes, Richardsons, Regans, Knights, you name them, and Nosher knew them.

He was even a minder to superstars like Frank Sinatra and Sammy Davis Junior, even the iconic John Wayne… and also starred in a dozen bond movies.

He was a decent fighter, and he knew my father going back years from the boxing game. Nosher was always around the gyms, especially the Thomas a Becket where he used to spar all the great fighters for boxing manager Jack Solomon and over the years, he sparred with Ali, Frazier, Jersey Joe Walcott, and even the Great Joe Louis.

When Roy started training at 'The Becket,' Nosher was there with boxing coach, Danny Holland, and he started to help out with Roy's training.

One thing led to another, and he then ended up being the Master of ceremonies (MC) at the boxing events, anyone who knew Nosher, knew he had this big booming voice!

A cockney accent spoke through his nose, which sometimes had the effect of making him sound muffled. You had to listen hard to understand him, but he had that showman quality about him, plus he could bring in his showbiz friends from his phone book full of celebrities.

Years later, I had him working for me doing a charity auction at a boxing show in Knightsbridge. The sound microphone we had, wasn't the best in the world, and with his deep cockney muffled accent, no one could understand a fucking word he was saying!

Nosher was up in the ring in all his glory, talking to the crowd...

"Ere we ave a mummid arli signed smudge. naa dart me off at undred quid!" he said to a baffled crowd scratching their heads. "What's he saying!" people are shouting out. "Is he fucking pissed?" another shouted.

It was funny, but the mike had too much bass on it, and that with his deep voice, it was never going to work, and sorry to say I pulled Nosher off the auction after a couple of items and got someone else up there to do it.

He was a good sport about it, he saw the funny side of it, and I gave him his wage for the job.

Nosher always had good things to say about my father. I remember him telling me once when he was on the door at Ziggis in Streatham that my father was, in his words, "A naughty bastard," back in the 60s.

He was the head doorman at Ziggis for the owner Tony Chaplin, and back in those days (the rave days and the M25 parties), it was a great club and the place to be on a Friday night, especially in South London. It was the days of acid house, and most of the people in there were off their tits on Ecstasy. But there were still a few local rivalries simmering, so the door team, even though everyone was high as kites, still had to have their wits about them. There were my crowd, the Rosehill and Carshalton boys, the Roundshaw estate boys, the Sutton Boys, Croydon, Mitcham and Tooting boys. We were all little firms, and we all had a history of fighting amongst each other.

Nosher also had a pub on Garret Lane, just behind the Wimbledon dog track. Id pop in there from time to time and have half a lager with him. I liked talking to him; he had a very colourful life and always had a story about some celebrity or villain.

One funny story was when we were at Zigis back in the day, and Nosher had been in an argument with a couple of my mates and slung them out! I wasn't happy, so I pulled him to one side and asked what happened. Apparently, he caught them smoking a joint. I said to him, everyone in the club is smoking a fucking a joint!

Nosher, though, wasn't listening to me as my mates gave him a bit of lip when he was slinging them out. I was half-drunk and in a bit of bad mood myself, so while we were talking, I reached into my pocket, and when he wasn't looking, I crushed two ecstasy tablets into his drink.

I'm not proud of what I did, but I was a lot younger then and much more reckless. About thirty minutes after I spiked his drink, Nosher was carried out the club by and ambulance - tripping his head off.' He was screaming out as he didn't know where he was.

He was okay, though, and years later, he would joke with me about it, "How the fucking hell do people take those pills? It was horrible, why would you pay money to feel like that?!"

Terry Marsh

Terry was a very good pal of my fathers and lived around the corner from him in Morden surrey. In the 70s, he was always around our house, and I looked at Terry as a second father. I was a kid at the time, but he was always taking me out like swimming and stuff. When my father was in prison, he sort of filled the gap for me, always being there if needed. Sadly. In June 1976, Terry was stabbed and killed when he got into an argument with his friend, mad Ronnie Fryer. That was a very sad time, and I remember my parents being very upset over it. Mad Ronnie was also my dad's pal and was a dangerous bastard back in those days, who many people feared. Ronnie, though adored my dad, he was fixated on him, and it was only my father who could tell him what to do. I think he was jealous of the friendship Terry had with my father.

When Terry was murdered, my father was abroad, but he rushed back as soon as he heard the news. Mad Ronnie went into hiding, but gave himself up after a few days and was remanded in Brixton charged with murder. While awaiting trial, he was found dead in his cell after being poisoned.

Peter Brayham

Peter was another good friend of my father. They grew up together around Morden and Rosehill, and Peter was very much a part of my dad's gang in those early days of the 50s. They were all young boys getting up to mischief, but Peter got out the 'game' he became a stuntman and was one of the most successful stuntmen in the UK. He was a technical advisor for a few bond movies and was always in TV series like The Sweeney and all those other period shows. Peter was usually the one driving the getaway car or being shot and falling down a flight of stairs. Even though Peter and my father went separate ways, their friendship didn't. They remained good friends right up to the times of their deaths.

Peter was like a general manager at the Roy fights; he was someone my father could trust. He was reliable and a good man to have on your side.

Greg Steene

Greg is a few years older than me and is Alex's son, we both carried the union jack flag into the ring when Roy beat Ron stander. Greg was like his father's right-hand man back in the days, and he was at all the boxing fights. He has a mind like an encyclopedia regarding the fights.

In the early 80s, he took out his professional boxing promoter's license and promoted shows and managing fighters ever since. Greg has managed and promoted countless champions, including - World, European, and British. Even to this day, me and Greg still work together in the boxing game.

When Dennies Andries fought Thomas Hearns in Detroit - USA, Greg was Andries manager and was in the corner. After the fight, he gave me his trainers top, which I still have today, and it still has blood on it from the fight.

THE MEN   THE FIGHTS   THE HISTORY

THE GUV'NOR
TITLE

#1. Best Seller
JOSEPH ARNIE PYLE
UNLICENSED
WHO'S THE GUV'NOR

CHAPTER 6
THE GUVNOR TITLE

The Guv'nor title.
(Roy Shaw / Lenny Mclean)

Now let me explain in this chapter the legendary belt that has caused so much conflict and debate. It has baffled me over the years how so many people are so mistaken.

Some people say the belt belongs to Roy, and some say it belongs to Lenny. But both of those comments are wrong!

The Guv'nor title was (our) belt, created as a tribute belt (to) Roy and Lenny in the early 2000s.

In this chapter, I hope to clear this up once and for all. I will try to be as thorough as I can in describing how this title began and what it means.

First and foremost, the label of being the (Guv'nor) is a terminology used in London, which simply means being the top man, the best fighter, or the boss. It's funny, but time and time again, I have had so many conversations with people who just don't seem to get it!

I am not talking derogatorily here, but it's mostly those north of Watford, who *get confused* about the name.

Let's just say, for example, Lenny McLean was from Liverpool?

When he beat Roy Shaw in the third fight and addressed the crowd, Instead of shouting out 'WHO'S THE GUV'NOR." (London - Saying)
He would have shouted out.
"WHO'S THE COCK!!" (Liverpool - saying)
Now, how would that have sounded? Or Norman Buckland screaming everywhere, "WHO'S THE FUCKING COCK!"
So The Guv'nor is a London saying, but in some parts of the country, it is also used in a similar fashion.
Another thing to get straight is, neither Lenny McLean nor Roy Shaw boxed for a title or a championship belt named the 'Guvnor title!'
They boxed for,

'The unofficial heavyweight championship of Great Britain' or the NBC British heavyweight title.

There was no Guv'nor title or (Guv'nor belt,) and when Lenny shouted out the ring, he was shouting a cockney term for who is the best!
It baffles at times, and now I hear stupid stories about Roy Shaw handing down his Guv'nor belt.... Its fantasy and makes me laugh at the lengths people go to trying to get credibility. What fucking Guv'nor Belt?
All these fantastic stories are all made up, and they're all bollocks!

If the term '*being the Guvnor*' was a title … then it would have been handed to Cliff Field when he beat Lenny after the Roy Shaw fight.

The original Roy Shaw documentary called *The Guvnor* by David Vaughn, it has a scene where my father's pal Micky Savage says a toast.
He toasts Roy by saying 'To the Guv'nor.'
It's the scene where my father, Alex Steene, and Roy Shaw are watching an amateur boxing show at the Cats Whiskers club in Streatham.
What Mick was saying is a term of endearment or compliment, Mick never said to the Guvnor title holder!!
In the same documentary, you can also see Lenny using the same words to, 'Be the Guvnor,' he never said I want to win the title, but what he was really saying is… I'll be Roy Shaw's Guvnor!
It's like someone saying, 'Wait until fight night, you'll see who the winner is.'
But a Londoner would say the following,
'Wait until fight night; you'll see who the guvnor is.'

Ronnie Kray said the following to the American mafia at a meeting in the 60s.
"The way it works is this, in America, you're the guvnors but over here, we're the fucking guvnors and were running the show Right!"

Another thing to consider is that both fighters once they retired went on to publish bestselling books. Before their life story books came out, there was nowhere near the praise as there is today.

And I'm not disrespectful to either man, but it was the **three** fights against each other, which cemented their legacies.

Those three fights between Roy Shaw and Lenny McLean were what, really made them.

Take away those three fights, and both men's boxing records were hardly spectacular. Both are infamous from those fights, but what you have to remember is at the time of those epic battles, this kind of boxing (Unlicensed) was brand new!

It was so different from what the public had been used to that it created a real underground feel, it was naughty, gritty, edgy, fights for the fella down the booza. It was even romantic for fuck's sake! It struck a nerve in every man who had testosterone flowing through his body.

Until these fights started, if you wanted to go and see a boxing fight, you had to go to the professional shows. At this time, the British champions were men like Joe Bugner, Danny McAlinden, Richard Dunn, and Bunny Johnson.

Not to sound harsh, but boxers who hardly got the blood flowing!

Roy Shaw and Lenny McLean came to the ring, already boasting big reputations for fighting. The men on the street knew who they were, and locals feared them. All of a sudden, there was a platform for them to fight each other.

Somewhere to go with your mates, have a bet, get pissed, and see two well-known men punch the *fuck* out of each other.

It was the talk of the town! Nothing like this had ever happened before.

There have always been local tough guys squaring off and bare-knuckle fighting at places like fairground, Fayres, car parks and fields, but this was different.

Fight posters were appearing all over London. There wasn't just one fight; it was a full evening of fights. (Just like the prfessionals)

Celebrities from the acting and music worlds were attending at ringside. There was music, and topless ring cards girls.

It was an event, the place to be, and the tickets sold like hotcakes.

With everything that was going on, it was inevitable that the national press wanted a piece of it. They came along and fell in love with these 'old fashioned' fighting men with names like, Pretty Boy Shaw, Donny The bull and Mad dog Mullins! They ran with these stories because it garnered interest with the public, Unlicensed boxing and, being the (Underground) Guvnor of London was a sure fire headline grabber.

WALLOP! WHO'S A PRETTY BOY THEN!

The much heralded punch up to decide the Guvnor of London was over in seconds last night.

That was the headline in the national press the day after Roy Shaw and Donny Adams. It didn't say 'punch up to decide the Guvnor title' it was the Guvnor of London.

In a way, it's a bit like saying you're the pride of London. Chelsea, Arsenal, Spurs, the Hammers, all say they are the 'pride of London,' but there has never been a trophy.

So I hope that clears up the so-called Guv'nor title...... as regards the early fights of the 70s and 80s.

And to reiterate the point,

THERE WAS NEVER A **GUVNOR TITLE OR BELT** THAT LENNY OR ROY BOXED FOR!

The Guv'nor Title
The Fights after Roy and Lenny

So let's now explain where the Guvnor title actually originated.
It was in the early 2000s me, and Ricky English started promoting unlicensed shows at Caesars in Streatham under the promotional umbrella of MeanMachine Promotions and Junction 5.
We also created a sanctioning organisation called 'The English Boxing Federation. (EBF) '

After a few shows, we asked Roy Shaw for his blessing to create a belt in his honour, and we founded a belt called the (EBF - Roy Shaw championship belt) this belt was available in all divisions, i.e., Heavyweight, Middleweight, and Welterweight, etc.
We also created a belt called the Joe Pyle championship, and as Roy and my father were always at the shows, it was customary to get them into the ring to present the belt to the winner.
All our championship fights were originally for EBF belts.
The tag of the *Guv'nor title* just evolved; it evolved once we started to stage regular shows. The history of my family promoting Roy and Lenny is my heritage, I even called my promotions company (MeanMachine) in honour of Roy Shaw's nickname (Mean Machine)

As My father and Roy were always at the shows, we started announcing the main events as a fight to see who the Guv'nor was!' We even had a super middleweight called Den Palmer, who we used to bill as the middleweight Guv'nor.
As the shows progressed, The Guvnor tag became more apparent, especially as fighters were being interviewed and filmed. Plus, social media was kicking off, and our shows were being more publicised.
That's when **other** people started to call them *The Guvnor.*
This is why I think over the years; it has caused so much confusion as it's not easy to document it on paper.
The Guv'nor title ended up being a **'tag'** that went hand in hand with our Heavyweight and then super heavyweight title fights.
Once people started calling it the Guvnor title, then we went with it and attempted to place some rules around it.

You could win the title, but you had to defend it against a decent opponent, look at Sven Hamer, Joe Kacz, and Garry Sayer; they all fought each other. All fought each other for the title.
The Guv'nor title wasn't like our other titles at lower weights. Which was like normal boxing, and you had to win an area title or eliminator; The Guv'nor title was available to anyone who wanted to make a challenge.

People would get into the ring and say they were making a challenge, and we would decide if it was a good fight and a money fight or a fight the public wanted to see. Over the years, we had loads of these challengers coming forward. Some were legit and went on to fight for the title, and other fights just didn't happen for one reason or another.

Welsh Phil, for example, was very unlucky, he won our Guv'nor title. He was scheduled to fight names like Garry Sayer and Decca Heggie. Unfortunately, the fights fell through. Welsh Phil also challenged Norman Buckland, but again that fight never happened as Norman retired.

That's a shame as a fight between Welsh Phil and Norman Buckland would have sold a venue out twice over.

Another example of how the title is so unique is - Norman Buckland being awarded the Guvnor title after beating a journeyman who had boxed 22 times for us and lost all 22 fights; we matched him against JJ when his original opponent dropped out (Dave Courtney)

Now that might sound ridiculous! But there is a method in our madness. Our heavyweight title (Guv'nor) title was vacant as Sven Hamer retired.

The plan was to have Norman Buckland fight Dave Courtney for it, but that fight needed building. What we decided to do was let Norman win the vacant title, (an easy fight) then a week or so after we would have a party somewhere (cameras on hand) where Dave Cortney and Norman Buckland would get into an argument (all staged for the cameras) there would be a small scuffle which would be broken up. Then the next day or so, the pictures taken of the skirmish would find their way into one of Dave's magazines. And then Dave would make a statement to say, "Let's settle our differences in the ring." We were going to turn it into a big thing, a big grudge fight, for the Guv'nor title.

So the first part of the plan was to get Normans first fight out of the way, I told Norman to really play up to the crowd! We had cameras everywhere, so he had to make a statement to make this fight with Dave exciting.

(This was the fight where Norman attacked someone in the crowd before the fight, I had loads of people on hand, so the place didn't go up in the air. If you watch one of the videos on YouTube of that fight, you see me and my brother warren walk into the changing room after the fight to see Norman, where I say, "That was perfect!")

That was me being happy about the fact he played the script well. He did what I asked him to do! I told him to make a statement, and he did, I never knew he would attack someone in the fucking crowd, but I wanted him to play up for the crowd!

The first part of our plan had worked perfect, now all we had to do was choose the time and place for Norman and Dave to have a very public fallout.

Me and Ricky was already looking at new venues to promote the future fight; we anticipated a crowd above 3000 people, so we needed somewhere bigger than Caesars. We were speaking to Dave about where we would have the fallout and then, WALLOP! Dave Courtney gets arrested and remanded in Belmarsh!

The fight, the plan, it's all off! We were sick, and there was fuck all we could do about it. At first, we were thinking, shall we hold on and see if he gets bail? How long will it be? Will he get bail? And then if does get bail, he is not going to be willing to be all over the papers for fighting in the street, and then promoting a bad blood grudge fight in the ring. It was over! We had no choice but to move on.

So now we have Norman as the new Guv'nor! and a load of fighters underneath him all eager to fight for the title. (Guv'nor)

When Norman won the title, I had a belt made for him online from a trophy shop in Birmingham, but the belt didn't turn up on time for the show.

So it was presented to him on the next show at Caesars. I asked Roy to come into the ring to present it., We made a big thing out of it!

The Courtney fight was off, so we had to make the best out of what we had, and that was building a future fight for Norman against Welsh Phill (The Welsh Heavyweight Champion) or Garry Sayer. (The London Heavyweight Champion) So that was the plan for Norman to defend it against either fighter in the not too distant future.

We had a couple of shows coming up. One was a small marquee show in Cambridgeshire, a three-fight dinner show. Two weeks before that show, I received a call from Norman asking if he could box on it, as he lived close by. There was no time to arrange a big fight for him, so I pulled in another journeyman called, 'Dolph.'

It was an easy win, more like a spar. So it was back to our original plan of getting Norman a challenger on our next Caesars show. Norman then asked me if he could have one more warm-up as he was still not a hundred percent fit. Reluctantly, I agreed, and we brought in Steve Yorath for his third fight, but said that's it, no more warm-ups, after this you have to box either Sayer of Welsh Phil.

Norman won against Yorath and then decided to retire, which pissed me off, to be honest. He had three fights for us, but he never boxed a 'live' opponent. There were big fights on the table, Garry Sayer and Welsh Phil, but Norman never fought them, so in my eyes, he was never a true Guv'nor.

That may sound harsh, but it's the truth, its documented on YouTube, and you cannot fight three journeymen and then hope to be mentioned in the same breath as fighters who boxed the best at the time they were fighting, or at least demonstrated they were willing to fight the best.

It's the same with Heggie, he boxed a journeyman when his opponent fell out, but in my eyes, he was never a true Guv'nor unless he beats Welsh Phil, his original opponent, and a man who would be coming to fight, not just get a payday.

Sven Hamer (2004 / 2008)

When we started doing shows at Caesars, there was a very good boxer who used to box professional for me called Sven Hamer, Sven boxed professional as a super middle / light heavy and actually had a professional fight at Caesars for me back in 1998.

He retired from professional in 2001, and when he came to box for me and Ricky in 2003, he had blown up into a full size heavyweight.

Sven had a couple of fights, then fought for the vacant EBF British super heavyweight title and won in the 1st round.

He then defended it a couple of times and we started to get challenges from other fighters, so we began to bill Sven as 'the Guv'nor, but he was still boxing for EBF titles, just like Roy and Lenny boxed for the NBC heavyweight title, the Guv'nor was a 'tag' but people began to say it was the Guv'nor title.

The EBF had other titles - like the London title, English, and regional titles. Ex-professional **Gary Firby** won a regional EBF title, and then we made a match against Sven for the EBF British title (Guv'nor belt) Sven won in the 2nd round.

Sven Hamer defended his belt until 2008 where he retired undefeated. His last fight in 2008 was on the 25th of May and it was for Super Heavyweight European title.

He then came back in 2009 and boxed against Joe Kacz, losing a hard fought bout on points.

Sven Being presented the belt by Joe Pyle Sr

He fought a lot of good fighters over the years at Caesars, he also boxed for us at other venues like, Oceanas in Kingston, and Tolworth and never ever ducked a challenge.

I have said over the years that Sven was probably the best Guvnor of them all, that's no disrespect to any others, but Sven was a good fighter, a former professional who went unbeaten for years.

Sven Hamer for me was a true Guv'nor! He was always professional both inside and outside the ring and was always willing to fight anyone.

He never courted publicity, he didn't need to, he just went about his business in the ring and let his fists do the talking.

He never let me or the promotion down and always gave the crowd value for money.

I remember my father once saying to me that Sven would have been too much for Roy and Lenny in the ring. He was an ex-professional fighter with heavy hands, good stamina, and a fantastic chin.

Even now, he doesn't brag about his boxing as some people do, we all knew he was the Guv'nor, he didn't have to say it once.

It was an absolute pleasure promoting Sven and I was lucky enough to promote him in the professional and unlicensed games.

He was the best! No doubt about that!

Below are a few words from Sven Hamer

Having boxed as a Professional for many years. I didn't retire due to falling out of love for the sport, but mainly due to injuries sustained during fight (mainly cut eyes). After two years out, and having set up my own Personal Training business. I was asked by a friend if I would work his corner for an unlicensed boxing match he had coming up. At that point, I'd never been to an unlicensed show before, and always thought they were dodgy illegal fight that took place behind closed doors.

After doing the corner for my pal, and watching some of the bouts, I couldn't help but be impressed with how well it was run and organised. I still missed getting in the ring and having a fight, and seeing the bouts that night made me miss it even more. Then I ran into Joey Pyle, who I knew from promoting a couple of my Pro fights at the Royal Garden Hotel in Kensington. We spoke for a while, and the next thing I was boxing on the next show.

As crazy as it sounds, but I used to make a lot more money doing the unlicensed fights, than I did in most of my pro bouts, due to ticket sales. And the fights only being 2-minute rounds, and a maximum of 5 rounds per bout. I could continue my personal training business and just add a few more rounds of training to be fit for the fights when they came up. It was always a great atmosphere, especially at Caesar's in Streatham, where most of the shows were held. I did them for quite a few years, and had some great times and nights there. It also gave me that adrenaline rush that anyone that has boxed knows too well. In the end, I had to stop due to my personal training business taking up too much of my time. I had a ball while I was doing it though.

Norman Buckland (2008 / 2009)

As Sven was retired, Norman Buckland then boxed for a title we named the (Roy Shaw, Guvnor title.) A brand new belt made as an interim until Sven decided what he wanted to do as he was saying he may return to the ring. Normans debut fight was a 3 x 2 minute round contest against one of our journeymen called JJ.

Norman won in the 1st round after hitting JJ in the balls. The fight is on YouTube, but it has more notoriety of what happened before the fight rather than the action that took place in the ring. Norman Buckland was in his corner when a group of fellas in the crowd started to call him names. Norman gave them a look before deciding to jump out of the ring and steam into the crowd, it caused absolute bedlam and it took fifteen minutes to calm everything down so we could start his fight.

I then staged a show in a large marquee in Cambridge, where Norman boxed another journeyman called 'Dolph', again in a 3 x 2-minute contest.

In early 2009, Norman boxed another journeyman, ex professional Steve Yorath for the EBF Super Heavyweight British title, Norman won on points.

In this fight, we stepped Norman up to the EBF super heavyweight title because there were some big heavyweights coming through the ranks and we were looking at a few big fights in the future for Norman, Garry Sayer boxed on the same show for the London title and was eager to fight Norman. Welsh Phil also defended his Welsh Heavyweight title on the show and was desperate ton challenge Norman for the British super heavyweight title but I kept stopping Phil from making the challenge.

I did this for two reasons, firstly Norman Buckland was a showman and a crowd puller, I knew if we kept him winning then somewhere down the road we could get a big fight and draw in a big crowd.

I also thought Welsh Phil would beat him in the ring quite easily, Norman was big and loud and had the charisma, but I'm not talking out of turn when I say he was limited in the actual boxing department.

When Sven announced he was retiring then we had our most prized title becoming vacant, Sven was a big crowd puller so we were looking for something similar. Me and Ricky English then came up with idea of Dave Courtney boxing for the title, Dave was always at our shows doing the auctions and stuff and had said on more than one occasion he wouldn't mind getting in the ring but it was difficult where to place him as Sven would have killed him inside the ring.

Norman Buckland was the perfect choice, him and Dave were friends but we were going to have a 'moody' very public falling out, it would be caught on film and a fight would start but be quickly broken up, then we would announce that Dave and Norman would settle their differences in the ring and have a massive fight that all of London would want to see. We even contacted Alexander Palace to get prices and date availability.

First, though, we had to build Norman up so we got his first fight at Caesars in October 2008

This part of the plan worked perfectly and we encouraged Norman to kick off before the fight, it's all on YouTube, where you see all the commotion and it was just what we wanted to get everyone talking about Norman.

Norman then had another couple of fights to build his profile which we had to make him look good, but just as we were going to stage the moody fight between him and Dave at one of our shows, Dave got arrested and remanded. That ended any chance of the fight taking place and we were now stuck with Norman as our super heavyweight champion.

Norman was a character, there is no disputing that, but we built him up for a big fight, a big fight that never ever happened. He decided to retire before fighting Welsh Phill or Sayer.

I respect any man who gets in the ring, but in my view, Norman never had that defining fight, he never boxed a challenger.

As the years have passed since he boxed for us there have been numerous stories going about that Roy Shaw gave Norman his Guvnor belt…… That is complete rubbish!

Roy Shaw or my father used to present the belts to ALL our champions. The reason it looks different on YouTube is because when Norman had his first fight for us there was no belt! So we had one made and said we would present it to him on the next show, we were trying to build Norman up so it was a staged presentation and it was me who had the belt made! That's what makes me laugh when people say it was Roy's belt…. It fucking wasn't as I had it made online from a sports shop in Birmingham and cost me £120 fucking quid!!

Welsh Phil Davies

Welsh Phil Davis was the EBF Welsh champion and was undefeated, he had been boxing on the undercards of Sven and was desperate to fight for the big title.

Phil was a lunatic and would give anyone a run for their money on the cobbles. I have been in his company one night when he took on four drunken rugby players and knocked three of them spark out. The other pest ran for his life, but was unfortunate to run straight into a left hook from me. (Lol)

But seriously, Phil is a bloody handful. He comes from an ex-military background and is someone I would defiantly want beside me when the shit hits the fan.

Now that the Buckland / Courtney fight was off, Phill pleaded for me to let him fight Buckland for the title.

He was dying to fight for the main title and was driving me mad about making the fight.

Finally, I agreed, and we were looking at staging the fight for the Guvnor, Super Heavyweight Title sometime in July 2009.

It was going to be a good fight; it was an exciting fight, with two big men and two big characters. They might not be the best in boxing ability, but it was a fight, and a fight we knew would put bums on seats. Me and Ricky were just about to start publicising the fight, and then Norman announced he was going to retire.

To say I was pissed off was an understatement! This was going to be a bloody big fight between two big larger than life scrappers but once again, because of matters beyond our control, we had no fight!

Me and Ricky were sick! Phill Davies against Norman Buckland could have been a terrific scrap, (that's if we could actually get them in the ring before they tore into each other)

When I told Phil that Norman was going to retire, Phil was livid; he asked me if I could set a meeting up so he could front Norman to his face. I said it wouldn't make any difference as Norman was adamant he was going to stay retired, so I agreed to let Welsh Phil box Buckland's former opponent Steve Yorath for the big title in July.

It wasn't the fight we wanted, but at least we had a fight.

Phil sold the place out and he went one better than Norman by managing to stop Yorath, to become the new Guvnor.

Sitting at ringside was a former ABA amateur champion Big Joe Kacz, he was a lump and a bloody good fighter who was in his prime and he wanted to get in on the action.

During the night, Joe spoke to me about Welsh Phil and boxing him on the next show; I said it might be a possibility once I checked out what he could bring to the table, Moneywise.

A couple of days after the show, me and Phill discussed a possible fight against Kacz and he agreed straight away to fight him, I said, let's get summer out the way and make a fight in September.

A couple of weeks after we spoke, I was preparing the fight posters and tickets when I had a call that Phill had broken his ankle while on military exercises in the Brecon's.

I was fucking sick! Once again, a big fight had been cancelled. I spoke to Phil and he said he would be out for a few months, so after a discussion I said I would have to strip him of the title and let Joe Kacz fight for it, and then once he had recovered from his injuries, Phil would have first option to fight for the title again. Phil wasn't happy and nor was I, but the show had to keep running. Boxing is just like life, and in life, people get injured or sick, I was sorry for Phill, but we had to keep the show moving. The title was our showpiece, our main event, and we couldn't put it on hold for months on end.

I knew one day, Phill would be back and the title would still be there.

It's like the saying ... The show must go on!

One funny story I would like to share was just after Phill had boxed at Caesars. It was a strange atmosphere that night. People were having a good time, but there was a more intense menace in the air that night at Caesars. Roy Shaw had just presented the Guvnor title to Welsh Phill, and then the three of us were standing on the stage talking as the music started for another fight. Phill was happy and excited and was posing with Roy for some photos when a fight broke out besides between two drunks.

Warren, Mitch, and Teddy came running over to us to break up the fight which had now turned into half a dozen people shouting and threatening.

Next thing someone threw a punch at Warren, and then it really kicked off! Welsh Phill jumped straight in and knocked one of them spark out, and then Roy chinned someone and sent them flying. Suddenly there was a massive gap where everyone jumped out the way! Roy grabbed another fella and threw him off the stage like a rag doll as Welsh Phill now lost it and steamed into the others.

It was just a matter of moments, and it was over. Roy, when he goes ... Goes! And he was looking for someone else to start on, but the drunks were either flattened or had run out the venue.

The security came over and just stood back, there was no way they were going near Roy or Phill.

Later that night Ricky jokingly announced on the mike that Roy was making a return and the whole place cheered.

It ended up being a good night and we all ended up back at my place joking about it.

I was joking about with Roy saying you still got it mate, he was laughing and I could see in his eyes he loved every fucking second of it.

Roy like Phill a lot, he knew, was Phill was with me and that to Roy was like family. A couple of years later when Roy was near the end and had lost a lot of weight and he had an argument with some arsehole, Roy said, Joe come up with Welsh Phill and were go down the boozer where these flash mugs are and we will smash the fucking lot of them.

Below are a few words from the man himself, Welsh Phill Davis.

I have known Joe for a lot of years, and we have had some good times, I used to run a lot of doors in the west end of London and would see Joe up around town all the time.

We got on straight away from the day we met, and over the years we have been through a few scraps together.

When I started boxing at Caesars, I fucking loved it! I loved the atmosphere, the buzz, and I loved the feeling of knocking people out!

Joe Pyle Snr and Roy Shaw always gave me good advice, and we would all drink for hours after the boxing, they made me feel like family, and I was dying to be The Guv'nor.

I wanted to fight anyone, anytime, and for nothing, I wanted to fight Buckland, and I was gutted when he retired.

But that was his fucking loss! I turned up, and he didn't, I won the title and he won fuck all. I was also sick when the Decca fight fell through, I hated that bastard, and I was going to rip his head off come fight night. I didn't care how I beat him just as long as I hurt the bastard. I told Joe that no matter what I have to do, I will put that c**t in hospital.

There are a lot of reasons that fight never happened, but me not wanting to hurt him was not one of them.

Maybe sometime in the future, who knows, I don't like, I've never liked him.

I have loads of promoters offering me fights, but I started with Joe, and I'll finish with Joe. Loyalty is everything to me,

Joe is my friend and family. IL end this by saying,

Roy and Lenny where the Guvnors, I'm a fucking guvnor, but the biggest thing we all had in common was we all worked for the man we called our boss.

Joe Pyle Snr and Joe Pyle Jnr.

Welsh Phill (Guvnor)

Big Joe Kacz

When I told Joe about Phill getting injured, he was gutted.

Joe was one of the fighters we had like Sven, Phill, Gary Sayer who wanted to fight anyone, he didn't want any easy fights, he wanted to earn the right to be the Guv'nor'

I said we had a couple of opponents lined up, but Joe wasn't interested unless he boxed someone very good, a fight that the public wanted to see.

Joe's first fight for me a couple of months earlier was against a lunatic heavyweight (A former Welsh Phill victim) who went under the name 'Temper.' The fight was a (test) and a slugfest while it lasted, but Joe won in the 1st round. The crowd loved it, and it convinced me that Joe was ready to step up. We had a show coming up in September, so we moved him to the main event to fight for the vacant title.

Sven Hamer was also scheduled to box on September show, but he was having a comeback fight before fighting for a title after having over a year out of the ring.

I was having absolutely no luck with matching Joe, so stuck for an opponent, I rang Sven, thinking fuck it, I'll ask if he wants the fight, expecting Sven to say, "No, not on this show' but to my surprise and delight he just said, yeah, why not, set it up, Joe'

So the fight was made, it was a massive fight, surprisingly a fight everyone wanted to see, and the tickets sold like 'hot cakes.'

'A former undefeated Guvnor against an exciting big strong former amateur star.'

As the weeks closed in, the fight began to get a lot of interest, and people from Joe Kacz were coming forward looking to lay more bets on their man.

Personally, I knew Joe was a good fighter, but I thought it would be business as usual for Sven, I couldn't see any other outcome than a big Sven Hamer win.

The fight took place at Caesars on September 13th, 2009, on an action-packed card that included former professional British and European champion Floyd Havard. Garry Sayer was also on the undercard defending his London title.

Steve Holdsworth was the referee, where he mistakenly announced Sven as the defending champion when he got into the ring with his championship belts. (The title was vacant)

The fight was very tough, and Sven just couldn't get going. After only one round, it looked like big Joe was in the driving seat, the fight went to a decision, and Steve Holdsworth announced Big Joe Kacz as the winner. Joe dropped to his knees as his corner celebrated.

We were a bit stunned by Joe beating Sven, but full credit to him he had pulled off a big surprise win and won in style.

After the fight I went to the changing rooms to talk to Sven and then congratulate Joe, Sven was choked by his first loss and more so his performance, he told me he just couldn't get going and by the second round was drained of his energy,

I asked him if he had been training properly, and he just sighed and shrugged, "Yeah!....... Fuck knows what happened, mate, I just couldn't put anything together......... I've never boxed so bad in my life!" he replied.

In Joes changing room, everyone was celebrating, Joe was hyper and full of energy, "Get me Buckland! Get me Welsh Phill!" he was shouting. I was with Warren Bammo, and together we laughed, Don't worry mate, there will be plenty of people to fight!"

I was disappointed for Sven, maybe he underestimated Kacz and wasn't fully fit from his year off, I don't know. (He certainly never looked his usual self) Like the fighting man he is, Sven never made any excuses, he congratulated his opponent and said well done. I did mention the chance of a return, but he was disappointed in his performance, which was understandable, and he wanted some time out to ponder his fighting future.

I could see what was going through his mind; he thought what thousands of fighters before him had to decide. Have I still got it? Have I got the time and desire to get my body into the shape it needs to be in?

Sven never said it, but I could see that he was nowhere near ready for a big fight on the night. His timing was off, the footwork was slow and his stamina failed him. I think Sven needed some time on his own, time to decide what to do next. He still had the ability and the strength, but the question was, does he still have the discipline?

There were a couple of big fights on the cards for Joe, but because of timing issues, we couldn't get them on our next show.

Big Joe defended his titles a few weeks later and beat the 6ft 6, tough as teak, Sheridan Davey in two rounds on our November the 15th event at Caesars.

Next for Joe Kacz was a fight against Dave Thomson on our February 28th show at Caesars, Joe destroyed Thomson in the first round, and as his hand was raised, Garry Sayer got into the ring and challenged him.

I knew Garry was thinking about a challenge, as he asked me earlier in the evening that if Big Joe won, then could he have a go at him next. Garry also slagged him off calling him a big poof and said he would smash him in one round. The crowd all cheered, and we had a very big fight for our next show. 6ft 4 Joe Kacz vs 6ft 10 Garry Sayer, both unbeaten and both wanting blood.

Big Joe Kacz Vs Garry the Viking Sayer

The date was set for the big fight, April 28th at Caesars. We then started to market and publicise it. We held a press conference at John Rooney's professional boxing gym near Tooley street, London bridge, so both boxers could face off for pictures. There was a bit of needle at the gym and me and Warren had to step in to keep them apart but it was nothing too bad.

I can remember that as the fight got closer the bad blood intensified, I encourage a bit of banter, but this one was getting nasty.

It was mainly the people around the fighters and not the fighters themselves. However, personal insults were being slung around. It got so bad I had to telephone both fighters and tell them to tame it down a bit, as I was now concerned that the verbal's could turn into crowd trouble on the night.

When fight night arrived, there was a buzz of menace in the air, you could feel the atmosphere as everyone waited for the main event.

I made sure that inside the ring, I had some big lumps with me, my brother's Warren and Mitch, and Teddy Bam Bam so we could keep them apart before the first bell.

The crowd was buzzing now they were both in the ring together. The bell went to begin the 1st round. Both boys went straight at it; they traded punches as Garry pushed Kacz, the lighter man, back to the ropes, both boys catching each other. The fight then turned nasty as Garry leaned on Joe and push him back where the pair of them went over the top rope, and crashed heavily onto the floor.

I ran over to Joe's corner men who ran to help their fighter or to attack Garry, but we luckily I had some men close by to separate them and I told the boxers to get back into the ring. Garry got back in, but Joe was shouting in anger and saying he was injured.

Looking back at now, it was lucky Joe Kacz never broke his back or neck, he went head first over the ropes with a 20 odd stone Garry Sayer falling on top of him.

Referee Steve Holdsworth called a time-out as he tried to get a grip of what was going on, Garry was in the ring shouting to Joe to get back in.

I also shouted out to Joe Kacz to get back in the ring, "Do you want to throw in the towel?" I shouted,

"DISQUALIFY HIM!" One of Joe's corner men Shouted back, pointing at Sayer.

"GET IN THE FUCKING RING OR YOUR DISQUALIFIED!" I shouted back at him before shouting out to the ref to tell him to get back in the ring. Joe Kacz got back inside the ropes but was rubbing his leg and didn't look happy at all.

Steve Holdsworth gave them both a couple of minutes to recover before starting the round again.

Both fighters went straight back at each other, both catching each other and then Joe caught Garry with a couple of big rights and Garry got pushed against the ropes. Joe was all over Garry, and the momentum of trying to avoid the onslaught made him turn his back briefly, Kacz carried on punching which angered Garry, the referee called break, but Garry pushed the referee out of the way, trying to get to Joe. Next thing all bedlam broke loose as Joe shouted something, which made Garry go to rip his gloves off to have a fight, bareknuckle.

At that point, the ring got invaded by loads of people trying to keep them apart. Warren was holding Garry back in the corner, yet he was going crazy, now there must have been over a dozen people in the ring, so I jumped up and spoke to Garry.

"Are you putting the fucking gloves back on?!" I asked him.

"Let's have it without the fucking gloves, Joe, I want to smash his fucking face in!" Garry Sayer shouted back at me, now completely consumed with rage.

Warren looked at me with a look that said ... The fights over brother.

"Fight with fucking gloves or the fights over!" I said to Garry now losing my patience, I then looked around and I could see the crowd getting restless, so I started to think about that, I went over to referee Steve Holdsworth,

"What do you think?" I asked him, stating the obvious that things had gone too far.

"Have to do it again another night." Steve replied.

"Then call it Steve… no contest… for fuck's sake." I said back to him.

Steve did as I asked and grabbed the mike, "I HAVE DISQUALIFIED BOTH BOXERS ... THIS FIGHT IS A NO CONTEST!"

Jesus! I can still hear the boos now, but thankfully it was the last fight of the night, so we raised the lights and called for security to clear the building. It was a horrible anti-climax to a fight that promised so much.

The result was definitely not what we wanted, but as a promoter, I thought it wasn't the end of the world. If we acted quickly and sensible, then we had another sell-out show on the horizon. And with the right bit of marketing and (fanny) ... It could be an even bigger fight the next time around.

The next week I was now buzzing and was thinking with my business head. I was going to turn this into a massive fight with press conferences, fight footage and promo reels, promoting the fight as two men who detest each other, even more so now!

Bad Blood would be the headline

or

'Now it's really personal.'

Everything was going well and I was in a really optimistic mood until I received a phone call from someone in the Joe Kacz camp. The conversation was not what I wanted to fucking hear! They went on to tell me that Joe was going to call the old bill over Garry Sayer.

I couldn't believe what I was hearing! Unbeknown to me, Garry and Joe had been exchanging abuse at each other over the phones, and it had got so heated that Joe was threatening to bring in the cozzers.

I called Joe to ask him what the fuck was going on, and he said he had been talking to Garry, which ended up in an argument where Garry said he was going to come around Joe's home and do him on the front door.

"I will fight anyone in the ring, but I'm a boxer, I'm not a gangster, I won't have my home threatened!" Joe said to me.

I then phoned Garry up to ask what had been said.

"Joe, I never threatened his fucking family, I said he could have it any way he fucking wants, in the ring, or I'll come to his front door, and we can have it on the fucking pavement!"

I spent the next couple of days on the phones trying to calm everyone down, but the damage was done, Joe Kacz then started suggesting to me that I report Garry to the police!

"Are you Crazy!" I said, "that would never happen, 'I sort my own business out!' Garry was also livid at being threatened by the old bill, and I just kept saying to both of them to calm down because we have the fight to sort out, but that was now the last thing on both of their minds. It just became too personal.

I knew the writing was on the wall; Joe Kacz was saying he will never fight at Caesars again, never mind fight Sayers. Feeling choked, I knew realistically that the 2nd fight was now, never going to happen.

I now also had a problem! I had a Guv'nor who I wasn't too keen on working with. Joe was a straight goer so I can half understand him threatening to call the old bill.

However, in my world that is a fucking big No No!

We had some thinking to do and how we could sort this out, Sven was still contemplating his future, Welsh Phill was still not fit and Garry was demanding that Kacz fight him for the title or I should strip Kacz!

It was a fucking headache! A headache I had to get rid of, but funnily enough, fate solved it for me.

Garry The Viking Sayer

After Garry's no-contest fight with Kacz, I was still trying to find a way to sort out our main title, Kacz was still the champion and Garry wanted the belt, but I couldn't get them to fight each other, I couldn't even have them in the same building, never mind the same ring.

What I decided to do was give them both some time and space, let time try to heal the wounds.

Garry was from Bexley (SE London - Kent), and I had been thinking for some time of staging an event at a club called Amadeus, which was on his manor. So the plan was, I would stage a show there for Garry and then another show in London at Caesars for Joe, where hopefully the months would have the effect of both of them seeing some sense and agreeing to sometime in the future having that second fight.

I met with the owners of Amadeus and agreed on a date for a show which was the 20th June 2010, Garry Sayer would be the main event, and Kacz would box on my London show around a week later.

In my head, I now had everything clear and a game plan to act on, but then I got a call from one of my business associates, Teddy Bam Bam.

"Joe, Joe, I just found out Kacz is fighting on a show in May." Teddy said, shocking me.

"What you mean, fighting on another show! Whose fucking show, he can't do that!" I snapped back.

"I don't know yet, I just got a call and called you, I thought you might know more about it."

"I know fuck all about it!" I said before telling Teddy I would call Kacz straight away and find out what this was all about.

I hung up the phone and spoke to big Joe where he confirmed what I had just been told. He had agreed to fight on another promotion, so I argued with him about it,

"No mate! That's wrong …. I gave you a fucking chance to fight for the title, our fucking title! You can't just go away and defend it on someone else's show!" I said.

"But we have no contract between us, "Kacz answered hesitantly.

"Joe …. Listen to me very carefully! ... You can't win **OUR** title and then fuck off to defend it on another show!"

"Why not? I can have this fight and then fight on your show after." Kacz answered.

"NO!, It doesn't work like that!... You won 'our' title, you can't take it anywhere you want! If I let you do that then I'll have to let all my fighters do it! It will be fucking chaos, and I'll end up with no shows!"

"I don't see what the problem is, I have bills to pay, I need to fight." Kacz replied,

 I have fucking bills as well!" I snapped back, now losing my patience.

"Who you fighting for? Give me his fucking number!" I added, now very angered.

"He's a mate. I know him down the gym."

 "WHAT'S HIS FUCKING NAME! … SO HE THINKS HIS GETTING A PAYDAY OFF OF ALL OUR FUCKING HARD WORK!" I shouted.

The conversation between Joe and me lasted about five minutes and followed the same tone, me saying it couldn't happen, and Joe arguing that he can't see the harm. No matter how I said it, he just couldn't understand what he was doing wrong!

I finally hung up, feeling pissed off, and called Teddy back and told him to find out the name of the fella who had approached Kacz, so me and Teddy would go pay this liberty taker a visit.

Over the next few days, we found out who the slippery bastards were, and I spoke to one of them and told them straight that they couldn't promote our title, No fucking way! But Joe Kacz was adamant he was still boxing on their show, I was put in a hard position. ... if I didn't make a strong stance on this, then I risked all my other boxers doing the same.

It was a decision I didn't want to make, but my hand was forced so reluctantly I stripped Joe Kacz of the Guv'nor title.

I didn't like or want to do it, Joe Kacz was a good fighter, and he won the title legitimately in the ring, by defeating Sven Hamer and then accepted the challenge from Sayer. But I had to remove my feelings of admiration for him as a fighter, and put my business head on. (If you are the Liverpool captain, you can't go and have a game for man utd next weekend.)

Our Super heavyweight 'Guvnor' title was now vacant and the automatic choice was for Garry Sayer to fight for it. I printed the tickets and posters and put my effort into the Amadeus show in Kent.

The show was a sell out and Garry boxed a very capable fighter Dan Lovett, stopping him in the 1st round. Garry Sayer after all this time and drama, got what he wanted ...He was the new Guv'nor!
The show itself was a great success and we had some fantastic talent on display, Pete the assassin Stoten, as well as Suki Dhami, the younger brother to the former professional British Welterweight champion Harry.

Below are a few words from Garry.

I first met Joe Pyle in 1997 at his boxing gym on Streatham. I had been to his legendary shows at Caesars where u would see all the faces of London. The atmosphere was electric and were some great fights in and out of the ring. I wanted to showcase my talent on his show, so I had a chat with Joe and he decided to put me on one of his summer shows at Caesars. Joe was always a gentlemen easy to deal with and I had no regrets. As the evening approached I felt a few nerves but no fear. The dressing room pumping with adrenaline and testosterone along with ten men who all had a survival instinct within them ready to go war, only no one had troops to go with them. Joe matched me up evenly with a solid southpaw. After stepping through the ropes we had a great first round and it was one of the best fights of the show. I won by KO in the second round and the crowd went wild. Joe was the first man to congratulate me and Wendy head of the ring girls. The afterpartys were legendary getting in at 9am.
Thanks to MeanMachine I have great memories to treasure.
Thank you Joe Pyle.

Sven Hamer (Comeback No.2)

It was an exciting year (Or, an eventful year) for our big lads. Joe Kacz and Garry Sayer, and now Sven Hamer came back into the frame. Plus, we had a few up and coming super heavyweights looking to fight for titles. Jamie Scarlett, from Brixton was one of them and had been looking very impressive in his last couple of fights. Jamie was eager to get into the mix.

The biggest kick in the balls was we finally lost our venue, Caesars. There had been talk of it being torn down and turned into flats for a few years, but when it happened, it was a devastating blow. It was part of history! MeanMachine Promotions and Caesars went hand in hand. Now we had to find another, but we knew it was a futile search, there wouldn't be anything like Caesars.

With our headquarters gone, we moved the shows to a club in Kingston, called Oceana, it was a lovely club, but didn't have the layout like Caesars, in fact, it was a bloody nightmare to arrange the venue for boxing.

Kingston was where Sven Hamer lived, so when he heard about us staging a show in his hometown, he gave me a call and discussed him possibly boxing again.

On 19th September at Oceana - Kingston, Sven Hamer had his comeback fight winning by KO in the 1st round. It was great to get him back again, and for his next fight after shaking off a few cobwebs, he was looking to fight for titles again.

In 2011 Garry Sayer fell ill, he was really bad. So I told him he could have a few months to recover, but it looked uncertain if he would ever fight again. MeanMachine Promotions were still trying to find a venue to rival Caesars. We promoted two shows at Oceana - Kingston, a dinner show at Heathrow, an event in Effingham park where we included a few MMA fights. In December, we booked Tolworth Recreation Centre.

Tolworth 2nd December 2011

As Sayer was now out of the picture, Sven Hamer received a challenge from Big Bill Buncy, a tough street fighter with a reputation, so it was like going back to the old days. It was a big fight and worthy of a Guv'nor tag, but one week before the show, Buncy dropped out. I searched around and couldn't find a decent opponent until someone called David Johnson from Scotland called me and said he heard Sven Hamer's opponent had dropped out and he would step in to fight him, I never heard of Johnson, who told me he had been fighting in Scotland and was unbeaten in 15 fights.

Me and Sven accepted the fight and by the sound of it, it looked a good match up.

On fight day, Johnson travelled down from Scotland on his own, I asked where his coach was and he said he never had one, which for a lad of 15 unbeaten fights sounded odd. Johnson then asked me if anyone could lend him some boots as he didn't have any. I was in fucking disbelief.

This was a big fight for a big title and here was a lad with no trainer and no fucking boxing boots!

My fears were proven right when he got in the ring, and Sven holding his punches back, absolutely destroyed him in one round.

All credit to Sven, he really pulled his punches, he knew full well if he let his shots go, then Johnson would have ended up in the hospital.

I was also shocked that after the fight when Sven asked Steve Holdsworth for the mike, and he announced to the crowd that this was his last fight, he thanked us and thanked the crowd. and said he is retiring for good this time.

It was a bit out of the blue, to be honest, but I couldn't complain as Sven had never let us down.

I was happy for him, he was a great champion for us, but I had lost two big heavyweights in the space of a year plus our venue Caesars.

2012

We started the year with a show at Tolworth on 18th February.

Then we took some of the lads on the road and co-promoted a show in Donegal, Ireland. Then it was back to Tolworth on 28th April where Welsh Phill Davies, after a layoff, came back to fight again.

Billy Isaac

When Manchester came knocking …

Billy Isaac vs Garry Sayer

In 2012, someone I knew local on the manner was driving me mad about some of the videos on YouTube and the Guv'nor title, Billy Isaac was a big lump originally from Manchester and was making a nuisance of himself in London.

Me and Billy knew each other well outside of boxing and we used to end up drinking together in a pal's club in Epsom. One day he began to pester me about fighting Garry Sayer, I told him Garry wasn't fighting anymore, but Billy started making snide comments all over social media against Garry calling him names until Garry phoned me up and said, who the fuck is this Billy Isaacs? Garry was fuming as Billy hadn't held back in the insult department. Billy called him a disgrace and a Pussyhole and said he would smash him in under one round. Garry said to me, "Tell the mug ill fight him," so I began to put the wheels into motion.

Billy Isaac continued telling everyone he would destroy Garry, so I phoned him up and told him he can have the fight. "You called him out and he said he will fight you." I told him!

Billy then told me he needed some training time and I said okay, I'll make the fight in two to three months' time, but Billy said he wanted six months to train for the fight?

I was a bit taken back and said to him, you have been calling him out saying he is fucking useless, and now you need six fucking months training to fight him.

To be honest, it was getting comical, and I told Billy to stop wasting my fucking time. (Either you want to fight him or you don't!)

About a month went by with nothing else being said, until one night when Billy turned up at our Tolworth show. He asked me if he could get in the ring and make an announcement. He then got up and publically called out Garry Sayer, calling him a 'Fat batty boy.'

After this, a month went past without hearing nothing again, until Billy called me and said he wanted a comeback fight first and then fight Garry Sayer in 2013.

At this stage I wasn't taking this too seriously as Billy kept changing his fucking mind, so I left it to see if he came back to me.

Surprisingly, he did come back and gave me a dozen fresh photographs of himself, so I made the arrangements and put a show together where Garry and Billy would fight on the same show against different opponents and then we would get them both in the ring to promote a big fight amongst them for 2013. The show was scheduled for July and I named the event - 'Welcome to Hell part 1' and there was a 'Hell' of a lot of interest as the tickets for the show were flying out, everyone on the manor was talking about Isaac vs Sayer, even though it wasn't going to be on this show, everyone just wanted to see them in the same room.

As a promoter, its fights like this that really get your blood pumping! You can sense the excitement on the street, I might be the one doing all the work to make it happen, but that doesn't make me immune to sharing the same excitement as everyone else.

But when you're promoting shows, you also have to take the rough with the smooth.

It's common for fights to fall out of bed and kick you up the bollocks, it's a fact of life you have to accept it and go with what you have left. This show was another kick up the balls.

One week before the show, I get a phone call from Billy saying he had hurt his back and would have to pull out.

At first, I was sceptical and I told Billy he had nothing to worry about as he had an easy fight on this show, it was a taster for the big fight to come later in the year, I even said I will have a quiet word with his opponent and sort something out for him.

However, Billy was adamant that he couldn't fight, so as an alternative I said he still had to come to the show, and after Garry Sayer's fight, he could get in the ring and challenge Garry, I would put some big lumps in there to keep them apart.

I remember telling Garry about how Billy pulled out and Garry just laughed, saying, "He won't fight me joe, it's all bollocks mate."

On the night, I was sitting at ringside with Shaun Sheehan, Warren, and big Barry when one of my workers came over to tell me Billy has pulled up outside in his Rolls Royce, and he is about ten-handed strong. I said okay, go out and get him in, and show them over to their table.

So I'm sitting there. Billy Isaac walks in with all his crowd and bumps into Garry Sayer, who is walking about with a couple of his mates speaking to some of his supporters, Garry sees Billy, and goes straight over to him,

"Oi! You got a big mouth, do you want to say it to my face!" Garry shouts at him.

I jump out of my chair as I can see this escalating as they both start shouting and shaping up to each other. Now the whole fucking crowd had stopped watching the fight in the ring and were watching the argument, (I think even the boxers fucking stopped to watch it.)

When I reach them, they are both being kept apart by their mates and security and then Billy breaks free and hits Garry with a left jab, Garry lunges at Billy where suddenly everyone jumps in to stop it turning into a real fight and then Billy shouts at his pals and storms out the venue.

Garry sees me and I ask him if he is alright, he just smiles back and laughs, 'fucking idiot, my mother's hits harder.' Garry said as I told him to go back to his changing room and let me sort this cobblers out.

A few moments later, me and Shaun walked outside into the car park where Billy and his mates were all still rowdy and talking about what had just happened.

"Joe, I'm going to fucking kill him.!" Billy says as he saw me.

"Not tonight you're not!" I replied.

"Fucking batty boy is dead!"

"Billy, this is my fucking show, I'm not having any cobblers in here." I answered.

I then pulled Billy to the side and managed to calm him down, before asking him if he wanted to come back in but if he did then he would have to behave himself.

"Joe, I can't come back in! If I go back in there and see him I'll just fucking lose it!" he said back to me.

We spoke for another minute and then I went back into the venue, Garry had his fight that night and won and we announced in the ring that he would be fighting Billy Isaac in his next fight with the date and venue to be confirmed.

The crowd went crazy and although the night didn't go as planned, it looked like we had managed to still *whet* everyone's appetite for the fight to come.

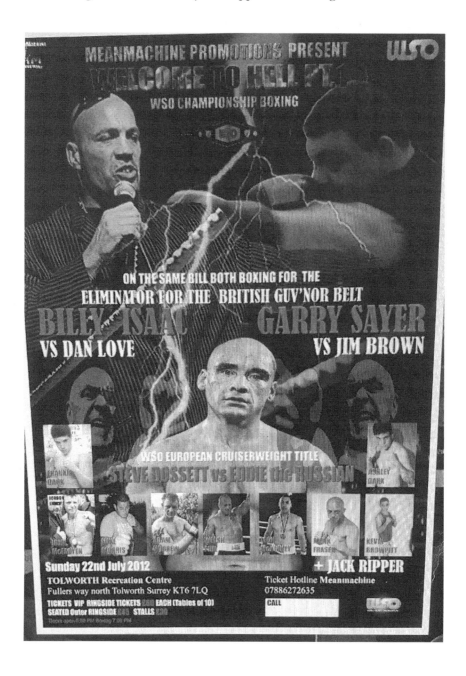

I left it a few days before calling Billy as I wanted to take the sting out of the argument, let both lads calm down and then talk about the fight (In the ring) which we were trying to make.

Billy had called me a couple of times, but I had ignored the calls, one was on the night of the show at around 2;30 in the morning and one was the next day. I knew he would be raging mad, so what was the point of talking when someone is drunk or angry? I wanted to talk to him about the fight and not listen to all the stuff he was going to do to Sayer. Or how much the hump he had!

When we did finally talk, I was hoping things would have calmed down, but now Billy was saying he wanted to go to Garry's front door and have it with him.

I told him to stop talking so fucking stupid and that it was going to happen in the ring, but Billy now didn't want it in the ring anymore, he wanted it on the streets.

To be honest, I was growing fucking tired of all this now, so me and Billy had a bit of a row over the phone and I told him I'm fed up with all the bullshit and basically I just can't be bothered wasting my time anymore.

Billy then said can I set him up another warm up fight and then next year he would fight Sayer in the ring.

That to me was the last fucking straw, I'm the promoter and I can't be having fighters dictate the fucking terms to me like this, I told him he had his chance for a warm up and if he wanted the fight with Sayer then it would be before Christmas, take it or fucking leave it!

So that was that then, it never happened, well it did slightly, all one bloody punch, it's a shame as I think the pair of them would have put on a good show or one would have been disqualified.

Sadly, Billy passed away in 2013, over in Ireland. I didn't mind Billy, sure he could be fucking hard work and he threw his weight about around the manor and me and him spoke heated at times, but that was all it ever was, two men talking to each other, talking like men, he didn't mince his words and neither do I at times.

We had a mutual respect for each other and I will leave it at that.

Tyrone Williams

First, I want to say, I respect Tyrone as a boxer and I think he would have been a real live contender in the days of Hamer, Kacz, Sayer and Welsh Phill, There have been loads of discussions and disputes on social media about Tyrone and Decca Heggie, so hopefully this will put it all straight as to what really happened.

Around the time Tyrone boxed for us, my old boxing partner Ricky English moved back down to South London, we met up, and Ricky talked to me about doing some shows again. I had been out of the game for a couple of years. I wasn't that interested in getting pulled back in, but Ricky told me about a venue he had heard of so we ended up going to have a look at it.
The venue was a smallish hall attached to Tooting and Mitcham football club. We met with the owners, agreed with a good deal to hire the venue, and ended up coming away with our own office at the club.
Like I said I wasn't that excited only Ricky's enthusiasm drew me back in. Once we had the office, we created a promotional company called London Boxing Club (LBC)
Me and Ricky then began going to the office every day. We kitted it out with computers and loads of boxing memorabilia; it was right next door to

Smallholdings amateur boxing club. Hence, we had loads of boxing enthusiasts right on our doorstep.

A date for our first show was set and started getting names down to fight, it looked good, except most of our old fighters had retired or moved on to box for other outfits. So, we had to start again. There were a few local boys who wanted to box, but we never had a main event or the main fighter, we needed something to sell the show.

Therefore, at this point, we decided to stage an eight-man heavyweight Prize-fighter event.

Ricky had already done this kind of event in Watford, so he knew the format and said it worked really well. The atmosphere was fantastic.

Next, we started promoting the idea and put the feelers out there to see who would come forward to participate. It was going to be a heavyweight competition called - The 'Guv'nor' Heavyweight Prize-fighter event.

It sounded like a good idea; an eight-man fight off to find a new Guv'nor! Someone who would then fight and defend the title on future shows.

Our thinking for this competition was to resurrect our old title.

We also had plans to stage Guv'nor Prize-fighter events at different weight divisions.

Tyrone, as we all know, won the Prize-fighter completion and took home the money and the title. The event was a success. Everyone had a great time and we once again had a decent heavyweight to start building the shows around.

I have only ever met Tyrone twice! Once on the day of the competition and then again a week or so later when I had to drop off the belt, we had made for this competition because it didn't arrive on time for us to present it on the day.

We then started planning for another show. I enjoyed the heavyweight Prize-fighter competition, so we wanted our next show to feature another Prize-fighter event but in a different division.

The main event for our next show was going to be Tyrone Williams against Stacey Dunn.

Stacey Dunn had been around the unlicensed scene for a few years and was a very decent fighter; he was scheduled to box in the Prize-fighter event which Tyrone won. Stacey would have been favourite to win the competition, but he had to withdraw because of injury.

This fight had the makings of a real tough fight. Ricky and I were excited at the prospect of promoting it. Everything was all set, and then I had a call that Tyrone was turning professional!

Now, this fucked everything up! Firstly, the BBBofC would not allow a professional boxer to fight outside their remit. Secondly, even if Tyrone wanted to fight before his professional application got processed, it was no good for us! We would be building a fighter where we knew we were going to lose him shortly after.

That just didn't make sense. It would be crazy to put all our time and effort into a boxer we would lose.

With our hands tied, we had to call the fight off, and our 'Guv'nor title would be declared vacant.

Once again, because of outside influence, I had lost another heavyweight, I was a bit pissed off at this stage, very pissed off to be honest1 it felt like we were cursed. So I said (Bollocks to it) and I pulled out of promoting again.

(I have often said that you have to take the rough with the smooth, but we were getting so much rough. I started to wonder if the smooth existed. Yet people still want to be a promoter! Welcome to the reality!)

Decca Heggie

It's amazing, but over the years, I have had more stick and questions over Decca Heggie than any other fighter I have ever promoted.
So it's time to put the record straight once and for all over Heggie and the GUVNOR TITLE.

A year or so after I pulled away from boxing, I had a phone call from Ricky English telling me about a fighter called Decca Heggie, I said I had never heard of him. So Ricky starts telling me all this stuff about a bare-knuckle animal who is the champion of Great Britain and all this romantic fighting stuff and then said there was a massive fight out there for him against Welsh Phill. But he had a problem, Welsh Phill wouldn't discuss any fight unless I was involved.
Phill was my pal and he was loyal to me, so Ricky was asking me to get back involved. With me attached to the fight, the Guv'nor title also had credibility.
I spoke to Phill told him what Ricky had said and he agreed to fight Heggie.
We arranged for him to come down to London to meet me and Ricky. We agreed on terms and took some photos and created a Facebook page for the fight, and put up a statement to promote the fight.
We decided to give Phill a warm-up fight first to build some real interest in the fight, Decca would attend, and I told Phill to call him out afterwards.
My pal, Teddy Bam Bam was staging a show at an old theatre in Crystal Palace, so I got Welsh Phill on the show.

It was on a good day to have it as there was a Kray reunion party at the Blind Beggar in the afternoon, that I was going to, I then arrived at Crystal Palace bringing loads of people from the party.

Everything that night went to plan, Phill smashed his opponent in the 1st round and then screamed at Decca Heggie who just stood there from the audience smiling, winding Phill up. Phill completely lost it, and it took a dozen of us to hold him back from getting at Heggie.

I had all the photographers and cameras arranged, so we got loads of footage and interviews.

Everything was falling into place, and we had laid the foundations and built up loads of interest.

That was the good part of the show, but what followed ….

Over the years, I have been in lots of shows that were a headache, however, this fucking Fight was without a doubt an absolute nightmare from start to finish.

The Fight was originally planned to take place at the Troxy in East London. We had loads of interest and it looked like being a massive event. It was going to be the biggest Fight in years as it had already set social media on fire.

Welsh Phill, we decided, would be walked out to the ring with his army mates with an army band playing his tune. Heggie would come to the ring like a Viking to the beat of drums. No expense would be spared. We had a fight! A huge fight, which everyone wanted to see!

Then everything turned on its head when Ricky received a call from the Troxy explaining they said they couldn't stage the Fight because of information received that there was a higher than likely possibility of crowd trouble.

Ricky spoke to the managers who were adamant they didn't want the Fight even though we had a signed contract and paid them a deposit. We threatened them with legal action as the excuse was so flimsy. They replied in writing that in any case, they wouldn't have bare-knuckle fighting there.

Ricky couldn't believe they were now saying it was bare knuckle, he sent them a reply saying it was a fight with gloves, but the venue wouldn't reply.

It was obvious to me that someone was ringing the venue trying to get the Fight stopped.

The managers even said to Ricky in one phone call that it was from 'anonymous information received.'

Finally, after two weeks of being fucked about we decided to bite the bullet and look for another venue. We had to postpone the show, which was a fucking pain as people had booked hotels and flights and start all over again.

But to find a venue big enough was now another headache, we contacted loads of venues and then after being turned down at all of them, we thought about the venue in Crystal Palace, it wasn't ideal, but it could house 1500 people and we could get it at the right price. I contacted Ted and told him we wanted to put the Fight on there and the dates we were looking at, a couple of hours later, Teddy called me back and said everything was agreed.

Great! We had a venue, not as good as at the Troxy but a decent venue.

But guess what happened next? The people at the Troxy found out our Fight was happening at a new venue and they knew the managers there, so they called our new venue and said why they halted the show at the Troxy. With a bit of spice thrown in like gangsters ran the event and there would be guaranteed crowd trouble.

The next thing we know, now we had another venue pull the plug on us saying they cannot stage bare-knuckle boxing!

Frustrating ay!! Two venues saying they can't have our gloved boxing event because they won't have a bare-knuckle event?? It's beyond belief, isn't it, but this is the bullshit we were having, trying to stage this Fight.

Once again … we were fucked! A big fight, but nowhere to stage it.

We then found a theatre like venue in Deptford, South London. Still, they had also heard about a bare-knuckle fight and possible crowd trouble, we tried to explain it was a licensed fight and we had staged hundreds of shows. Still, they weren't having any of it either.

By this stage, as you can imagine, id pretty much lost interest, all these venue cancelations were making us look like a bunch of fucking amateurs or idiots, Ricky kept me involved by saying it wasn't our fault and no one can blame us when we sign a contract with a venue and the venue have second thoughts. Regardless of what Ricky said, it was driving me mad now, and I couldn't really care less if the Fight happened or not. At this point it was only my friendship with Welsh Phill and Ricky which kept me involved.

While all this was going on, social media and Facebook was having a fucking field day with us, endless comments like, 'not again, 'and 'what the fuck are the promoters up to?'

It was driving me mad. I even put up a post saying sorry for all the delay and that if you had bought a ticket, you would receive a private message. If you never bought a ticket, then just Fuck Off and mind your own business!

Stuck between a rock and a hard place, Me and Ricky decided our only option was to use a venue we had promoted at before, 'The Grand' an old theatre at Clapham junction, it wasn't perfect for this Fight, yet it was a venue with friendly managers, who wouldn't listen to all the rubbish being spread around London, rumours like the plague going around about gangsters and bare-knuckle boxing.

So once again, we set a date and kept our fingers crossed that we wouldn't have any worse luck.

The Fight at last was back on, the interest started to gather momentum and we made arrangements to have the fight live streamed on YouTube PPV at £4.99, we had a terrific undercard who all sold tickets and we were looking at a sell-out show plus a lot of PPV buys on YouTube.

We were just ten days away from the show so what now could go wrong? We had really ridden our luck and somehow we had managed to get this Fight to happen when there were so many people out there trying to sabotage it.

Then I get a fucking phone call from Welsh Phil's trainer Brendon who hesitantly told me that Welsh Phil had collapsed in the gym and had to be taken to the accident and emergency.

"Is he alright?" I asked, concerned.

"No, mate, it's not good!" Brendan replied, "I'm on my way to the hospital now, I will let you know more when I'm there'" he added.

I called Ricky to tell him the news, at first he thought I was on one of my windups.

"FUCK!..... No, Joe, what are we going to do?" Ricky then sighed as he realised I wasn't fucking joking.

"I don't know Rick......can we postpone the show for a couple of weeks?" I replied, thinking out loud, although I knew the answer.

"What again! We will be fucking crucified if we pull the show again.!" Answered Ricky telling what I already knew.

"Maybe it's not so bad mate, maybe just heat exhaustion or something?"
"Rick! It sounds a lot worse than that mate, Brendon sounded fucking ..... I could hear it in his voice that he was saying its serious." I added.

Later that night, after speaking to Brendan I got the news I didn't want to hear and that Welsh Phil was definitely out, he had been kept in hospital and there was no way he would recover in time. I'm not going to say what was wrong with him as that's not my place, but there was no way he could fight.
I spoke to Phil the next day and he said he might be okay for the Fight, but when I heard what was wrong with him, I said no fucking way! He's my friend and I will not risk his life for a poxy promotion.

Me and Ricky was now in a right bloody situation, I asked Brendan and Phil to keep his illness quiet so we could get our heads around the release a proper press statement.
The show was just over a week away and all the undercard had sold their tickets, people had booked hotels and flights, plus we had paid out all the deposits and was put in a position, we just couldn't win.
In situations like this, you have to just tell the truth!
We would announce that the main event was off, but Decca would still box, if we could find an opponent in such short time, and then if he wins, he would fight Welsh Phil at a later date, if welsh Phil recovered.
(It was a nightmare, but we never had a choice, no matter what we did, we would be criticised, so we bit the bullet and did the best we could.)
Ricky phoned around everywhere to get an opponent, but he couldn't get anyone to accept at such short notice, there were a couple of journeymen floating about, but it didn't feel right for us to pull in a complete mug, especially after all the dramas and build-up we had had with this show already.
I then called Julius Francis on the off chance he might accept it, I knew Julius had been having a few fights in the unlicensed scene in London, so I thought id give him a try. Julius was a 'name' he had fought and lost twice to Mike Tyson and was a former British Heavyweight Champion. I called him and he sounded interested, so I made a meeting with him in Croydon the next day with Teddy Bam Bam.
At the meeting I managed to get Julius to agree the Fight but at a big price, (the biggest price I have ever paid an opponent on the unlicensed scene) but I wanted to get this show done and not let any more people down, and hopefully, sometime in the future, we could have another go of putting the Fight on with Welsh Phill..
The next couple of days we had to announce what had happened and announce the Fight would now be against Julius Francis.
We got the usual stick from loads of arseholes on social media, the ones who have never been involved in promoting boxing shows, who think everything

runs like clockwork, and any fuck ups has some kind of sinister conspiracy theory about it. Morons I call them, the kind of people who probably think all the world leaders are aliens or some shit like that.

'Shit happens!' but we don't run away, we try our best to please those that matter.'

They forget we had our hands tied! We never had a choice as to pull the show would be unfair to all the undercard boys who were all ready to fight and had sold their tickets, the show had to go on.

The show itself was still a sell-out, even with us offering to refund anyone because of the Welsh Phill / Decca fight not happening.

I was looking forward to the main event, Francis was nowhere near the fighter he once was, but I thought he would still be a test Decca.

When I got to the venue I went to the changing room to see the fighters, I went to see Decca first. He said he was a bit worried about how good Francis was, he was flapping a bit. Still, I thought it just prefight nerves, he kept saying he was just a bare-knuckle fighter and Francis was a real boxer, having won titles. I told him not to worry about it, just do his thing and everything would be okay.

I went to see Francis and had a quick word with him, he had turned up without a trainer and was just relaxing in his changing room listening to some music.

When the Fight began, Ricky English was Mc and he introduced both fighters.

The Fight was originally for the vacant Heavyweight Guv'nor Title, so on the night, Ricky announced it as that.

From the first bell, I saw immediately how this Fight was going to pan out.

Decca looked far too hesitant, respecting his opponent way too much. Francis spotted this and went straight into complete journeyman mode, just going through the motions, keeping his chin out of the way and just coasting through the Fight as easy as he could, so to just pick up his money.

After the 1st round, I went over to Decca's corner and shouted at his trainer to tell him, to let his fucking hands go!

"He's pacing himself, Joe." They replied.

The 2nd round was just like the 1st, both fighters not looking too interested in having a proper row!

This pissed me off, and after a third round of the same I went to Francis corner and told him if he doesn't step things up, then I won't be fucking paying him.

He came out threw a little flurry then went back into his shell, I was shouting to Decca's men for Decca to fucking do something to wake him up, hit him up the balls or stick the nut in! Anything to liven this poxy Fight up.

The rest of the Fight was exactly the same, Decca showing him too much respect and Francis just looking to survive by using the least amount of energy possible.

I think after the fifth round I went to the bar, I'd seen enough.

That was it then, Decca was announced as the new Guv'nor by fighting a journeyman, not that much different from when Norman Buckland fought, JJ, the journeyman, back at Caesars.

But in my mind, Decca could not call himself a Guvnor until he fought Welsh Phill, until he fought someone who wanted to have a real tear up.

That has always been the criteria for the Guv'nor title,

It's the same as in professional boxing, you can win a title against a very easy opponent, but you don't really become a champion until you defend it against someone decent.

After the boxing show we went to the after-party and I was exhausted mentally, everyone was saying it was a good show, but I knew the main event was a let-down. I had a good drink and stayed off the phone and social media for a couple of days.

When I did check out social media I saw what I expected. Loads of people coating the Fight, 99% of people who had something to say wasn't even at the show, they just took their opportunity to slag of Decca Heggie and the performance of Francis.

There was a lot of needle at Heggie, usually I don't take any notice of keyboard warriors, but I will admit it did get to me a bit and I private messaged a few people telling them to come and see me face to face if they had something to say.

I took a few days to think things over and then contacted Ricky to say I was calling it a day with promoting, I had lost the flavour and wasn't enjoying the shows anymore, so feeling this way, it seemed pointless for me to carry on.

After this, I did hear that Heggie boxed Tyrone Williams in Tooting, I gave my blessing, but that was nothing to do with me. I knew about it at the time, and I wished 'Jeff Gadsby' the promoter, all the best.

In November 2019 Jeff did contact me and ask if I was interested in making the Decca vs Welsh Phil fight which I said straight away that I wasn't interested. Jeff asked me to make the call and said he wouldn't contact Phil without me as that wouldn't be right. I did call Phill and like the fighter he is, he said yes he would fight Heggie but it had to be for the right money, he told me to ask what Heggie would bring to the table.

Around this time, there was a lot of bad things being said about Heggie on Facebook, stuff which I wasn't aware of. I asked Jeff about it and he told me it was all lies, he said Heggie had sworn to him he was innocent and it was all a witch hunt against him.

(I was told there was a page on him called 'tumble dryer' or something? But, I don't know, and I can swear I never took a look at it.)

I was then contacted by someone who told me Decca had been arrested in a nightclub for pinching a girl's backside.

Okay! I don't know what the circumstances were, and I'm not condoning it, but if that was all it was, pinching a birds arse, then it doesn't make you a 'sex fiend' as people were calling him.

I did say several times that if there was any truth in the accusations against him, then show me the proof, and I won't get involved in promoting the show.

This went on for a couple of weeks as me and Jeff discussed venues and dates until I finally pulled out.

I'm not a person who judges easily, and I'm certainly not a person to condemn someone without seeing proof with my own eyes, but the weight of anger against Heggie was clawing away at me. It just wasn't a risk I was prepared to take, so I told Jeff I was out.

Summing up the Guv'nor title.

The Guvnor title is not about a title that has a descended history, but more of a tribute title, which has evolved over time. The Guv'nor is a term to say who was the best at that time. I like to compare it to what we call in professional boxing, the unified or undisputed champion. You have to earn the title and fight another champion or beat the current champion. You can't be a Guvnor by beating just journeymen! You have to be willing to accept challenges, win or lose, and have the balls to fight the men around you.

I have seen people say they are the Guvnor by beating a couple of payday fighters! No, you weren't a Guvnor! You may think so in your mind but to be the best, to be (The Guv'nor) …. you have to have that defining fight or at least be willing to have that fight.

Roy Shaw was the first Guv'nor and he fought tough men, all challengers who came to fight and wanted to beat Roy. Men who put the money down to fight! Lenny then became the Guvnor when he beat Roy.

Cliff Fields and Johnny Waldron were good fighters, but they got their names from beating Lenny. They never boxed Lenny for a Guvnor title.

The so-called Guvnor title as it's known today, was created by myself and Ricky English as a tribute belt to Roy Shaw and Lenny McLean.

The belt was first contested by Sven Hamer in 2003 at Caesars, South London, and was defended and fought for over the next ten years. Many people have asked me over time so many different questions. One question that keeps on popping up was, shouldn't Cliff Fields be the Guvnor as he beat Lenny McLean, who beat Roy Shaw! He did indeed beat Lenny, but it wasn't for a Guvnor title! You could say he was the Guvnor of the times, as he beat the man, who beat the man.

But again he never won anything, called The Guv'nor title.

Asking 'who' the Guvnor is has become a strange question and misunderstood so much, that fiction and myth have become what some people think is the truth.

There is a clip, on YouTube with the title - ROY SHAW HANDS DOWN HIS GUVNOR BELT TO NORMAN BUCKLAND..

People look at that and think Roy is handing down his own Guvnor belt, which is not the case. The headline was created by the guy who shot the film and not the people who promoted the show, (US) or organised what happened that night in the ring. But, because it's on YouTube, people believe the headline and fail to see what was really happening.

Of course, Norman and his people milked the clip, it was a great headline for him, but it does not reflect what really happened. The simple truth is that I asked Roy to present a belt to Norman as his belt didn't show up in time for Norman's fight on the last show. It was us who made a big thing of it as we were building Norman Buckland up. We were trying to make as much publicity as we could, so we could have him in big fight in the future against Welsh Phill or Garry Sayers.

But as is life, those fights never came off! To be honest, it pissed me off they didn't, it was a kick up the bollocks for us after we had spent so much time and effort preparing everything behind the scenes, only to learn we had been wasting our time.

After Norman decided to retire, we then got back to business where Sven Hamer, Joe Kacz and Garry Sayer all held the title again. The Decca situation didn't help the legacy of the title either. It was too much bad publicity. Now I don't know really know what was going on with Decca. I never looked on the pages on Facebook that was created about him. I trust people, and a close person told me it was all bollocks, so I believed them.

It was also a time when I went back into the professionals, so I wasn't promoting the unlicensed shows anymore. Things got a bit lost because of the lack of my leadership, but what happened, happened, we cannot turn the clocks back.

I am proud of the fights we staged; some good men boxed for the title, and to this day, they are very proud of winning that belt. I am hoping soon we can resurrect the title and get some great fights in the future. Some people have called the Guvnor title, 'Royalty'

With me back at the helm, then I will get it back to where it once belongs.

CHAPTER 7
THE TWO JOES'

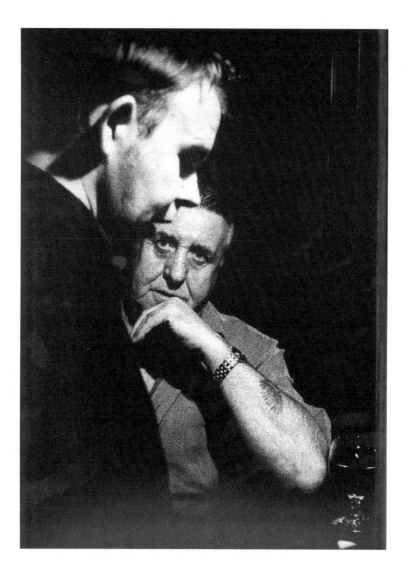

It is almost impossible to write a book about unlicensed boxing without talking about Joe Pyle Sr & Jr.

If you mention unlicensed boxing to the general public, then most of them would reply with the names of Roy Shaw and Lenny McLean. However, If you mention unlicensed boxing to those involved in the game, then the name, Joe Pyle will come up on countless occasions.

Joe Pyle Sr was the Godfather of unlicensed boxing. He created it and set the standards for what came after. In chapter one, we explain how everything began. But if you Google search unlicensed boxing, then click - videos, the page is littered with clips from YouTube featuring boxing from MeanMachine Promotions, the promotional company of Joe Pyle JR.

Boxing and the Pyle family seem to go hand in hand. Between them, they have decades of knowledge; both were boxers, managers, and promoters.

Both were very skilled boxers where people say they might have gone all the way to the top, but like so many men before and after them, the bright lights and lure of easy money pulled them away from the fight scene.

There is an old saying that goes - once boxing is in your blood, then it's there for life.

Just like his father before him, Joe went into the promotional side of things at an early age after realising he was too old to box professional.

in fact, Joe Jr was one of the youngest ever professional promoters in the UK and is still to this day the youngest promoter ever to stage a World title when he promoted Mark Baker against Ali Forbes for WBF World Super Middleweight Championship at a packed York Hall back in 2000.

(Mark Baker was also the first traveller to win a professional world title and not Tyson Fury or Billy Joe.)

Below is his own words is how Joe Pyle JR got into promotions.

"It started as a conversation down the Pub.

Nearly every Friday night I would join my Father and Uncle Ted for a drink in the Red Lion pub in Sutton, on this night I was talking to my father and said how much I regretted throwing all the years away and not turning professional as a boxer, it was at this time I was training every day and proper fit, but to be realistic, I was too old to go over, I was 29 years old and had just got out of prison.

'Why don't you do promoting then? my dad said,

I was a bit taken back as I had never even thought about this side of boxing, not even for a moment.

"Start putting the shows on, a promoter is a good job and it makes you something," Joe Sr added, hinting subtlety that he was keen to see his son get into something that would not take him back to prison.

So that was it, the next day I phoned Harry Holland, who was a friend of my fathers and he gave me the phone number for the British Boxing Board of Control. (BBBofC)

I called the board and they set up an appointment for a couple of weeks' time. I went to the meeting at their offices, situated at the Borough, London. I can remember having to wait upstairs until I was called downstairs to the conference room. I had to sit down in front of the committee of around ten people.

Once inside I can remember feeling very intimidated, I was given a barrage of questions to which I didn't have a clue what most of the answers were,

I can remember thinking they were so hard on me because of the links my father had to the 'unlicensed' scene, but regardless, I tried my best to answer their questions.

Robert Smith, who was then the Southern area secretary then threw me a lifeline, he suggested that I go away and prepare myself for a second interview as it was obvious I was unprepared at this meeting, I was given a British Boxing Board of Control rule book and advised to learn it thoroughly.

So I had a month to prepare myself for the second meeting, I went off to Fuerteventura in the Canary Islands where I laid on the beach every day reading and learning the rule book.

At the next meeting, I was ready now, and I was bang on form, I remember Roy Cameron waiting to see the committee over something, and he said he would come into the meeting with me. When we entered the room, Ron was asked why he was with me and he replied he was just with me to offer support, they replied something like that is very nice of you, but it is his interview and not yours.

So again, the committee started throwing questions at me, things like medical procedures at the event. This time I answered all their questions with newfound confidence. When you know the answers, it is easy to sound confident. After about twenty minutes of being interviewed, they usually ask you to go outside the office so that they can decide. With me, they never do this. I answered all my questions correctly, so they told me that they could not fault me on my answers, congratulated me, and said I would be permitted a boxing promoter's license. So that was it, I was now a professional promoter, the youngest in the country.

I went straight outside, punched the air in delight, and then phoned my fiancée and father and told them the good news.

Over the next couple of weeks, I spent all my time looking for fighters and visiting venues. I finally decided to stage my first show at The Royal Garden Hotel in Kensington, London, the show would be on the 17th of March, St Patrick's Day.

I joined an association called the (PBPS) the Professional Boxers Promoters association, a group of promoters who helped one another and created their own championship belt called the British Masters belt which was originally an official eliminator for the British title.

On the PBPA were Bruce Baker, Harry Holland, Jim Evans, Jon Feld, John Ashton, Jimmy Gill, Roy Cameron, Jonny Griffin, Pat Brogan and Greg Steene, Greg was the son of Alex Steene.

The PBPA was a great organisation to be a part of, especially when you're starting out. Eventually, I grew away from them, but I will always acknowledge the help they gave me in the pro game.

With the show planned, I went flat out promoting the event. I pulled in my pal Dave Courtney to help with the publicity, and I confirmed Mathew Barney

against Simon Andrews as the top of the bill. I had also sighed a good amateur, Karim Hassine from Balham for his first professional bout on the show.
For entertainment, I booked Alexander O'Neil, the American soul singer to perform on the night.
The show was a massive success and was packed, on the night, I even had to squeeze more tables in. We had Roger Daltrey from The Who there, and even the England cricket team turned up as they were staying at the hotel and heard about the boxing downstairs.

So that was that I was now promoting and was off to a flying start with, many people saying it was the best boxing dinner show they had been to for years. My next show was scheduled at the same venue in a couple of months, and I wanted to improve the boxing standard.   The promoters association I belonged to (PBPA) had created their own title, The British Master's Belt, which the (BBBofC) had just approved after months of discussions.
And as luck would have it as I was the promoter with the closest show scheduled, so it fell onto me to promote the first-ever British Masters title. It was just what I was looking for, a ten-round title fight for a belt and it was only second promotion.
The title fight was made between Mathew Barney and Bobby Bangher. It was not a fight to set the world on fire, but it was a good southern area standard fight and an excellent top of the bill for a dinner show.
Once again the show was a great success, and we managed to throw in a few laughs too, we had decided to have a laugh with one of my best pals Rob Davis, so I asked him if he wouldn't mind getting into the ring before the fights and saying a thank you to all who raised money on the last show. He was apprehensive, but after a minute, we finally convinced him. But poor Rob had no idea we had two microphones, so when he got into the ring and got the attention of over three hundred people, we killed his mike and my pal Lee, who was hiding behind the DJ booth started talking, it was at the time when the Budweiser ad was out where they used to shout WHHAAASSSSUUUUPPPPP. So when Rob put the mike to his mouth we switched Lee's mike on and he gave a massive, WWAAASSSUUUPPP, Rob nearly died as three hundred people in the middle of their meals looked at him like he was some kind of nutter.
Now Rob was a big fella, six feet two and around sixteen stone. Still, in that ring, he shrunk with embarrassment. Lee, however, was just getting going and he wasn't content to end it there, so Lee decided to have another go at him and started talking like a German porno star, Lee was grunting and groaning in this mock German accent, and poor Rob was looking more and more like a raving loon. it was fucking hilarious when Rob realised the laugh was on him so he jumped out the ring and came flying over to me and Lee, who were in stitches. "You fucking bastards", he said now himself laughing
Another funny thing happened on the show that night, we were just about to start the first fight. I looked around and asked where the ring card girls were, I

was told they were having trouble parking so we're going to be a bit late. The boxers were already on their way to the ring so we would have to go ahead without ring cards for the first fight, but as I was still a new promoter and the British Boxing Board of Control officials were present at ringside I was eager not to be seen making any mistakes. I saw the late Davy Lane sitting at ringside, quickly I called him over and asked him to step in and do the ring cards, Davey accepted, but what happened next turned into the best laugh of the night and totally backfired on me.

Davy Lane was around sixty and an ex-fighter who was a bit 'punchy.' When the boxers went back to their corners after round one, Davey got up and started trying to get into the ring with the ring card, but what Davy had not told me was he suffering from a bad back, it took the poor bugger around fifty seconds just to get into the ring! Now the referee is just about to start round two and Davy is hobbling about with the card, the referee turned to Dave and asked him to leave. Davey told the ref to fuck off, and he was doing the cards for Mr. Pyle and the ref should mind his own fucking business. It was nearly another minute before Davey got out of the ring. The board officials were having kittens! I can remember Mick Collier, the southern area rep looking at me with daggers as I was trying my best to hide my laughter. The crowd could now see the funny side of it and began to applaud Davey, Davey punched the air like he had just won the world title and then shouted out bollocks to the referee just as he left the ring, I was hysterical with laughter. Mick Collier ran over to me

"Joe, he is not doing round three as well is he?" Mick asked

"No Mick, I think we will leave it!" I answered, still cracking up with laughter.

Talking about Mick Collier I always liked and got on well with Mick, he was out of Battersea and was a boxing man and had a bit more common sense than some of the board officials. He did his job well of supervising the shows, and he realised that hick-ups can and do happen at boxing shows. I can also remember one night with Mick where we had a show on at the Equinox Leicester square, it was the second fight of the night and the first fight had stunk the place out, this fight was not going to good either, and the crowd was getting restless, so I decided to give them a bit of a lift, I was sitting close to one of the ring card girls so I called her over.

"Listen, when you take the card for the next round, I want you to get ya tits out and flash them at the crowd."

"What!" she said

"Just do it, it'll be a right."

So at the end of the round, the card girl gets into the ring. Just as she gets in front of the board officials she pulls up her top and flashes at the crowd, the look on Mick's face is a sight I will always remember, it was like he had just been hit with a brick, the crowd went crazy. They were laughing and joking with the girl and then Mick flew over to me.

"What the fuck was all that about, Joe?"

"Fuck knows Mick, I didn't tell her to do it, wait here I will go and see her," so off I went and knelt down beside the card girl.

"That was blinding, but don't do it again, listen just make out your talking to me, alright," I said to her before going back to Mick.

"Fucking hell, Mick, someone in the VIP seats bunged her fifty quid to do it, she didn't know she couldn't do it, mate, I've told her not to do it again."

Mick shook his head.

"I'm gonna have to write you up on this, Joe."

"Oh fuck off, Mick! It's not my fault that could happen to anyone."

Mick looked at me, squarely.

"Alright, Joe, but just make sure it doesn't happen again," he said before returning to his chair with a wry smile and slight shake of his head.

Somehow that little stunt of mine worked, the two fighters upped their game, and mood of the crowd improved.

When the next round ended, the girl got back into the ring. I remember Mick looking over at me with a smile on his face. I think he saw what I did, Mick was no fool, and I smiled back at him as he gave me a sneaky wink.

Another laugh we had at a show was at a promotion we did at the Royal Lancaster hotel when I booked Kim Bridges who is a great Elvis impersonator to sing at the event, I had also booked a DJ who was an old pal from the manor. Kim was in the middle of his singing set when the DJ who had been slinging pints down his neck all evening, began trying to hurry Kim up, so he could begin his DJ set. It started with the DJ using his own mike to mimic Kim in the middle of the songs, Rob Davis, who was a friend of Kim's saw what was happening and marched over to Barry the DJ to tell him to cut out the piss-taking, I then saw Rob have a heated discussion with him and then come flying back over to me with a mad look on his face.

"What's the matter?" I asked him,

Rob bit his lip and snarled.

"That c**ts pissed; he told me to fuck off."

"What!" I said, laughing.

"Year, he told me to fuck off."

"What'd you say?" I said, now getting Rob at it.

"I told him I'd break his fucking jaw," Rob snarled just as Tony Lambrianou walked over to us,

"What's the matter, Rob?"

"That saucy mug."

"Who?"

"The fucking DJ, he is pissed as a fart."

"What you got agro with the DJ, Joe?" Tony turned to me and said with his serious look.

"No," I said, laughing my head off.

"Elvis and the DJ don't like each other." I said which made Tony crack up laughing.

It's funny as I write it, it doesn't sound so funny, but it was hilarious. Tony was ready to pull the DJ and Elvis.

Anyway, as I started putting on more shows and my reputation as an up and coming promoter began to grow. I was now getting lots of offers from managers and other promoters wanting me to work with them.
I had a couple of meetings with Frank Maloney, where I even took him to a PBPA meeting. He told me his brother, Eugene was starting to promote shows, and that it might be a good idea for me and him to do a few joint shows together. I like Eugene, but this was at a time I had struck up a good friendship with Jon Feld at the (WSO) The World Sports Organisation. Jon was a good businessman and came from a wealthy Jewish background, but I found Jon to be a bit of a rebel, he hated any kind of authority and was always being called up in front of the board for mostly trivial little arguments. Still, I liked his style and so it was me and Jon and the WSO who began to do shows together.
One of the first shows we did together was back at the Royal Garden Hotel where we brought over a group of fighters from Africa, we named the show, 'The Lions of Africa' and the boxing was fantastic! We featured Israel Ajose in his pro debut who is now the unbeaten commonwealth champion and is ranked no 4 in the WBC ratings. Another fighter we featured had a name which you just couldn't pronounce, so Jon asked the boxer who his favourite fighter was? He replied, George Foreman, so we changed his name to George Foreman, I was tempted to change it to Ronnie Kray.

We then promoted a show at the Royal Lancaster Hotel in Bayswater and featured boxers from the Kronk gym, Manny Stewards famous gym in Detroit USA. The Kronk had just opened its first gym in London and we're looking to stage a show, so they came to Jon and me and we staged a fantastic show, we booked out the whole top floor of the hotel and we partied away until the next morning.

One of our biggest promotions just after this was when we staged the WBF World light-heavyweight championship at York hall between Mark Baker and Ali Forbes, the show was a complete sell-out. Even the staff at the venue said they could not remember when the hall was so packed, Mark Baker won the title and became the first UK gypsy ever to win a world title and I became the youngest professional promoter ever to stage a world title.
We had Larry Merchant from the American TV network HBO at ringside and had a good chat with him about the possibilities of gate-crashing the USA market.

In 2001, we started to promote shows at the Equinox nightclub in Leicester Square, London. A was a fantastic venue, situated right on the square, smack bang in the centre of London. Our reputations were now growing and we were always in the Boxing news as being the new kids on the block. It felt like we were just on the verge of securing a major TV deal. We started to be more innovative, looking to stage over ten fights on our shows, I remember us coming up with the idea to stage two shows at the same venue on the same day, one in the afternoon, and then a show in the evening but we had problems with the logistics, so in the end, we just went with the evening show.

Our stable of boxers was now growing and was a great mix of seasoned pros and prospects. Some of the fighters on our shows included, Cornelius Car (the WBF World champion) Sam Solomon, Geoff McCreesh (the British champion) Pele Reid, Floyd Havard (former British and European Champion) and our prospect stable was second to none; Martin Lindsey, who is now the British Champion, Ashley Theopane, also now a British Champion, Gary Buckland, who recently won the British title and Prize-fighter series, Michael Grant, former ABA Champion, Anthony Small, Toks Owah, Mickey Steeds, Sven Hamer, Ossie Duran.

The list can go on and on.

Around this time, we staged an absolute classic, Pele Reid was signed to us, heavyweight puncher, Michael Sprott was just coming onto the scene, Jon Feld had just become the President of the WBF, so we made a fight between the two fighters for the vacant WBF European Heavyweight championship.

When we announced the fight, we had a lot of press coverage and we staged a press day at Stringfellows nightclub a week before the show. The R&B singer Wyclef Jean, (a pal of mine) was in London, so I invited him along and we had some great pictures taken. It was a win or nothing fight for Pele as he was on his comeback. We had already promoted him twice, getting him two wins. Michael Sprott was a dangerous fighter, but he held a high ranking in the British ratings. We wanted to take that rating position, so it was a decent opportunity for Pele and a massive fight for the public. Both boys could bang and both boys could go over when hit. Therefore, on paper, the fight had the makings of a classic.

On the evening of the show, I can remember standing outside the venue greeting people and looking at the crowd stretched out over a hundred yards up the road. It was a great buzz and then one of the reporters from the boxing news arrived. He asked me how I saw the fight.

"This is a dangerous fight for Reid" he said,

"Well, he's got to move up, if he wants to go anywhere, then he has to get past the Sprotts of this world, how do you see the fight going" I replied.

"I can see Pele knocking him out in the first three rounds, but then if Sprotts still there in round four then I can see him knocking Reid out."

"They're both dangerous." I said.

"You know, Joe, as well as I do, if Pele could take a shot he would be world champion, but if Sprott hits him…. Its Goodnight!"

When the fighters came to the ring, the atmosphere was electric. It was just after the interval where we had the soul singer Jocelyn Brown in the ring singing her smash hit, 'Somebody Else's Guy' which had got everyone going wild. The place felt like Las Vegas in London as the boxer's ring entrance music started playing. Michael Sprott got into the ring first, and then me, Rob Davis and my brother Warren and Gary Page walked Pele Reid into the ring, we had an American announcer and he really whipped the crowd into a frenzy.

Round one went pretty much as expected with Pele going after Sprott and throwing absolute bombs at him; Sprott covered up and fiddled about, just keeping his chin hidden. Round over - a good round for Pele.

In round two, Pele came out and began where he left off, he called Sprott in, challenging him for a scrap, and Sprott opened up for a brief moment. The two fighters traded bombs until Pele forced Sprott back onto the ropes after a crushing right hand hit him in the temple, Sprott was in trouble. He tried to grab, but Pele threw him off. Sprott went down, which the ref ruled a slip. Pele then went after him and, at the end of the round, caught him with another devastating right-hand flush on the jaw. Sprott went down like a sack of potatoes, yet somehow he managed to pick himself up. The ref ordered them to fight on, Sprott covered up as he tried to clear his head and just as the bell went he caught Pele with a good left hook which had him in trouble, Pele staggered back to his corner. The crowd was going wild, and the fight was shaping up into the classic everyone was expecting.

The second round started with Sprott coming out and going straight for the kill, both me clashed in the centre of the ring and traded bombs, Sprott caught Pele with a big right hand only for Pele to laugh and shake his head saying *'the shot didn't hurt him,'* both continued to trade blows till Pele caught Sprott flush with a right uppercut, Sprott staggered back and then went down, he took the eight count but was still on shaky legs. The ref called for them to start boxing again. Pele went for the kill, Sprott was now in desperate trouble as he tried to survive. Pele caught him again with a right uppercut and then followed it with a flush straight right to Sprotts chin, Sprotts eyes closed and he fell to the canvas and rolled onto his back. I ran to the corner and was just about to get into the ring to congratulate Pele, when somehow Sprott rolled onto his knees and unbelievably was trying to get to his feet, I had one foot in the ring when Sprott staggered up, he warily raised his hands as the ref looked at him, I shouted out to the ref.

"He is gone ref, stop the fight!"

The ref Marcus McDonnell looked at him and asked him to walk forward, then the bell to end the round rang and Sprotts cornermen jumped in and helped him back to his corner. The look on Pele's face was one of disbelief. When he caught Sprott with right hand, Sprott was gone! He was completely knocked out. I honestly believe the force of the fall and the way he hit the canvas, woke him back up. Pele didn't come straight back to his corner; instead he confronted the ref.

"Do you want me to kill him"? Pele said.

"Back to your corner Reid, I am the referee."

When the next round started Sprott hardly took three steps forward, he just covered up as Pele hit him around the head and body, Pele was calling the ref to stop the fight while I was shouting at Pele to end it, Pele just continued to club Sprott, I am sure he thought in his mind the fight was going to be stopped, so for some reason he was not throwing the punches with all his might, then about half way through the round, Sprott began to fight back. The crowd began to go wild and rose to their feet and cheered Sprott for the courage he was showing, then at the end of the round he caught Pele with a wild right hand and Pele fell back into the ropes, Sprott sensed blood and began to throw punch after punch as Pele struggled to stay on his feet. The bell went and Pele went back to his corner, now he was out of it.

Rob Davis ran over to me and put his arm around me.

"What a fucking fight!" he shouted.

"Pele's fucking gone!" I replied, sensing the worst.

It did not long for me to realise my fears as Sprott came flying out for the next round, Pele tried to fight back but he was now just going for broke and had no defence at all, he was getting caught with big wild right hands and a few moments later he went down, Pele was hurt and only just beat the count, his legs were stiff, he tried to move but his legs just gave way, and he touched down again just as Sprott was throwing another right hand. Pele got up slowly, but we could now see that just one more good punch would end the fight. Pele tried to fight back, narrowly missing Sprott with a big right, but then a body shot and left uppercut hook struck him flush. He fell to one knee, he grabbed the ropes and pulled himself up but the referee then stopped the fight. Michael Sprott was the winner and fell to his knees in exhaustion and celebration. I bit my lip and applauded Michael, I acknowledged the heart he showed but in my heart, I was sick, Pele had just been knocked out and with it went my chance to manage and promote the Heavyweight British Champion and the prospect of securing a lucrative TV contract.

On a promotion side of things, the show had been a great success and the fight ended up being voted the third best fight of the year in the boxing news, it would have probably received the best fight if it had been on TV, but as usual, the boxing News gave preference to the TV promoters, they enjoyed their free ringside passes at the big fights like Hamed and Calzaghe, so they returned the favour as often as they could

After the Pele loss we dug our heels in and just got on with business with the rest of the boys that we were promoting and managing. The shows were going well, even though behind the scenes I was getting more and more frustrated with the politics of professional boxing.

There was a lot of hypocrisy about some of the decisions the board was making, especially the favouritism when it came to the TV promoters, Warren, Hearn, and Maloney.

When you are promoting without TV, you are branded a 'small hall promoter' this term I hated as I was promoting shows at the same venues as Frank Warren and Frank Maloney, (York Hall). Why were my shows small hall? Or any less important! I contacted the boxing news about this to complain, I explained to them that what they are doing by giving me a tag like this was affecting my ability to sign good amateurs. I was given a promise and then two months later they did a report on my show, which had the headline 'A great night of small hall boxing.'

I called the Boxing news office and had a heated conversation and almost put a bar on the boxing news reporting at my shows, but I had to bite the bullet as doing this would almost certainly make things harder for us. (This was before the boom of social media)

I was also growing more and more tired of some of the BBBofC regulations, the year was 2001, and we had already staged more shows this year than the so-called TV promoters which is no mean feat, but we wanted to show the powers that be that we can and will compete at any level with whoever we had to do.

In June 2001 we brought over Butterbean from the USA and staged a massive show at Wembley Conference Centre, this was at the time when Butterbean was featured on all the big HBO undercards in Vegas and Atlantic city in the USA. We had some fantastic press for the show and we fly posted all of London with massive posters of Butterbeans neck. We even had BBC and ITV staging interviews with the big man himself.

Butterbean won on the night, beating Shane Woolas in stopping him in the first round. The venue was sold out! Promoting a show at Wembley was another great milestone as we proved that we can stage 'big shows' without the pillow of TV revenue coming in. And in my book that makes you a better promoter because you have to work your balls off not to lose money, when SKY TV come in support a show they basically promote it themselves, over the years I have seen some promoters sit back and just put the show on, some dont even bother going that extra mile because they know on the night their money is secured by the TV.

Me and Jon Feld, often spoke together on our progress in the boxing world. It was up for debate that we were the fourth biggest promoters in the country at the time, but believe it or not the BBBofC instead of acknowledging our hard work, seemed to get more and more agitated by us, we were constantly being called to appear at the southern area meetings to answer silly misdemeanours. On one occasion, we were called up because Jon Feld had had an argument with the board appointed timekeeper and told him to fuck off. At the meeting you would have thought we had shot the Pope. It was ridiculous to call us in for such a trivial thing. It could have been dealt with a phone call after the show. Jon was livid as we sat down before the board; he took off straight away by saying what is wrong with saying fuck off! One of the board officials said that nothing was wrong with fuck off, but it was how it was said, and in what context, so now we are sitting here (at our costs) discussing the context of the saying, (fuck off,) I began laughing which I think made some of the board officials see just how ridiculous this was, we sat there for a further fifteen minutes arguing about what had happened, I was not that bothered as I knew the real reason why all this had happened, but I kept it to myself. What really happened was that the timekeeper turned up with two guests and expected them to get free VIP ringside seats, Jon argued with him that they should pay and the timekeeper threatened to walk off which would have left us without a timekeeper for the evening. So Jon resentfully agreed to let the Timekeeper's guests in, but would not give them VIP tickets, instead he gave them stall tickets and when the Timekeeper came to complain, Jon just told him to fuck off as he was too busy to deal with it.

I was still laughing and finding the funny side of things as I had this up my sleeve which, if I told the board would in fact get the timekeeper in trouble. I did not want to do that; (two wrongs don't make a right!)

I thought if the board started taking the piss then I would pull Robert Smith to one side and tell him exactly what had happened. In the end, we agreed to be more tactful and that was that, though it had stuck a seed in Jon's head that the board was prejudiced against him. To be honest, I took it with a pinch of salt, but to Jon it was something bigger, maybe it's a Jewish persecution thing, I don't know really, Jon however, convinced himself that the board wanted him out.

As the months went on, our relationship with the board deteriorated further. The more shows we put on, the more we were getting summoned to appear before them. It was like a constant struggle with us having to keep explaining ourselves for various actions.

For me, it was the boards interfering that was annoying me. We were also called up before them because we were paying some boxers with tickets rather than purses. The board did not like this as it could cause them a problem with working out their commissions. Especially if the boxer wanted to lie about how many tickets he sold, I can understand the reason why they showed concern, but what annoyed me was their total lack of understanding of just how difficult it is promoting shows without TV.

What we created was called a **'ticket deal.'** The BBBofC hated it, I wasn't keen on it, but promoting shows without sponsorship or TV was extremely hard. In the past, we had booked fighters to box on our shows and they had shown little interest in selling tickets or helping us to promote the show - the ticket deal solved this issue.

It's funny how, almost twenty years later, the **'ticket deal,'** is used by almost every promoter and promotion in the country, the BBBofC even questions and gives advice to boxers about it when they apply for their professional license.

Many people frown on the dreaded ticket deal, but although unpopular, it changed the way boxers were paid and how shows were run.

Thank me or loathe me for it, but the **'ticket deal'** I nearly lost my pro license for - was down to us.

Another occasion that caused more friction was when I signed up former British and European champion Floyd Havard. We had spent a lot of money promoting him for his return, but because he was based in Wales, he was weighed in the day before by the Welsh boxing board and appeared on the day with a signed certificate of weight. This was not something which was that out of the ordinary, but when he turned up to fight the next day at the Equinox, he weighed over a stone heavier. The board officials at our show were suspicious and said the fight couldn't happen. We had already paid for his opponent, Rachael Minghaliev to fly in from the Ukraine but the board were complaining about Havard's weight and saying something was untoward, I offered Minghaliev an increase in his purse to fight Havard and he agreed. Still, the board was refusing Floyd to fight! I argued that he weighed in right in front of the Welsh board and that he had a signed certificate of weight by an appointed board official, and his opponent is willing to fight. However, still they dug their heels in and were not letting the fight go ahead.

I thought this decision was outrageous, the bout was over six rounds and not a championship bout so it could be boxed at a catch-weight, but no matter what we did, the board would not budge on their stance. We had spent hundreds of pounds promoting this event and had hundreds of people turning up to see Floyd's return. If the fight did not go ahead, we would (look like idiots) I told the board, I tried to be as flexible as I possibly could and even suggested we drop the fight down to a four round bout, but still, the board would not budge. This was the beginning of the end with me, it made me realise the hypocrisy and the politics involved in the sport, I knew full well that if this fight would have been scheduled for TV, then it would have gone ahead, but with us, it seemed we were getting no help at all.

I was also called to appear before the board for a misconduct charge because I had had an argument with another promoter, to cut a long story short, I was owed a thousand pounds and the promoter was messing me around so I sent someone to his office to collect it, sure enough he got the cheque but I was reported for threatening the promoter. When the board summoned me, I more or less told them it was none of their business and that they had only heard his side of the story as I don't go around telling tales. I was reprimanded and threatened with a license suspension which made me livid! The truth of the matter was that this promoter had my money and was then going around to my venues and trying to get exclusive rights at the venue, which would have stopped me promoting there, now what am I supposed to do when someone is trying to sabotage your living? The other promoter was not hurt, or punched, but he was told very firmly to back away or there will be a problem, again the board did not take my side or even take a neutral view, instead I was in the wrong, and now had a mark against my license and was one more reprimand away from being suspended.

The final straw came just after I had promoted an event at the Marriot hotel. On the night of the show I had had a lot of problems with the hotel manager. During the day I asked the hotel staff for a safe location to store some auction items and was told to store them in a secure room, about an hour before the auction was due to begin, I sent one of my ring whips to fetch the items but he returned with three items short. I went myself to the room and found it empty, so I called the hotel general manager and told him that three items were missing, he scratched his head and said he did not know so we began to argue with me telling him I placed the items under his supervision and if they do not show up pronto then I would be billing the hotel for them.

At the end of the night once the boxing had finished, I had prior arranged to meet the hotel manager and pay the balance of what was owed for the hire of the hotel. I then discovered that certain members of the public had run up tabs and then left without paying and they were now asking me to pay over £800 more. I argued that when I booked the hotel I insisted that no tabs be allowed, I even asked them to include it in the contract, I looked at my paperwork, and sure enough, it was in there but they replied that it must have been employers of me who had run up the tabs. I told them it was their incompetence and not mine and refused to pay, and I also told them I would be withholding £1000 back because the auction items went missing.

Over the next few weeks I had a few more conversations with the hotel where I put the matter in the hands of my solicitor to find a compromise, as far as I was concerned the matter was being dealt with until I got a phone call from Simon Block at the board.

I had just submitted a list of boxers who would be appearing on my next show in two weeks' time at the Equinox, when Simon rang up, at first I thought there may had been a problem with the list of boxers, but when he started talking about the Marriot hotel, I just couldn't believe it.

I was told that unless I pay the Marriot in full, my show at the Equinox could not go ahead, I told them my solicitor was dealing with the matter and that I had already released hundreds of tickets and posters for the Equinox show. Simon told me that the Marriot was on a list of board venues and that he could if he wanted to take the money from my bond, which would mean I would have to top it up, I protested that this was outrageous as the board were finding me guilty without hearing any of the facts. I then told Simon that as a license holder of the board, I should be the one who should be being protected and not the hotel, I ended up slamming the phone down as the conversation was getting more and more heated.

I just sat there in total disbelief, I was being blackmailed, if I did not pay the hotel, then I had no Equinox show. Simon suggested I pay the hotel first, and then I can pursue the lost items and see if I can work out a compensation. But once they had my money, I knew full well there would not be any compensation, I would just get a letter saying they have reviewed the situation and that they would not be paying any compensation, and that would be that! And thanks to the board who are supposed to be looking after me (A license holder) I would be a grand out of pocket!

I spoke to my solicitor and he agreed with me that the boards stance was totally prejudiced against me and what they were doing was almost certainly 'restriction of trade,' I called the board again, once I calmed down and tried to have a civil conversation with Simon Block but it was like talking to a wall, all I kept hearing was this regulation and that regulation. I said this should be a precedent, then, but it just fell on deaf ears. Simon apologised and said unless I pay the Marriott in full which included the tabbed drinks (even though I had contract insisting for them not to run up tabs) then my show at the Equinox would not be granted permission to continue, I said then I would run the show independently (unlicensed) but was told that the board would then suspend any boxers appearing on the show.

Ultimately, this debacle ended up with me paying the hotel in full just so my equinox show could continue, I was livid... But I had no choice, if I cancelled the show, then it would have caused me untold aggravation and the loss of more funds.

The equinox show went ahead but for me, this was the last straw, I could no longer be dictated to like this, I actually liked some of the members of the board especially Robert Smith and Mick Collier, but the constant regulations had struck a nerve with me, I can remember at this time feeling like I was an inconvenience to them, when I phoned them to ask for permission to a championship fight or something like that, I began to hear groans from the other side of the phone, like I was being a nuisance or something.

In 2004, I decided enough was enough and after a conversation with my old pal Ricky English, who had been promoting a few unlicensed shows in Watford, I joined forces with him and we started….

The legendary Caesars boxing events.

CHAPTER 8
CAESARS – THE LION'S DEN

Caesars

**Wot an Era you created it gave so much to so many people community spirit London as one. Take a big bow .X **
PAUL BARTLEY

A few words from my dear friend Clive Black.
My mate Joey and his Dad the great Big Joe used to invite me 'down to Caesars in Streatham for the boxing ' and it was an invitation I never declined.
The worst bit for me was getting there parking up and getting past all the nutters outside.
As soon as I got within eyesight of Joe's security I would hear a loud scream ' of move out the way, let Mr Black through' ....I suddenly felt like Sinatra !
Usually Big Rob would give me a hug and a kiss on either side of my face and take me around the side , avoiding the metal detector and venues paid security.
Up the stairs and suddenly there were the bright lights the regal looking boxing ring and many tables of 10 covered in crisp white table cloths.
'I will take you to Joe's table , he wants you on his table' was the usual line as I was walked through the younger boxing fans and local hard-men until I reached the VIP AREA.

'Sit er mate'…..Bottle of vodka and a jug of warm flat coke were usually on the table , getting a beer wasn't easy and I used to go to the bar to get one , it was always a tasty crowd and the safest place for me was on either Joe Seniors table or Joey's table…there I sat between legends of the underworld , blokes the size of houses all with knuckle-dusters , all who I got on great with , they loved hearing about my world of 'music biz life' and when they found out my dad wrote Diamond are forever , well let's just say that sealed the fucking deal !

The venue was special , the fights were often brutal but what made it magical were the characters all under the same roof sharing stories planning their next moves , all being a big naughty and have a great time. Laughter was everywhere until a fight broke out !

Joey asked me to write something about 'nights at Caesars' but I can't without highlighting that his dad was the biggest draw for me and many who went to there. Having 'an audience with Joe Pyle was like sitting by the side of Brando in Godfather , softly spoken he would tell me a few things, no words were wasted, short clear easy to understand observations made by a man who irrespective of criminal nonsense had a mind sharper than anyone I have ever sat with.

He was a giant and is missed every day by those whose lives he touched.

I met so many feared men (I thought some of their other halves were a lot scarier !) on these night. Some made a big impression on me. Tony Lambianou had such great Italian style and class, Roy Shaw was just hard as nails, Freddie Forman and Charlie Richardson I was nervous to look at but when either one spoke to me, they always whispered a little too close to my ear that I used to shiver! They all treated me like family.

While all the old boys drank and enjoyed themselves Joey was always rushing around like a lunatic , he did everything on those nights to make them magical. His energy and drive and his this ability to being screaming at a boxer one minute and next auctioning something to raise money for the local children's hospice was unique.

He was and still is the most fearless person I have ever met – if I ever need a one man army , he is who I will call.

I had some amazing nights there, exciting times , terrifying times but I was always treated by Joe and the firm as one of their own.

With my family and in everyday life I feel like a normal sized bloke , tall enough with big strong arms but whenever I was in their company I always felt small , I still do when I meet up with 'the chaps' , I used to leave with a rash from their stubble kisses on my soft skin!... Most of them have two things I will never have – Big rough hands and very cheap cologne !

They were great times , times I will never forget…..the memories will live on forever.

Clive Black

When we started promoting at Caesars in Streatham, south London, it was like the kids who had been given the keys to the sweet shop, after six years of being regulated by the BBBofC, we were now totally free to do what we wanted to do. we could make our own titles up, weight divisions, round duration or even scrap rounds all together, the gloves were off so to speak and our only regulations were what we felt were right.

In these early days we broke just about every rule going, I call them our 'wild west days.'

We were frontier men doing what we liked, when we liked…. And we had the largest dance hall in London as a stage for our imagination.

Caesars … a brief history.

For over 80 years the building had been one of Streatham's most popular nightspots. It started life as the Locarno Dance Hall and its opening night on 1st October 1929 was a glittering occasion attended by over 1,500 dancers. The Locarno quickly established itself as one of the premier dance venues in London with many of the country's top bands performing there.

The building underwent a £100,000 refurbishment in 1970 and reopened as the Cats Whiskers. A further £500,000 was spent on improvements in 1984 when it was re-launched as the Studio Nightclub.

The building was subsequently acquired by Rank who opened it as the Ritzy in 1990 after a £1m face-lift. However, this venture was short lived and the hall was taken over by a private consortium in 1995 and after yet another refurbishment reopened as Ceasers Nightclub adopting a Roman theme.

Caesars Nightclub Streatham Hill London: A Tribute 1929 – 2010

It seemed fitting to pay a tribute to Ceasers Night Club Streatham Hill London here on Tribute To Most Haunted as it had featured in Most Haunted Series 2 in search of the ghost of Ruth Ellis and of course was owned by demonologist Fred Batt. Reports of dark shapes which move across the room, a ghost of a woman, hearing footsteps and doors opening on their own.

Caesars started life as the first purpose built Ballroom in England opening in 1928 as The Locarno Ballroom.

Many stars appeared here in those days including: Glenn Miller – Laurel & Hardy – Charlie Chaplin and a host of others. In the sixties bands such as: The Rolling Stones – The Small Faces – Rod Stewart Ect.

Miss World and Come Dancing (now Strictly) started there

The Last Owner Fred Batt held the First Pro Female Boxing at Caesars and introduced Cage Fighting to Caesars

When the doors closed in 2010 an article in the Local Guardian advertised the auction of the chariot and horse that once adorned the entrance.

For sale: one Roman chariot, four horses, featured in a Spice Girls video – price on application. Preferred buyer local to area.

Love it or hate it, the giant statue rising over Streatham High Road from Caesars nightclub is one of the defining images for those passing through Streatham.

And a once-in-a-lifetime opportunity has arisen to purchase it, as club owner Fred Batt strips the club of its contents, ahead of it being passed over to developers in three weeks.

Mr Batt said: "If no one buys the statue it will have to go in my back garden, but I'm hoping someone locally will buy it, to keep it in Streatham as part of the club's history."

To give a little inspiration to potential buyers, the Streatham Guardian has taken the time to imagine what it could be like displayed on another local landmark – Streatham Ice Arena.

But for those who are not interested in the chariot and horses, Mr Batt is also selling the rest of the club's contents, with everything from a stuffed Siberian tiger to tables and chairs going under the hammer.

Mr Batt said: "It's sad to finally be going, it's the end of an era."

Developers have bought the club and have permission to knock it down to build a 243-flat residential and shopping development.

The club was built in the 1920s as the UK's first purpose-built ballroom.

It was one of the premiere south London nightspots of the time, with Glenn Miller, Audrey Hepburn and Charlie Chaplin among the top names to grace its stage.

It later became the Cat's Whiskers club, with a revolving stage.

Mr Batt took it over in 1994, it then became home to events by Lap Attack – London's first lap dancing club for women – and a boxing venue, where Brad Pitt was filmed in Guy Ritchie's movie Snatch.

Mr Batt blamed the loosening of licensing laws on the failure of the club, as drinkers could stay in bars rather than move on to clubs.

Unlicensed Boxing – MeanMachine Promotions – Caesars.
Above are three names that go hand in hand with one another.

Without a doubt, Caesars was the main venue to fight at!

The Mecca of Unlicensed Boxing! It was full of history, boxers who boxed for me stood under the same spotlights where Lenny McLean fought years earlier. It had a gladiatorial feel to it, like walking into a roman battleground.

When you walked through the entrance, past the stuffed tigers and wax models of gladiators, you could feel the atmosphere. Then you walked down the stairs into the main hall where a lone boxing ring sat surrounded by tables and chairs. People looked at you as you walked in, wondering who you were with or who you was with? You never knew who was at Caesars, little firms congregated in separate corners, it was a knife-edge, where anything was possible. There was fighting in the ring and fights in the crowd.

(Fuck, I miss that place so much!)

It wasn't by chance that the producers of the hit movie **SNATCH** chose Caesars to film their fight scene.

Ex-MeanMachine fighter, Colin Wilby - once said in an interview, "Until you fought at Caesars … you are a nobody."

Dave Courtney, a regular to our shows, said, "Caesars … the place just smelt of battle!"

It's funny when you look back at things, at the time you don't realise what kind of impact you are making. But now the dust has settled on Caesars, I often see and hear people talking about the memorable shows that went on there.

They were more than shows, they were local events where everyone looked forward to them. It was just a crazy mix of fights in the ring, fights in the crowd! The stage would be a who's who of London's gangland where you might be sitting next to Joe Pyle Sr, Roy Shaw, Charlie Richardson, Freddie Foreman, Howard Marks, Tony Lambrianou, Dave Courtney, Paul Ferris, Tommy Wisbey, Bruce Reynolds, or even a mobster from New York or Los Angeles. They were crazy times! Then we always had celebrities on the stage, like Brian Harvey from E17, soul singer Mark Morrison, Jocelyn Brown, actors and actresses from EastEnders, ex boxers like Frank Bruno and Nigel Benn. Wycleff Jean even turned up once with his entourage, arriving on a dozen Harley Davidson motorbikes which roared down the street outside.

I remember Rob Davis come running over to me and telling me that loads of bikers were pulling up outside and there could be trouble. I called a few pals and we went out to see what it was all about and then I saw Wycleff taking his crash helmet off and smiling.

I laughed, and then Rob took them all downstairs, found a table for them on the stage and waved out to Ricky who was in the ring with the mike, to announce Wycleff was here, Ricky looked over and nodded and then announced "Look, Bob Marley has just arrived! … I thought he was dead!"

Me and Ricky had a fantastic team working for us at Caesars, the owner Fred Batt, Colin and Dave Burns ran the venue and then we had my auntie Lorraine at the box office, who was very good at her job. You would be surprised at the amount of people who turned up saying they were a pal of mine or Ricky's and ask if they could they talk to us. I always told Lorraine to tell them I was busy running a show. We had a guest-list and if their name wasn't on the list, then they had to pay for a ticket and talk to me or Ricky about it downstairs. Lorraine was brutal at this, she had to be. It's surprising the amount of people think they should get in free because they know you, I don't know what it is with boxing, but people think they have a right to enter for free if they know the promoter. We would let a few 'freebies' in but we had bills to pay! Boxers and officials on the night needed paying. We weren't being horrible or nothing, but we had a show to run, sure we had fun, yet on the nights me and Ricky were working, it was our job!.

We were a good team though, both of us knew the promotions game like the back of our hand and we bounced off each other well. Ricky would usually sort out the books and collect the ticket money and we would play 'good cop, bad cop.' Usually, when a fighter would come in well short on his ticket money or fuck us about with excuses. Ricky would sit down with them and go through how many tickets they sold and what they were handing back. If the fighter had done shit, then he would give me the nod, and I would come over, being the bad guy.

"Ar, that's a fucking joke! ... You're taking the fucking piss!" I'd tell the fighter.

"Well, he's boxing for nothing then!" I would add angrily before Ricky would soften the blow.

It may sound harsh, but over the years, I have heard every excuse going from fighters. I'm not a callous man, but I can see when someone is talking bollocks. There was this one occasion some fighter had to pay us money to box. He had his tickets and we got him a 'Set-up' fight, (a fight where the opponent had been paid to lose.) Anyway, this kid comes in and says he has only sold **two** £25 tickets. It was a fucking joke, fifty quid and we had to pay £250 for his opponent. Now remember this fighter had £1500 worth of tickets and promised us before the fight, that he would sell them all. So I made him box for nothing and then collected £500 off him out of his wages for the next two Fridays. My old pal Johnny Essex who was a ring whip for us was standing and shaking his head, smiling when he heard me telling the boxer, I'll be wanting my money from his wages next Friday. John came over to me after and sighed, "You're fucking ruthless Joe, I've never seen anyone so hard on fighters like you."

"You have to be that way sometimes, John, you want your wages tonight, don't you, and so does everyone else want paying tonight, this c..t could have called us a few days ago and said he hadn't sold any of his fucking tickets. But he didn't, did he. He's s fucking idiot and only has his own stupidity to blame."

"Yeah, but that was fucking strong, Joe."

"John, fuck the fighters! Some of them are alright, but the others are a fucking joke ...You have to treat some of them that way, mate."

That reminds me of another time when we had this lad from Brixton fighting for us, he came through Teddy Bam Bam, so we called down to him to come up to the office to sort out his ticket money. He walked in like he thought he was Mike Tyson, a real attitude on his face, he slumped down in front of Ricky and threw a full book of tickets on the table. Ricky looked at the tickets and then me, "How many you sold?" Ricky asked the fighter who just kissed his teeth and said,

"Me, no sell no fucking tickets!"

I was standing close by and I heard what he said and couldn't believe the flash c**t. I walked over and picked up the tickets and looked at Ricky who was looking pissed off at this mugs attitude. "He sold no fucking tickets." I said in disgust.

"No, nothing, joe, fuck all," Ricky replied.

Then he ain't fucking fighting! Tell his opponent the fights off!" I said sternly before walking off.

That was that! The idiot never fought and later on in the night he had the gall to come over to me complaining about the people who came to support him, saying they weren't happy because he wasn't fighting.

"What fucking people? … You never sold a ticket!" I snapped back at the clown.

Wendy was another important person working for us, her jobs were arranging the ring card girls and helping out doing managerial tasks.

My brothers Mitch and Warren were always on hand, like an extra pair of hands if we needed them. Plus, they were always in the middle of any crowd trouble, helping to quiet things down. Rob Davis was another good pair of hands and Teddy Bam Bam.

Talking about crowd trouble, it was crazy how we just expected it to happen, it was normal and we just got on with things, didn't take any notice of it, unless we had to.

One show, there was me and Ricky does an interview just as the doors had opened. Then half way through the conversation we heard a great big bang, we looked over and noticed that someone had been thrown off the top balcony onto a table below, he hit the table hard and then rolled off before jumping to his feet and ran out the door. I just carried on doing the interview as nothing had happened. The look on the interviewer's face was a picture, he couldn't believe what had happened and interrupted the interview,

"Did someone just get thrown from the balcony?" he said in disbelief.

"I think so." I replied before getting back to what I was talking about.

"Someone just got thrown off the balcony!" he repeated in shock.

"Yeah, it happens … this is Streatham."

That was Caesars! ... Crazy! ... We just got used to it! It happened every show, so we just dealt with it.

Another mad time was when Colin Burns fought and brought with him all his West Ham ICF firm, and us being us (and not giving a fuck) had a Millwall boy fighting on the same show who brought along loads of his firm. The two boys weren't fighting each other, but nevertheless we had a venue full of football hooligans who both hated each other.

It did kick off, but my brothers and I sorted it out, a few had to leave, and the others all said they would behave, so we gave them another chance. A lot of them were my pals, as well, so it was dealt with amicably enough.

Another time was when three masked men burst through the doors looking to rob us. I was in the box office in the middle of having an argument with someone when I saw my auntie Lorraine shout out, I turned to see three men in balaclavas and one of them was waving a machete, he tried to jump through the window of the box office, but I grabbed the baseball bat we always had under the window and swung it in his direction, he backed off and tried again, but he couldn't get in, not unless he fancied having a bat smashed around his mouth. We shouted out, and then a few of my mates came running up the stairs, so the dopey idiots in masks ran back out the doors empty handed.

I put the bat back under the window and carried on with my argument as nothing had just happened.

"Joe, you alright, mate." One of my mates asked through the window.

"Yeah... I'm good." I replied.

"Someone just said there was a c..t with a machete up here!"

"Yeah, there was, he's gone now."

It was just a typical night at Caesars! That was how the shows went, and we never batted an eyelid or gave a fuck.

If that sounds crazy outside the ring, that was nothing to what usually went on under the lights. Fights would often end up on the canvas having a wrestling match where everyone would jump in to separate them. I would laugh all night at the antics, it was bloody funny.

Ricky would Mc the evening, but he wasn't just any MC, he was good, bloody good at getting the crowd going.

Regular MCs, only announce the fighters and then get out the ring and sit silently at ringside, but not Ricky! He would sit at ringside and keep his mike on... (Giving the crowd a running commentary)

"C'MON.... Let's GET THESE BOYS GOING!" he would shout on the mike.

Or make a joke to the crowd if someone was getting a beating, Ricky would say, "FUCKING HELL! HE SAID HE COULD FUCKING FIGHT!"

Ricky was the *bollocks* on that mike, and he always had the crowd in stitches. I can honestly say he was the best, and over the years, I have seen countless MCs all try to copy Ricky's style, but they never come close!

It was like a running commentary during the fights as Ricky would shout out things like "WOW... WHAT A FUCKING SHOT!" and "CMON YOU TWO.... ITS NOT A FUCKING HUGGING CONTEST!"

The crowd loved it and it lightened the mood, made everyone smile.

I remember one night where we had a good kid turn up to fight who had sold over 150 tickets, but his opponent had let us down. The kid was going mad as this was the second time this had happened and he was saying if he wasn't fighting, he would be leaving and wanted to refund for all his crowd. That was a big chunk of money and there was no fucking way I was doing that! We already had the money in our pockets so there wasn't a chance in hell he was getting it back. Me and Ricky walked outside for a quiet chat and a cigarette when I saw Ricky looking over the road.

"What you looking at?" I asked him

"What do you think he weighs?" replied Ricky.

"Who?"

"Him over there." Ricky said and then nodded at some poor fella standing in a doorway trying to sell the big issue.

"You taking the piss!" I said, laughing,

"Worth a go mate," replied Ricky.

We both walked over and spoke to this trampy looking fella selling the big issue, "It's an easy £200 quid mate." I told him.

Ten minutes later and we have walked him into the changing room trying to find this poor fella some boots and shorts, he's smiling as I give him a pint of lager. (Talk about thinking on your feet! we had no opponent, now we had the big issue man)

The fight, well it wasn't a fight ... The poor bloke got sparked in the first round, but we told the ref to look after him and then Ricky being Ricky got on the mike.

"GIVE THIS MAN A ROUND OF APPLAUSE! ... HE NEVER KNEW HE WAS FIGHTING TONIGHT, HE WAS OUTSIDE SELLING THE BIG ISSUE..... BUT HE GOT IN HERE FOR YOU LOT."

The crowd went absolutely crazy, bursting into laughter. But I wasn't laughing! I had my head in my hands, thinking, 'Ricky, what the fuck have you done mate... I've now got to go to the fighter, who is going to be moaning his head that he has just sold loads of tickets to his friends to come and support him bash up some poor bloke who sells the big issue."

I gave Ricky a look to say (fucks sake turn it in). Ricky clocked what he had done so, he raised the mike to his mouth, and tried to make good his blunder,

"THIS KID HERE WAS A FORMER RUSSIAN AMATEUR CHAMPION! HAD OVER 200 FIGHTS BUT HE GOT IN THE RING FOR YOU! AND YOUR MAN BEAT HIM!" I just started laughing and shaking my head....

Fuck it; this was Caesars!

When I look back at it all now, we just didn't give a fuck! We had the license to do what we wanted and we played up big time.

Ricky was great on the mike, he always had the crowd in stitches. Another funny moment was when a big heavyweight came to fight and I mean big, he had a few extra pounds around his waist, this fella had been driving us mad at the last couple of shows asking to fight, he wouldn't stop telling us how good he was.

So we gave him a shot and he was fucking terrible! On the night he got stopped in the first round and looked awful... when he went down for the count, Ricky started on the mike from ringside.

"CMON GET UP! ...... GET UP!" he was saying as the referee counted.

But the lad was gone and the count got to ten and he was counted out.

"WELL THAT WAS FUCKING GOOD! ... SORRY EVERYONE, HE SAID HE HAD BEEN IN FIGHT CAMP FOR A MONTH ... WHERE WAS THE CAMP, FUCKING PIZZA HUT!" Ricky said over the mike.

It was crazy when I looked back at it, and crazy how we got away with all we did.

Later on that night I was talking to Ricky about the big heavyweight.

"You might have overmatched him mate," I said,

Joe, it's his own fucking fault! You were there when he said he could fight! If he told the truth, I would have matched him up to someone his own standard, fuck him, it's his own fault for being a lying c..t!" Ricky answered.

The fighter left that night and never came back, Ricky was right though... Don't come to us, giving it the biggun.. You WILL come unstuck!

In the early days of Caesars, we would always have a strip show in the ring during the interval, we would put a chair in the ring and the card girls would pull someone out the crowd and give him a lap dance in the Centre. That was always funny as all the fellas sitting with their wives pretended not to be looking. I used to have women coming up to me complaining saying it was a sex show, but I would just laugh it off.

That's got me thinking about behind the stage; there was a small passageway that we nicknamed, 'Blowjob' Alley. I'll leave it up to your imagination what went on there.

Dave Courtney would always be at our shows, and I would ask him to get in the ring to tell a few jokes, he would have the crowd laughing and it usually always ended up with him auctioning one of his knuckledusters.

Dave is and was a funny fucker, in another life he should have been a comedian. He would be in the ring doing a charity auction, pulling this duster out of his back pocket, and saying who will bid £250 for this! If you buy this, then I will also invite you to come to stay at my house where I guarantee you get drunk, drugged and have your dick sucked, all for £250! (people did actually go and Dave lived up to his promises)

Another funny thing we would do, usually before the fights began, was to go into the DJ booth where they had a spotlight, the lights in the venue would be dim, so we would find someone at the bar and just hit them with this blinding spotlight and then change the music to James bond or the pink panther. The fella would take a second to realise he had the light on him and then move to the side, but we would follow them with the light as the music played. It was comical watching them trying to duck out the way as the pink panther tune played. (Da doo, da doooo, da dooo, da dooo, da dooo, da da da dooo,!!!!) It was funny.

Another trick we liked to play on the fighters, was change their chosen ring entrance music half way through their ring walk. One time we had this big, arrogant prick who me and Ricky didn't like, and he came out to his heavy rap music trying to look mean and tough, he was a proper arrogant c..t, so just before he got in the ring I changed his song to Cyndi Lauper's 'Girls just wanna have fun.' The look on his face was worth paying a grand for, I was in stitches. After his fight, later in the evening, he came over to me moaning. I was standing with my brothers and was half pissed.

"Oh Joe, I ain't happy bout what you did!" he said.

"It was a joke, mate, relax," I replied.

"Well, I never found it funny!"

"LISTEN YOU SOPPY C..T...FUCK OFF! ... TAKE A FUCKING JOKE WILL YA, YOUR'E LUCKY I DIDN'T CHANGE IT TO TELETUBBIES!" I said back to him before we fucked the clown off.

Idiots who can't take a joke! Fuck sake, why do some people take themselves so seriously?

The stage area at Caesars was the VIP section, and you couldn't get up there unless you were invited or had a wristband, but sometimes you would get an idiot who would find their way to get amongst us. On this one occasion someone, I won't say who was a bit pissed and go to the stage and was annoying some of the VIPS, I pulled him to one side and told him to behave himself, but he was too pissed to listen, so I told one of my brothers to take him behind the stage where there was a small cupboard.

They took him there, and we then threw this idiot in the cupboard where I locked the door. I was just going to leave him there for fifteen minutes as a laugh, but we forgot all about him. It wasn't until after the show when we were on the stage packing up to go home that we heard a "HELP" only then I twigged, so we let this poor fucker out who had just spent the last five hours in a mouse-infested hole.

Warren is going to me, "You c..t, joe, how the fuck have you left him in there all fucking night!"

"Wal... I forgot bruv," I said laughing,

"The poor c..t!" Warren said, trying to sound compassionate, which made me laugh even more.

"The poor c..t?? You were fucking standing next to me when we banged him up! You forgot as well, didn't you!" I said back.

"I thought you were going to let him out,"

"Well, I thought, YOU were going to fucking let him out!"

Nazi Boxing at Caesars....

Now this really was a fucking classic! Unbeknown to us we had a boxer who wanted to fight on our show who we later found out to be an active EDL fund raiser. At every show we used to have application forms at ringside and throughout the evening Ricky would announce that if anyone wanted to fight on a future show then should come to the ringside and fill out a form. We would then call them and have a chat and get them on a show.

On this occasion, one of the lads unbeknown to us had agreed to fight and then decided to use his fight as a fundraiser for the English Defence League. (EDL) Me and Ricky were totally in the dark until we got a phone call from Fred Batt the owner of Caesars, who was worried out of his head,

"Joe what the fuck have you done?"

"Hold up! What's the matter, " I interrupted.

"Joe, I have the council calling me, the old bill, and the press! They are saying there is to be a march outside the club with over a 1000 protesters, the law are saying they are shutting us down."

"Fred!, what the fuck are you on about!"

"You got all fucking Nazis coming to the next show!"

"NAZIS!... are you fucking mad? I don't know anything about this."

Fred then told me to google it, where I found the following bullshit.

"Fumble For The Fatherland", Boxing's Fascist Fight Night

Muhammad Ali Fan | 23.02.2010 16:57 The sport of legends Muhammad Ali and Amir Khan, is being hijacked this weekend at the world-famous Caesars Nightclub venue at Streatham in South London. This coming Sunday, the 28th February 2010, a team of eight fascist-friendly semi-professional English boxers will supporting the neo-Nazi EDL, entering a boxing ring displaying EDL logo shorts and flags for an official EBC prizefighter contest.

This far right boxing night promoted in conjunction with Mean Machine Promotions, in the nation's capital, is designed to raise the profile of the cowardly racist political organisation whose last rally in England involved storming through a predominantly Asian area of Stoke, smashing up cars, windows and passers-by in what has been described by onlookers as an anti-Muslim pogrom.

Rather than being being a cage-fighting event in a derelect warehouse akin to criminal hoodlums, the EDL's event is being held in one of London's most famous boxing venues, Caesars, advertised as "London's largest and most luxurious nightclub", and is sanctioned by the European Boxing Council (EBC). Caesars has hosted the likes of Lennox Lewis, Lloyd Honeyghan and Gary Mason, and outside of boxing, has been used to film scenes Footballers Wives (ITV) fight sequences from the movie "Snatch" starring Brad Pitt, chat-show goddess Trisha, Big Brother's Big Mouth (Channel Four), and Most Haunted (Living TV), with their legendary Christmas parties regularly featured on Sky. Caesars is indeed a celebrity-frequented venue, and not some backstreet dive, all the more shocking when you consider that the BNP have to make do with the less than glorious surroundings of the New Kimberley Hotel for their shenanigans.

On their social networking web pages, self-confessed boxing fan and psychotic fascist thug Liam Pinkham devotes plenty of space to the merits of his "Great White (Supremacist) Hopes" of boxing, aiming to prove to the world that Aryans pack the best punch. Following the EDL's showcase sporting event, Caesars are laying on an "exclusive afterparty" where hardcore neo-Nazis Pinkham and steroidal busom buddy Wigan Mike can chase around siliconised Page Three models all night long, demonstrating the pro-active feminism of the EDL.

Over forty EDL members have already bought tickets. Tickets for the "Fumble For The Fatherland" are being sold on Ebay through the EDL's "merchandise shop" alongside their paramilitary hoodies and assorted nationalist and racist tat at £45 each, as well as other outlets. (Like their "multiracial nationalist" idol Nick Griffin in the BNP, the EDL seem happy to rip off their own members by charging £5 for postage per ticket).

From Bolton to Sheffield, Cardiff to Brixton, boxing gyms all across the country pride themselves in offering sports and fitness training to young people from under priviledged backgrounds. Go in any inner city gym, and you will see black, Asian and white kids training together with mutual respect and admiration. The ethos of equal competition is one sadly lacking in most other sports, and for that reason, boxing is part of the government's sports development strategy to coincide with the forthcoming 2012 London Olympics.

Despite the EDL's recent setbacks, organised racism and religious hatred is steadily increasing year-in, year-out with the spirit of fervent Islamophobia fostered by politicians, state institutions and the scaremongering tabloid media who worryingly have turned their attentions from hooked-handed foreign bogeymen to British Muslims (the "enemy within"), to shore-up public support for the War On Terror and silence critics of an extremely unpopular and bloody Afgan war with casualties on all sides.

It is the misguided belief fostered by the rightwing newspaper industry and black ops foreign office "leaks" (the whole of the Taliban have Brummie accents) that has created the environment for a resurgence of the British far right exploited by violent neo-Nazi groups such as the EDL.

Egotist and publicity whore of the EDL Trevor Kelway sees mileage in turning media attentions from race riots to ringside aggression. Eight shameless racist boxers will be taking to the ring this Sunday in London for what the EDL leadership see as both a moneymaking opportunity and a cynical PR exercise, a chance to appeal to a wider fan base who might not otherwise warm to their hardcore Hitler loving British Freedom Fighters or the EDL's violently destructive racial football hooliganism.

Whilst a handful of potential boxing starlets of tomorrow fritter away hopes of fame and fortune through mutual association with English fascism, sweating tears of endurance as lackeys for an Islamophobic masterplan, spare a thought for Alan Lake and the EDL's other weathly far right backers who will be sipping extravagantly on champage on ice, playing millionairre war games with people's minds while the cancer of organised racism takes a foothold within the grassroots sporting world.

Since the defeat in the rematch of Max Schmeling by Joe Louis (Schmeling himself refusing to join the Nazi party or sack his American Jewish manager, and hiding two Jewish boys in his apartment during the Kristallnacht pogrom), with the rise of Jewish, black and Asian ring fighters, boxing has had an estranged relationship with fascism, and may seem like an unlikely target for the EDL.

Since the New Millenium, the Lonsdale boxing brand became momentarily popular with the European far right in the Netherlands, Belgium, northern France and Germany, especially because a carefully placed outer jacket leaves the letters NSDA showing; an acronym of Nationalsozialistische Deutsche Arbeiter (National Socialist German Worker), and one letter short of NSDAP, the German acronym for the Nazi Party, however the boxing world has generally embraced non-white people and immigrants (including Muslims) into its gymnasiums, alongside the white working class.

One thing's for sure, the undeniable patriotism and steadfast patriotism of Amir Khan who dedicated his victories after 7/7 to the victims of Islamic terror, will be affronted by the poisonous bile and misdeeds of the EDL, who, despite claims of being "only against religious extremism", regularly create disorder, race hatred and chaos in the city centres of England, Wales and Scotland with straight-armed Hitler salutes, banners calling for the banning of mosques, incessant racist chanting, and behind the scenes, plotting deadly large-scale race riots.

During recent invasions into British cities masked paramilitary followers of this violent anti-Islamic far right gang have physically and verbally attacked innocent (non-extremist) Muslims in the street, vandalised Islamic gravestones, and threatened Muslim taxi drivers with death, (hardly the behaviour of a genuine anti-religious extremist group).

Whatever are one's personal thoughts regarding boxing, with the Olympics approaching, it is important that anti-fascists everywhere show our massed opposition to hate-peddling British fascist bootboys infiltrating the corporate sporting world.

You can register your disapproval of the EDL hijacking boxing by contacting the venue direct and asking them to cancel the Prize-fighter event (please be polite and courteous in all correspondence!!! Thanks!):

CONTACT:
Mr Fred Batt (Owner)
Caesars Nightclub,
156-160 Streatham Hill
London
SW2 4RU

Or speak to Club Manager Vickie on 020-8671-3000
Fax: 01306-711660
(no email address, sorry!)
Mean Machine Promotions:
NO PASARAN IN SPORT!
Muhammad Ali Fan

"What the fuck is this?"

I said to myself in disbelief at what I just read.

For fuck sake, now we had councils, protestors, the old bill and every labour lefty wanting to sabotage our show, and all this had sod all to do with us.

I called Fred back up and he was still sweating.

"Joe I just got off the phone with the council and they are telling me there will be over a thousand protestors outside the club on Saturday night, trying and shut us down! This is really bad!"

This was a bloody nightmare and it took me two days nonstop on the phones and emails to put out the fire. I found out who the lad was and we took him off the show, he took a liberty using our show to raise money, so it was only right we told him he wasn't boxing.

I then had to ring around to find out who was organising the march and tell them this was one massive fucking mistake and nothing to do with us! The fighter has been removed, and it wasn't us (the promoters or the club) raising money for the EDL.

The show did go ahead and there were no boycotts or protestors outside so it all worked out well but it shows how precarious it can be promoting boxing shows. There are so many angles or things out of your hands that can seriously damage all the hard work you put in.

We still laugh at even now as the kid who caused all this trouble, came through Teddy Bam Bam, who is black!

I still take this piss out of Teddy even now, calling him 'The Black Nazi.'

I promoted shows at Caesars for over 14 years, but all good things, sadly must come to an end. The club closed down in 2010 and in my eyes that was the nail in the coffin for the old school unlicensed boxing.

We tried to find other venues and export what we did at Caesars, but the atmosphere wasn't there. I think I lost the flavour when I lost Caesars.

Roy Shaw and Fred Batt

Fred Batt the owner of Caesars said the following about the days at his club.

When I was asked to write a few words about my London nightclub, Caesars, I thought, yes, ok, as I am often asked to talk about the history of the place either for books or documentaries, after all it had been there since 1928 when it was called The Locarno.

But this time it was different, it was about a phenomenon that was created there by Joseph Pyle Jnr and although I had to think hard as to whether I should put this type of thing into my club, mainly because I had the reputation of the club to think of and I had already gone through the longest licencing hearing in history with the police trying to put 21 conditions on my licence, but with the best licencing barrister in the country and finishing at 2am in the morning, I won the case! So, I thought ok, let's do it and the Sunday Night Unlicensed Boxing Nights began.

So, I had a meeting with Joe and his dad, Joe Snr, and talked about the way it would work.

Now I had known Joe Snr for a few years and so I didn't need any contracts or similar as Joe was very old school like me, your word is your bond and we shook hands on it.

It's strange really but the last time I had seen Joe Snr was when he asked me if I would go for a licence for him at a premises he had in Kennington so I went to see the Licencing Officer at Kennington and as soon as I walked in I didn't get a chance to say a word, he said, "Right I know why you're here but you have two hopes, Bob Hope and No Hope, that will be a watering hole for villains". I spent half an hour trying to convince them that it wasn't the case, but I had no chance.

Anyway, The Unlicensed Boxing started and we never looked back, it was something I think of with great affection, especially the amazing charity nights where many well-known stars would come and help to raise thousands for charities.

There were some funny times too, such as when somebody didn't agree with the decision of a fight, the fight would end up out of the ring with my security trying to break it up.

Joe Jnr was very professional in his outlook towards the nights and the fights were very well run, I couldn't have asked for anything better.

I used to set VIP tables on the stage for guests and it usually read like a who's who of gangland and celebrities. Always there were Roy Shaw, Tony Lambriano, Joe Pyle Snr, Charlie Richardson, Dave Courtney, Charlie Breaker and many more.

Joe's dad, Joe Snr, was very proud of what his son had done with the boxing nights and just before he died, I went to see him in St Thomas's Hospital and he thanked me for everything and I gave him a medallion that belonged to the champion boxer Joe Louis.

I know your dad will be looking down on you Joe with everything you do, and he will be so proud of you and is probably guiding you along with the writing of the book.

Good luck to you Joe, you are, and along with your dad, were, two of the best!

Fred Batt – CEO – Caesars London Limited

CHAPTER 9
THE FIGHTING MEN OF CAESARS

The fighting men of Caesars
I've already mentioned the Guvnors, but in this chapter I want to mention some
of the other boxers who fought regularly for us at Caesars.
Our memories of Ceasars would not be the same without them.

EBC PRIZEFIGHTER PROFESSIONAL CHAMPIONSHIP BOXING

MEANMACHINE PROMOTIONS WHO'S THE GUV'NOR

BAD BOY   COLIN
                           WILBY

MMK1

THE NEW GENERATION OF FIGHTING

FRIDAY 23RD APRIL 2010
CEASARS SOUTH LONDON
TICKETS VIP TABLE TICKETS £80 EACH (TABLES 10 & 8)
UNRESERVED £45 BALCONY £30

Ticket Hotline Meanmachine 07886272635
or Teddy Bam Bam 07853184408
or Warren Bamford 07544574608

WWW.MEANMACHINE.BIZ   WWW.MMK1.BIZ

Colin 'Badboy' Wilby

Colin had loads of fights for us, and loved fighting at Caesars and even had MeanMachine tattooed across his back. He fought at Light Heavyweight and was as tough as they come and didn't mind throwing a few 'dirties' into the action when he fought.

Colin was from Dartford and he always brought a good crowd with him. He featured in the documentary we had made about us called 'Unlicensed' where he said on camera that, you have to fight at Caesars, until you fight there you're are nothing.

Colin won a load of titles at Caesars, The Roy Shaw championship belt, The Joe Pyle London belt and he also won the Light Heavy and Heavyweight British Title belts.

When we had an MMA show, he also fought on that, winning in the first round. The crowd loved Colin, he always came to 'Fight' and always gave the crowd good value.

I saw him lose his temper a few times in the ring, one where he jumped on top of his opponent and continued to hit him while he was on the ground.

Another good fight was when he took a challenge for his British Heavyweight title from a fighter called 'One Punch Steffen' Steffen was a tough kid from Mitcham, who had done a bit of boxing, but he was a local street fighter with a big reputation for having a row, he challenged Wilby and the challenge was accepted, so we made the fight. Colin was a big favourite, and when the bell rang for the first round, Steffen just came out swinging, he looked awful, but he kept steaming in, only for Wilby to tie him up when they got close. I thought it was just a matter of time as he couldn't continue to steam in like this, he would fuck himself, blow himself out.

Then right near the end of the round, he swung a right hand from his boots, and it landed with a thud on Wilby's chin! BOSCH! Wilby fell backward and was asleep before he hit the ground. The ref immediately called it. Then, the ring was invaded by Steffen's cornermen celebrating, followed by the doctors and Wilby's people helping their man who was still completely out of it. Thank god, Colin was okay, and he got to his feet and sportingly congratulated Steffen. We did arrange a rematch for the next show, but unfortunately, Steffen was arrested and remanded so it never happened.

Colin's legacy, though is still intact as he never let us down, he won numerous titles at numerous weights and for us will always be…

A Caesars legend.

Pete The Assassin Stoten

Pete Stoten is, without a doubt, one of the best boxers I ever promoted in the unlicensed game. I actually used to promote and manage Pete when he turned professional in 1998. He used to train with me down the Park Tavern gym in Streatham where Brian Hill coached him.

Pete won a lot of titles for us, and he was unbeaten on the circuit. It was unlucky that Pete never got amongst the real heavy lumps and fought for the Guv'nor title, he was certainly good enough but just wasn't big enough at the time he boxed for us.

He was also just too good for his own good! I know that sounds funny, but it's true. He was the same weight as Colin Wilby, who was a massive crowd puller, and I think Colin would be the first to admit he would have got beaten by Pete. It's how we did things in the unlicensed, and it isn't so much different from how things are done in the pros. We kept our fighters away from each other; we built them up and got the crowd used to them, and then once we thought the time was right, then we would make a big fight.

After Caesar's finished, Pete went on to fight on other shows and started to promote his own events, he has done well and his shows in Kent are really good shows, with great fights and great atmosphere.

I think Pete the assassin Stoten would have in time gone on to win a top Guvnor title. I know he was interested in challenging Norman Buckland, but that never happened as I didn't allow it.

Pete 'the Assassin' Stoten will always be …

A Caesars legend.

I first met Joe Pyle at his gym 'scallywags' in the late 90s, we were just starting on his journey as a professional promoter and he signed me as one of his first pro fighters unfortunately my road took a different journey not long after. The next time I saw Joe was as a guest at one of his unlicensed shows at Caesars.

I couldn't believe the atmosphere, ring walks and the savagery of the contests it was unbelievable I made up my mind then I was going to enter this world and make waves.

Having boxed all my life, I wasn't too bad in the skill department, but a little small for the heavyweights so I started in the cruisers, winning all but one of my fights by KO I always brought in a crowd and had some awesome ring walks with Wendy Samuel's very own Mean Girls we were a great team

Under Joe's guidance I won titles at Cruiserweight, super cruiser, and a Roy Shaw title and I was the world sports organisations first heavyweight champion.

I learnt so much from joe and fighting at Caesars which stood me in good form for the next 10 years fighting around the UK and aboard.

Pete the Assassin Stoten

Glenn The menace Reynolds & Gentleman Jimmy Cann

Glenn was a real character around Sutton; he was called *the menace* as he was hard-work once he had a drink inside him. Glenn had half his ear missing, from a street fight, so we used to play the song from the film Reservoir Dogs for his ring entrance. The song they played in the scene where the fella cut someone's ear off.

Glenn started fighting for us right at the beginning of our Caesars shows, and soon became a regular and a main event fighter. He was crude in the boxing department and often just threw his shots from any position, but he could bang! He would also fight dirty if he needed to.

Glenn went unbeaten for a year or so, and then he got challenged in the ring by a Sutton doorman called - gentleman Jimmy Cann. These two boys knew and hated each other, and it almost kicked off in the ring when Jimmy got in to make the challenge.

Jimmy was a doorman at a club that Glenn had been barred from, and we had word that Glenn was thinking about going back to the club and having a row on the door. And Glen was one of our biggest draws so we didn't want that happening.

Who knows what would have happened, fighting in the street with things to pick up, use, or even arrest? We got hold of Jimmy Cann and suggested that he and Glenn settle their argument in the ring on one of our shows. Jimmy liked boxing, so we invited him to come along to our next show, where Glenn was fighting. I told Glenn to not go to the club until after the show and to let me sort it out.

Anyway, on the night of the show, Glenn won by knockout, so we got Jimmy Cann up into the ring. I was standing inside and ready to grab Glenn in case he made a lunge at Jimmy. There was a little bit of needle and I pulled Glenn back and told him to behave himself, it was good really as it was just what I wanted to gain interest in the next show.

Ricky let both boys talk on the mike, and the match was set for our next show. Five rounds for the super middleweight London title.

The fight didn't let us down and was an absolute slugfest which ended in a draw... Jimmy wasn't happy as he thought Glenn should have been disqualified because he tried to butt and kick him a couple of times only to get a stern warning from the referee.

Jimmy immediately asked for the mike, where he demanded a return on the next show. Ricky got the crowd going and asked who wanted to see this again. The crowd all cheered as the fight had been a blinder. Glenn then took to the mike and said to Jimmy, "LETTS FUCKING DO IT AGAIN RIGHT NOW THEN!" which got the crowd even more excited. We pulled them apart and made the return.

Once again, they boxed over five rounds on the next show, and it was just like the first fight, brutal from the first bell till the last with both lads punching themselves to a standstill. Again there was nothing to separate them, so it was called another draw.

A decider was a no brainer. The crowd wanted it, the boxers wanted it, and me and Ricky wanted it.

But the decider had to be beefed up a bit, there was nothing between these two, and they both really wanted to beat each other, so me and Ricky came up with a new title.

It was called **'The last man standing' belt**. It was a fight to the finish, three-minute rounds, but with no limit or rounds, basically, the fight would keep going until there was a clear winner.

The buzz around the fight was fantastic, and the whole of the area was looking forward to seeing this fight where there had to be a clear winner. It would be by either a stoppage or if someone said they had had enough.

On the night of the show, the crowd's buzz was electric; all the chaps were there in the audience, my father, Roy Shaw, Tony Lambrianou and Freddie foreman.

As there was no clear winner from the last two fights, we decided that they would both come into the ring together.

Caesars had a lift on the stage where we used to bring the boxers down, so we put both boxers on either side and separated them with myself and loads of mates, there must have been twenty of us coming down on the lift. The DJ then started playing. Frankie goes to Hollywood song - Two Tribes. The crowd went crazy as the tune come on, and the lift started to come down.

At the beginning of the song, there is an intro with sirens, and then the music blasts in and the lyrics 'When two tribes go to war' it was the perfect song for a double ring entrance. The fight was on, and the place just went crazy.

Glenn was sitting on the ledge smiling and calling out to the crowd as Jimmy on the other side was deadly serious.

This was a fight to the finish where this time there would definitely be a winner, both boys knew it and so did the crowd.

In all the time I promoted shows at Caesars, I can't remember a bigger buzz for a fight than this. We had the big heavyweight fights, but this was something special, they had boxed each other twice with nothing between them and both times punching themselves to a standstill. There was a real buzz in the air, a real excitement that anything could or might happen.

I made sure I had a chat with both boys in the dressing room before to remind them that this was a fight to the finish. There would be no limit on rounds; you would just keep fighting until we get a winner.

They were both really focused as they came together in the middle of the ring. The ref reminded them of the rules and the fight length and then sent both boxers back to their corners to commence the fight.

Round one and Glenn came straight out looking to land bombs, jimmy covered up and looked like he was trying to pace himself for the fight. I remember thinking at the time that this was his game-plan, to hope Glenn would blow out. Glenn went looking for him all the first round until the bell went, and Glenn shouted at his opponent to fight!

There was a bit of 'after's' when the bell rang, which got broken up by the corner men.

Round two started with Glenn shouting once again at jimmy to fight, Jimmy called him on and once again to the delight of the crowd the fight took back off where the other two ended. Both boys now swinging shots at each other.

It was toe to toe stuff, and soon, we passed six rounds, they were both tired, but they just kept going, it was amazing how two boys were fighting at this pace over a fight duration that only seasoned professional fighters fought for.

We then got to round nine, and I walked over to Ricky English at ringside, "We got to call this mate … these two are going to fucking kill each other.!" I said, now worried about the two boys who were running on pure courage.

"Good shout, Joe, I agree" Ricky answered.

The round ended for round ten, so I quickly ran over to each corner.
"THE FIGHT ENDS IN TWO ROUNDS." I shouted, "TWO MORE ROUNDS AND THAT'S IT!"
Both boys boxed to an absolute standstill the next two rounds, they were absolutely knackered, too tired for defending themselves, they just stood in the ring putting everything they had into their punches.
As the final bell went they both fell into each other's arms; even the referee started applauding their bravery, the crowd was cheering and clapping, I could hear people around me saying … "What a fucking fight!"
Once the excitement of what we just saw eased, I then started to think about who the winner was, Ricky was now in the ring, and he was looking for me. Remember, this fight was arranged as a fight to the finish, so we didn't make any arrangements for a points decision. Both boxers' corners were also asking us what was going to happen.
I pulled Ricky to the side, "You call it!" I said to him, meaning he decides the winner.
The crowd was now getting reckless at the indecision, so we had to think of something quick, Micky Nana, Jimmy's trainer, came over to me, "Not another fucking draw please Joey." He said to me.
Ricky spoke to the referee and the timekeeper, and then he came over to me and whispered in my ear.
"Glenn by one point, mate."
"Glenn's the winner," I replied
"Yes mate, I've spoken to the ref, and the timekeeper and both reckon Glenn nicked it on aggression." Ricky said, "What do you think?" Ricky added, asking my opinion.
"It was close … I couldn't say who won it; I wouldn't moan either direction."
"We can't do another draw!" Ricky said.
"I Know!" I replied.
Ricky then nodded and told the referee to bring both boys to the middle of the ring before getting on the mike to address the crowd and announce the winner.
"LET's GIVE THESE TWO A FUCKING ROUND OF APPLAUSE …..
WHAT A FUCKING FIGHT THAT WAS …right after 12 unbelievable rounds of boxing, we went to the scorecards and the winner by one point is …………….. GLENN THE MENACE REYNOLDS!"
The crowd cheered, and Glenn fell to his knees as Jimmy applauded him. It was one hell of a fight, a fight which would go down in history as two unlicensed fighters stood toe to toe for a mammoth 12 rounds of boxing. It was unbelievable. I was happy for Glenn but choked for Jimmy, to fight like that, and walk away with nothing. But he walked away with all our respects that night … He put on three epic fights with Glenn, three fights that whoever witnessed them will never forget them. Glen Reynolds and Jimmy Cann, both, will always be, **Ceasars's Legends.**

Colin Kane

During our early days at Caesars, Colin was another regular on the shows. He was a real entertainer who frequently ended up on the canvas in some kind of wrestling match with his opponent, one time with both of them trying to bloody bite each other.

Colin was another local lad from Sutton and good pals with Glenn Reynolds, where they often did each other's corners.

I used to love watching him box as there was always a surprise in store, he would usually enter the ring wearing a mask or sometimes a batman cape.

Now, I'm not talking out of line here as it was common knowledge that Colin ended up, dating one of the ring card girls. In the picture above, he actually started to snog both card girls in the interval of a round.

One night, however, springs to mind was when Colin came in to see me and Ricky to sort his ticket money out, and he told us that his ex-missus, angered at him being with the card girl, was coming to the show to kick off.

"It can't fucking happen here, mate, this is our show; if you have problems indoors, then fucking deal with them there mate", I said to as thought about the possibility of having some angered ex-bird screaming and fighting at ringside.

"Yeah ... ill deal with Joe." Colin reassured us.

"You better mate, I'm telling you that if she kicks off, then she is getting slung out! This is our show; we can't have that shit happening here." I added as he got up.

When Colin left us, me and Ricky started laughing … "Fucking hell, we got every mug in the world wanting to kick off at our shows, now we got ex old women as well," I said laughing.

 "Yeah, he should tell her to stay at home, Joe" Rick said before smiling. "Don't worry about it, leave it to me." Ricky then added with a mischievous look in his eye.

Anyway, when the fight came round, Colin was on his way to the ring with his usual ring walk song, and then the song suddenly changed to Louis Prima's hit song - 'Just a Gigolo.'

I looked over to ringside and saw Ricky laughing his head off along with a few of Colin's mates, Colin got in the ring and then leaned over to me and Ricky, "You fucking bastards!" he said shaking his head.

Colin didn't really give a fuck though, so it all light-hearted fun, he bashed his opponent up and then snogged the card girl in the middle of the ring as Ricky told the DJ to put the record on again.

I can remember another fight where Colin and his opponent kept going to the floor and fighting on their knees, it was mad. One minute they are boxing, the next they are on the floor with Colin in a headlock while he is punching his opponent's balls. The referee kept on getting them up, but as soon as they got on their feet, they would end up back on the canvas. At one point they even ended up fighting outside the ring amongst the crowd!

A few years later we heard he went to live in France (With the ring card girl) Colin Kane will always be …

A Caesars Legend.

Hughie the Banger Robertson

Hughie was another regular on our shows, and he always gave a good account of himself. I remember him when he turned professional and had his pro debut at The Elephant and Castle leisure centre on Frank Maloney's show. However, the pro's didn't suit him, and he came back to the unlicensed shows.

He had a few memorable fights for us, one of which was against Manny Clark. Hughie won a couple of belts 'The Roy Shaw London title' and what I always liked about him was his willingness to fight anyone, he never ducked a challenge. We had some good nights with Hughie, some good wins, and a few shocks like his fight against Matty Ross.

There was no doubt about it, Hughie could fight, he was always exciting to watch and the crowd loved him.

Hughie the banger Robertson will always be …

A Caesars Legend.

Manny Boom Boom Clark

A REAL FIGHTER ... springs to mind when you talk about Manny Clark, he has been fighting on the circuit for what seems forever and is still fighting today. He has boxed all over the country, and was a regular at Caesars and the Circus Tavern with the Mortlocks. Manny has done boxing, MMA, and now BKB (Bare Knuckle)

He fought anyone! He wanted the best fights out there and when he took on Hughie Robertson we all expected a loss for Manny but he ended up the winner after a brutal fight.

One fight we was working on but never came off was Manny against Colin Badboy Wilby, we had the press photo's done at the Embassy club in London and it was going to be a terrific top of the bill on our next show but for certain reason the fight fell through.

Manny was and still is a good pal of mine, he will always be ...
A Caesars legend.

CAESARS
Nightclub, Streatham
Sunday 22 May 2004
MAIN EVENT
For the vacant
EBF English Light-Heavyweight Title
4x2 minute rounds

TATTOO JOHN
(Kickboxer/boxer/streetfighter/
EBF South London Champion)

Wade 'the kid' Garrett
(Boxer/Cage fighter/Thai boxer)

"I've heard all about Wade. He's a
dangerous man. But that's exactly why
I'm fighting him. I fully intend to seek out
and beat the hardest guys in this game.
I am avoiding nobody. I am going to
show London exactly what I'm made of!"

Tattoo John

"This guy's got a reputation as being a
tough nut to crack.... so what? I am bigger,
stronger and fitter. He's going to regret the
day he ever asked to fight me. I'm going to
be too much for him!"

Wade 'the kid' Garrett

Ringside seated table tickets available for only £20
For more information on this fight contact
TATTOO John on
07977 796649

Tattoo John

John was another champion in our early days at Caesars, he was a good fighter
and had some memorable bouts for us. He was called tattoo john as he was
smothered in tattoo's. John was also a born show man who would often get on
the mike after a fight and call out a fight or fighter. John, grew tired after a few

easy wins so he set up his own fight against a kid called Wade Garrett who in later years turned out to be more known by his real name, one of the UKs most successful MMA fighters, Tom Kong Watson.

John even had his own posters made where he donated all his ticket money to charity.

He won a few belts for us where he became the Middleweight London champion and the English champion.

John will always be…

A Caesars legend.

Steve Dossett

Steve was and still is a proper fighting man. Steve will fight anyone and doesn't want weeks and months' notice. One of the best fights we ever had at casers was featuring Steve against marc Woolf. It was an absolute war and would be well met at any professional show. Both lads could box and it was technical as it was savage! (Watch it on Youtube)

Steve lives in the gym and is very dedicated to his training. I have said on numerous occasions that he would have made a really good professional boxer. He definitely has the dedication and courage for it. I wish Steve all the best and Steve will always be

A Caesars legend.

Steve Yorath

Steve has been with us at Caesars from day one. In his day he was a tidy professional boxer and would fight anyone. At Caesars he did fight anyone, in fact he fought everyone. Sven Hamer, welsh Phill, Garry Sayer, Norman Buckland.

He was always good value for money and the crowd loved how he would take the piss out of his opponents. He was another who knew his way around the ring and he would tie his fighter up and wink at the crowd or laugh as if to say, "you can't fucking hurt me."

Steve never let us down when we asked him to find opponents or the promotions. We would also get Steve being the referee from time to time.

Steve was without a doubt,

A Caesars Legend.

Den Palmer

Den was a tough little fighter and a regular on our early shows winning and defending successfully one of our early title belts. he always came with a decent crowd and always had tough fights. Den worked his way through the titles, winning the English and the British Super Middleweight titles.

Den was also a world champion kick boxer

A Caesars Legend

Rocky Muscus

Rocky was a former professional boxer but decided to go on the road (be a journeyman) as it paid him more money. He would turn up and fight anyone and he could fight!

Just like all other journeymen he knew how to slip punches and move in and out of range, tie you up and had that natural instinct for staying out of trouble. Rocky was one of the bravest fighters I have ever promoted. He would honestly fight a lion if the money was right. Rocky would also help out behind the scenes and be an extra pair of hands or help out with the fighters in the changing rooms. Even when he was doing this kind of work he would turn up with his boxing kit. (Just in case an opponent failed a medical or didn't turn up and he would jump in)

Rocky was as game as they come and only five foot six but he will always be,

A Caesars Legend.

Dan Cassius Connor (Dan Marsh)

Dan was another fighter who ended up turning professional and winning the Southern Area title and boxing on some big undercards at places like the O2. I've lost count the wars he had at Caesars and would always turn up with his kit, even if he wasn't boxing. he was fearless and would fight anyone without any notice.

Dan boxed a couple of times for after Caesars when I went back to the professionals, once at Tolworth where he won the British Challenge belt over eight rounds. Dan will always be

A Caesars Legend.

Paddy and Ginger

These two fighters were two of the toughest kids to ever put on a pair of gloves at Caesars. They boxed for us on almost every show from 2003 till 2011 and both of them between them, never won one fight!

They were journeymen, who turned up to get beaten up for £100 or £200.

I used to laugh or sigh at Ricky when he would say, put that boxer against Ginger… I would say, "He's two stone heavier than Ginger, he will fucking hurt him, Rick,"

"No, Ginger can deal with it!" Rick would reply.

One night in particular, Paddy boxed at around 8;30 and got knocked out in the first and then went back to the changing rooms and changed his shorts and boxed again about two hours later. The doctor was going crazy! I ran over to the doctor and said, "don't worry, doc, it's a fix, its pantomime, he is going over in the first."

Sure enough, Paddy was hit with a body shot and he fell to the ground like he had been shot. He rolled around as his opponent and his supporters celebrated and then once he was counted out hobbled back to the changing room holding his stomach in pain. It was funny about an hour later when he was showered and changed with his money he was at the bar dancing with some bird.

The pair of them really made us laugh and ricky would be ruthless at times. One fight Ginger was told to go over in the 1st round, so he takes a shot and falls to the ground and the ref counts him out, but Ricky starts shouting out on the mike, overruling the referee.

"NO, HES ALRIGHT REF! LET HIM FIGHT ON!"

The ref, said alright and waved for them to start boxing and Ginger goes down again.

"GET UP GINGER… YOUR NOT FUCKING HURT!" Ricky is shouting again on the mike… it was a funny night.

They were one hundred percent Caesars legends.

Above are just a few of the boys who made the nights at Caesars so memorable, if this book was just about Caesars then I could easily add another hundred names to the list above.

All the boys who boxed at Caesars have my respect and thanks, it takes balls to get in that ring and it takes 'BIG' ones to do at a place like … Caesars.

Other worthy mentions are ..

Mickey Oliver, Suki Dhami, Ricky Boylan, Lee Bates, Scott McDonald, Andy Roberts, Piwi Adams, Steve Surin, Lewis Pinto, Lee Cook, Steve Cook, Paul Bartley, Matty Ross, Dan Lovett, Mickey O'Sullivan, KO Kitsen, Rocky, Sniper, Ricky Greenidge, Magic Mo, Rocky Lee, Trevor Smith, Jonh Brennen, Stan Wilson, Luke Morris, Leon McKinney, Erkan Ibraham, Aaron Hodgeson, Tony Owen, Lee Owen, Liam Bucko, Danny Anderson, Daryl Setterfield, Jabz, Frannie, The D Man, Sheridan Davey, Reece Stewart, Shaun Rogers, Jermaine Grant, Malky, Michael Soteriou, Remi Stewert, Darren Jerrom, Danny Coleman, Jim Power, Andy Wallace, John Pema, Stuart Leray, Dolph, JJ, AJ, Damian Pavey, Phill Todd, Ricky Miller, Calvin riley, Steve Holder, Des Holder, Kyle Chambers, Marc Rice, Sam Chesney, Big Fritz, James Cox, Jake Dowsett, Marc Smith, Ryan Crawford, Robin Deacon, Mark Harvard, Craig Flynn, James 2cute Deans, Randell Mendez, Jamie Scarlett, Joe Rock, Troy K, Dynamite Jack K, Richie Glaysher, Mo Holloway, Sam Butler, Danny Grainger, Carl Sayer, Jimmy Riley, Liam Conroy, Ryan Corrigan, Craig Amer, Wayne Abdullah, Jamie Brittle, Ben Hurr, Philip Stephensen, Jordan Fowler, Ryan Fields, Alan d, Gary Barcelona, Glenn Bodan, Luke Jones, Ryan Weland, Lesley Smith, Ben Achmpong, Jack Hamer, Fred Loudis, Mark Thornton, Wayne Heffer, rob Chapman, Harry Russell, Dean dodge, Tony Clemmy, Jordan Waynes, Ashley Walsh, John Hutchinson, Hughy Doyle, Ross Parker, Dave Morris, Khalique Miah, Frank Sadler, Danny Boardman, Joe Miles, Sid Jeffries, Dan Bolt, Freddie, Cook, Dave long, Dave Smith, Keiran Mcdonald, Sidney Fitzpatrick, Anthony Mullins,

CHAPTER 10
HAMER FIGHTS TWO MEN

"He gets killed, were in fucking trouble!"

Those were the words spoken by Ricky English which can be heard on camera just before Sven Hamer fights someone from the crowd.

December 2006.

It was a crazy and tragic night, a night just before Christmas which sadly ended in a callous murder at a party in the early hours of the morning.

The show was a complete sell-out, it was our Christmas show and we had all our top fighters on.

Sven Hamer's original opponent did not turn up after challenging Sven from the audience on our previous promotion. Luckily we found a stand in on the day, it wasn't the fight we wanted, but at least we had a fight for Sven and his supporters.

The fight itself, though turned out to be a farce as Sven was just far too strong and destroyed his opponent in seconds of the first round. Ricky got into the ring and told the crowd about the original opponent who challenged Sven not turning up so everyone gives the stand in a round of applause for taking the fight with one days' notice.

I was standing ringside keeping an eye on some supporters who had brought tickets for an earlier fight, but by now were getting pretty rowdy, there were about 200 of them and they were all Chelsea supporters.

Someone then pulled me to one side and said one of their fellas will fight Sven now.

Foolishly, I entertained it, I shouldn't have but it was now late and I had had a few beers, so I had that carefree attitude and said 'fuck it, why not, let's get him gloved up."

Ricky was furious, I could see it in his eyes as we both knew that doing this could have serious consequences.

"He gets killed, were in fucking trouble!" Ricky said which can be heard on the footage. (Worried that Sven was going to hurt him)

On all our shows, the fighters had to sign insurance waivers on the day have a medical, but now there was a lad who was drunk getting out of the crowd to fight our undefeated champion.

There was no time for a medical or signing waivers. Our doctor went crazy and threatened to walk out, but by now the challenger was in the ring and Rob Davis was shouting out for someone to get some gloves.

Anyway the fight was on and the Chelsea boys were shouting songs for their man. Everyone was getting excited.

The first round started and the challenger flew at Sven but didn't have a clue how to box, he was game, but there was no way he could beat Sven. He swung a few shots and then fell to the floor and then a few moments later Sven knocked him clean out of the ring.

That was it and the fight was over, "FIGHTS OVER!" Ricky called out over the mike, sounding proper pissed off, and you can also hear Ricky saying, "fucking stupid" over the mike.

The Chelsea supporters didn't like what they saw and then they all started to move to the ringside where another one of their lads jumped in to challenge Sven, to be honest, I was getting the hump and was almost on the verge of shouting out to Rob Davis to give him a fucking pair of gloves as well.

Ricky then took to the mike and calmed everything down, saying if everyone doesn't calm down then the nights over.

By now I had a few of my boys in the ring, Rob Davis, Terry Dixon, big Chuck and we managed to get the Chelsea boys out of the ring and calm things down. We had another couple of fights to go and the atmosphere was still rowdy but that happens sometimes at shows and anyway we had two more fights to put on, one of which was Glenn the menace Reynolds, whose opponent, had not turned up.

I was going to call the show and just apologise to Glenn but word had got out that his opponent hadn't turned up and guess what… the Chelsea lad who had gotten in the ring after his fellow Chelsea boy was beaten by Sven, now wanted to fight Glenn.

I was like, for fuck's sake, but then I called him over and I had a chat with him and he seemed alright, Glenn wanted the fight so we took the lad into the changing rooms and gloved him up. I was joking about with him and he was laughing saying to me, "you're not setting me up Joe, I'm not going to get knocked spark out am I?"

At this point we were laughing and joking, Ricky wasn't happy again and threatened to walk out, but, it was going to happen so we went along with it. It was now around 11 at night so I was half pissed by now, so I thought fuck it, let it happen.

Looking back at it now, it was crazy as Glenn the menace Reynolds was a lot different to Sven, Glenn didn't mind fighting dirty, hitting his opponent on the floor or throwing in the odd head or elbow. I did tell Glenn to take it easy and just go through the motions, but as the first bell rang, his opponent just ran across the ring and started a street fight with gloves on, the first clinch they got into he tried to bite Glenn but was thrown to the floor and then Glenn went to stamp on him but was pulled off by the ref.

"NO! NO! NO!" Ricky shouted on the mike as he could see it was spiralling out of control. The Chelsea boys were now getting agitated and were trying to get closer to the ring.

The fight in the ring was getting ugly as Glenn was trying to behave, but was getting butted and bit and was losing his temper.

As all this in the ring was going on, I was keeping an eye on the Chelsea firm and with the security we were stopping them getting to ringside.

Glenn then decided he had had enough of his opponents dirty tactics and just let his hands go, moments later, the fella was knocked spark out.

I was standing with a few of my crowd by the corner of the fighter who has just been knocked out, and the venue security was now pushing the Chelsea lot away from the ring, then I heard a loud crash and I saw that one of the security had been hit round the head with a bottle. Then the whole place just went up in the air.

I was pulled by some of my mates away and we ended up on the stage as over 200 of the crowd started fighting, bottles were flying everywhere and so was tables and chairs and those who weren't fighting made a frantic rush for the exit.. The security also ran out the building which left just members of the crowd fighting.

We were now on the stage looking after our VIP guest and just fighting whoever was trying to get near us. It was bedlam and it went on for a good fifteen minutes. I was told that even the old bill, refused to come in and stop it. I later found out that over two hundred people ended up at accident and emergency at the local hospital St. Georges in Tooting.

Once everything had quietened down, me and a few pals and family went back to my house which ended up looking like a doctors surgery with all the white towels covered in blood. The women tended to the men's wounds (I never had a scratch) and then we opened a few beers and relaxed after one hell of an evening.

If memory serves it was around five in the morning that I received a phone call that one of the spectators at our show had been shot and killed at a house party of one of the boys who boxed on the show.

It was horrible news. I wasn't friendly with the man who was tragically murdered, but I had been introduced to him a couple of times.

Sean Jenkins or stretch as he was known was well known around Earlsfield and Garret Lane areas, and I have only ever heard good things spoken about him.

As the promoter of the event it's staggering news when something like this happens.

I just put on a boxing show and one of the people who came to the show was murdered. I know that once a show is over then what happens has nothing to do with me, but you can't help feeling guilty.

There was another terrible time where one of our fighters died in a car crash on the way home from the fight. It's horrible and you cannot help thinking that if I never staged the show then maybe these two men would still be alive.

The next couple of weeks after the shooting was also a very stressful time for me as my father was very ill from his motor neuron disease, he was struggling to speak now and had lost so much weight and then I had the old bill calling me saying they wanted a word about the shooting.

They asked me to come into the station but I told them to fuck off, adding it's got fuck all to do with me. They had already arrested someone for the shooting, so why did they want to see me or my father.

But being old bill, they just kept calling asking me to come into the station, but I said no way. In the end I met two of them in the Woodstock pub one afternoon. They walked in and introduced themselves and before they started to question me I said,…

"This has fuck all to do with me! Fuck all to do with anyone I know, so that's all I'm fucking telling you!"

When I finished I walked out and never heard from them again.

Being a promoter when things like this happen is always a horrible thing to accept. I just put a show on and people come along to enjoy the evening and then stuff like this happens after the show.

Below was a news article from The Evening Standard.

Friend of Krays faces quiz over gun murder

Last updated at 10:51 15 January 2007

One of London's most notorious gangsters is to be questioned by police investigating a south London murder.

Joey Pyle, a legendary underworld figure and associate of the Kray twins, promoted an unlicensed boxing event attended by Sean Jenkins, who was shot five times at a party hours later.

Mr Pyle, 69, is one of the few surviving former "godfathers" of organised crime from the Sixties.

Detectives will question him about the boxing match as a witness and not under caution.

The murder of Mr Jenkins, 36, has caused tensions in south London.

Police believe up to 15 people, including three teenage girls, witnessed the shooting at the party held at the Carshalton home of one of the boxers.

Witnesses have told the Evening Standard that some people at the party were snorting cocaine. They claim the killer became "out of control" and stormed off.

He returned just after 4am with a gun but no one is telling police his name.

One source said: "It's a classic closed-shop underworld thing and the police keep hitting a wall of silence."

Mr Jenkins was killed on 4 December after attending the boxing match at Caesar's nightclub, Streatham, where police were called after a fight broke out among the 300 fans. Unlicensed boxing is not illegal.

In 1992, "Big" Joey Pyle was jailed for drug trafficking. He was freed in 1997 and has since said that he has "gone clean", working with his son Joe Jr behind the scenes in the music industry.

Mr Jenkins, whose funeral was attended by up to 2,000 people on, leaves a son Ronnie, four, and girlfriend Lindsay.

A source close to his family said: "He was a really popular guy known by almost everyone in Earlsfield because he used to do the windows of the businesses, shops and homes.

We knew him as 'Stretch' because he was so tall he didn't need a ladder.

"He was a real gentle giant, a guy so inoffensive I can't believe that anyone would not like him.

"It's a tragedy he was shot down."

CHAPTER 11
SET-UPS & PRANKS

If you're a big-ticket seller and a possible star in the making, then, since boxing began, promoters and managers will find a way to protect you. The manager must protect you.

Protect your health, your winning record, and protect his investment.

What people have to accept is ... Boxing is a sport, but to those involved, it is very much a business.

Set-ups - fixed fights - journeymen - easy fights - in the bag - a walkabout.

Call them what you like, but these are various names associated with the boxing game, which means the same thing. The home boxer is winning the fight.

Love it or hate it; it's an integral part of boxing happening every single weekend throughout the world. Over the years, I have put on hundreds of these fights in both worlds of boxing, ... professional and unlicensed.

Personally, I have neutral feelings about it as it's just part and parcel of the game, and you would be shocked at some of the well-known people who had called me a couple of weeks before a fight and asked if they can have an '*easy night.*'

I have heard boxers use every excuse in the book to get an easy night's work, things like - I haven't been training, I've hurt my hand or bruised my leg, or even someone has died, and I don't feel right. I've even been told that its mother's day the weekend before, and he's taking his mother out for a big meal. (Fuck knows what that's got to do with fighting the weekend after)

Great big men, who scream and shout, have asked me to arrange them an easy fight, some even asking me for a 1st round knockout win.

People moan and say, 'Joey Pyle puts on fixed fights!'

Yes, I have! But nine times out of ten, it has been at the behest of the fighter coming to me. It's ironic because the ones who moan have usually bought a ticket off the fighter who has asked for an easy night and hasn't told his mates his opponent will be taking a dive.

Set up fights are not so pronounced in the professional side of boxing, but every week it goes on.

The only difference is, in the professionals, it's called fighting a journeyman. It isn't so blatant as unlicensed where you tell the fighter he has to lose, in the pro's it's an unspoken understanding.

Journeymen turn up knowing they are boxing the local favourite or ticket-seller and its easy money for them. They move around for four rounds, just avoiding being stopped, pocket around £1200, and then go home and do the same thing next weekend. However, I have been asked a few times to have a chat with the favourite to take it easy on the journeyman, not to stop him, so he doesn't get suspended for the 28-day ban imposed by the boxing board.

In the unlicensed game, it's much more blatant where I tell the away boy he has to lose in a specific way or specific round. Sometimes it works well, and then there are others where it goes awful.

On one occasion where a pal of mine, Charlie Breaker got a few local lads to box on the show, one lad called Soldier sold a fistful of tickets, but he couldn't fight to *save his life*. I was asked to get him a set-up, so I agreed, but I said the opponent would have to go over in the 2nd round. They asked for the first round, but I said no, bollocks, at least giving his crowd some action.

Soldier agreed, and I told him the fight is fixed, so just go out there, have a fucking good time and enjoy yourself, put on a show for your fans, and the fight would be over in the 2nd.

Anyway, the fight started, and both boxers wouldn't throw a punch! The crowd started booing, and Ricky shouted out on the mike for them to get stuck in.

The fighter who was going over in the 2nd was now almost shouting for Soldier to hit him; it was so fucking embarrassing.

I'm screaming at ringside for him to let his fucking punches go, but he hardly threw a punch!

It was looking so bad as everyone could see that the journeyman fighter was holding back.

When the round ended, I ran to the corner, "Fucking hit him! What's wrong with you, he wants you to fucking hit him!" I shouted at the fighter.

Round two started and the same thing happened, Soldier came out plodding about just throwing a few silly arm punches that were missing by a mile, I had my head in my hands and couldn't watch it anymore. Soldier couldn't have made it more obvious the fight was crooked. His opponent was now getting the hump so he pressed Soldier hoping it would make him fight, then Soldier clipped him with a right hand that wouldn't have hurt my grandmother, and he went down for the count, the crowd booed, and I looked at Ricky, and we just both started laughing. It was **so** terrible, but thankfully it was over.

Ricky got in the ring and took the piss straight away,

"Right put your hands together, what a great fight ladies and gentlemen …

definitely a contender for the fight of the night! … or strictly come dancing"

I was laughing with Warren and Mitch and then Soldier got out the ring he came over to me, "thanks Joe, he was a tough kid, how did it look, did it look good."

he said to me which made Warren crack up laughing

"Yeah, it fucking looked blinding!" Warren said, shaking his head.

The funny thing is … It didn't really matter because this was Caesars! The crowd expected a few joke fights as they knew anything could happen next.

Some of the set-ups were so bad that they actually made the night more entertaining as it got the crowds in fits of hysterics.

Another funny instance was when we were promoting a show at Crystal Palace. We had a local kid fighting who could actually fight, but he was so worried about losing his reputation as a local hard nut he always begged me for a fixed fight.

On this occasion, his opponent hadn't turned up, so I told him the bad news. He was really upset as he sold a load of tickets and didn't want to let his crowd down.

Trying to salvage the situation, I spoke to one of the fellas who worked with us, who usually brings a few journeymen along, I told him we needed another fight as he always had a couple of spare fighters come in the transit bus with him. He told me he had one lad around the same weight, but this kid wouldn't take a dive.

"Can you have a chat with him, it's against our best ticket seller, and if he beats him, then the place will go up in the fucking air."

"He won't do it, Joe, he's a stubborn c**t and won't go over mate."

"I'll pay him fucking double! Just ask him, will you, and explain to him I'll tell my boy to go easy, it will be like an exhibition bout." I added.

Around half an hour passed and I still hadn't heard anything. On another occasion, I would have just let it go and got Ricky to announce that the fight was off and apologise to the crowd. However, my fighter was really giving me agro as the same thing happened to him last time, he sold his tickets, and his fight fell through, and now for it to happen again, it would be a complete piss-take on the people who had paid twice now to see him fight.

I was under pressure to get this sorted, so I went back to the fella I spoke to.

"Have you spoken to him?"

"Yes, joe, and he won't do it, mate."

"What a wanker! It's a fucking easy payday for him."

"I know, but he just won't *take a dive* .. he's a funny c**t like that."

"What's he like then, can he fight?" I then asked, thinking about making the match anyway.

"He's a right handful, punches like Tyson!" my mate James replied.

That's all I wanted to hear, and now I was in a right predicament.

If I didn't make the fight, then I would certainly lose the ticket seller on future shows ... And If I do make the match, I might be getting my ticket seller knocked spark out!

I thought about it for a moment and then knew I had to make this work somehow.

"Alright, the fights on, let me have a chat with him, though." I said to James as we both walked off to see the fighter where I could see by the look of him, that he could fight. James told the kid he was boxing, and then I pulled him over to a quiet corner.

"Did James explain everything to you .. My man has to win," I said sternly to him as I looked him in the eyes.

"I ain't taking a dive, I don't do that!" he replied.

I gave him a strong look and then thought I would turn the tables and tell him a little lie.

"Look! … This can be an easy nights work for you or a trip to the fucking hospital with a broken jaw! … My man isn't happy, either. His original opponent broke his hand, so the only fight I can get him is with you and now I have to tell him will have to take it fucking easy! … He is not fucking happy, he wanted to put on a right show for his crowd and keep his knockout record going, he's had six fights and won all of them in the first two rounds…. He's an ex ABA champion, and I've got to tell him to have a glorified fucking sparring session. So fine, if you won't play ball, then I'll let him off the leash, and he'll knock you out the fucking ring!"

The kid suddenly looked down at his feet and looked confused,

"I've never taken a dive before," he said quietly.

"It's not a fucking DIVE!" I snapped back at him.

"Both of you are just having a move around, it's like a fucking spar, only the ref will say he won. What fucking difference does it make to you? You got no crowd here, and we can even call you by another name." I now tried to push the kid into accepting my offer as I could see he was cracking.

"Alright." He then said quietly.

"Alright, good… now don't worry, he will go easy, and I'll pay you another £50 on top okay… but listen to me! If you try anything, you start trying and land a big shot then he will take your fucking head off your shoulders, this kid is fucking good, but he will be holding back."

"Alright, Joe, let's do it."

So that was the first part done, and I've just lied to the kid saying he is fighting an ex Aba champion when the truth of the matter is that he is fighting someone who has had a few amateur fights and someone he could beat quite easily if he wanted to.

Next, I had to tell my boy he would have to take it easy. Now my boy was a bag of nerves so I had to tell him that the kid he was fighting was useless and he would have to take it easy.

"Listen, I found you someone, but you can't knock him out, alright."

"Fuck sake, Joe, I wanted to put on a good show."

"What do you want me to do? It's either fight this kid or fight no one! It's his first-ever fight, so you will have to go easy on him. I gave my word. Otherwise, you weren't getting a fight tonight."

"So he can't fight?" he then said as I saw him warm to the idea of an easy night's work.

"Mate, he's fucking useless, just move around for three rounds with him, get the win and then get pissed with us lot."

"Thanks, mate, I love you, Joe." He said, now smiling and giving me a hug.

So the job was done and fight matched, I told the good fighter he was fighting an animal and the not so good fighter he was fighting a novice.

The fight went ahead, and it worked out well as both boxers did as they were told and it turned out to be, not a bad fight. I did tell the referee what was happening beforehand, so he helped keep things on a good-tempered basis, and I also told the timekeeper to cut the rounds short slightly; the first round, he rang the bell around 1'45 of 2 minutes and just keep an eye on the action. (Ring the bell if it looks like it's going off-script)

That was another way of fixing fights using a bit of psychology.

There were loads of different ways we fixed them, and I can't think of one show in twenty years and over a hundred promotions where some (kind of) fix wasn't used on a show.

Another time I remember a big heavyweight we were promoting. Now, this heavyweight was a big lump. And he had a big mouth where couldn't stop himself shouting out that he was the best or how he could fight. It actually got annoying in the end, but on this occasion, I was asked to go see him in the changing room before a fight where I found him shaking like a leaf.

"Joe, it's definitely fixed, Isn't it, mate," he said to me after he cleared the room.

"Yes, mate, I told you, he's going down in the first." I answered, feeling a bit embarrassed at how the fella in front of me was worried.

"Honestly, mate, I haven't done a day's training for this."

"Look, stop fucking worrying, it's sorted … I promise you." I replied.

It amazes me now that when I look back some of the fighters I promoted, some of them never had one straight fight. Every single fight they had was a set-up.

The Russians

This was a funny situation that we had in our early days when we started using Russian fighters on our shows as opponents (Journeymen)

Ricky English told me had a contact who could get fighters to lose, Russians, and Lithuanians. They were cheap, so we booked half a dozen of them for our next show.

On the day of the show when they turned up, I took one look at them and said to Ricky, what's this mate? These kids look fit as fuck and hungry as hell.

Straight away, I said to Ricky, do this c**ts know the score?

Ricky replied to me that everything was okay and not to worry.

I wasn't that convinced, I could sense something was in the air, and when the first bout got underway, and the Russian kid knocked out one of our best fighters, believe me, I was fucking livid! I went straight to the dressing room to talk to the Russian trainer who himself was a big six-foot-something Russian, I was mad at him and read him the riot act but I calmed down when he promised me it was a fluke.

Fucking fluke!! It wasn't any fluke as over the night's space, the Russians knocked out another three of our boys, including our top fighter and champion Andy Roberts.

I told Ricky they could go fuck themselves, and they weren't getting paid. I was just about to gather up a few of my lads to go up into the changing room to have a row with them when Ricky pulled me back and calmed me down. We ended up paying them, but I wasn't happy.

A few weeks later, I heard the Russians had some of their lads on a Tel Currie promotion at Hammersmith Palace. (Tel was a pal of mine and he did the right thing by giving me a pension from the show, he was promoting in our area, so he thought it best to give us a slice and work with us, rather than against us) I was in the red lion pub in Sutton when Warren walked in, so I told him I had to drive up to Hammersmith to collect some money and come with me.

We got to the venue, sat down with Tel Currie and a few of the lads, and watched the boxing where I saw that a couple of the Russian boys had done what they did on my show and beat the home lads. It was annoying me that they thought this was okay, so after another beer hit home, I thought to myself that this is a fucking liberty, they tried to ruin my show and now ruined Tel's show (And they were getting paid!) I then asked Tel Currie what dressing room the Russian kids were in.

I then nodded to Warren and we walked up the stairs to the room. I walked in, and I saw this big Russian fella in there so immediately I grabbed the c**t around the throat and pushed him back against the wall. I then told him I want half the money he earned tonight, or he will be fucked.

Warren was jumping about as I never told him I was going to have a row; his eyes were all over the place, and he laughed later on saying to me 'Thanks pal for the fucking warning!'

I got my money out of the Russians and told him to behave himself, this is London, our fucking town and if you fuck us about then we will have the lot of you fucking deported.

Right hand Alley
I don't know what it is with boxing shows, but over the years you don't half get some weird funny fuckers come to the shows. Maybe it's all the adrenaline inside the ring that makes people act like idiots. Then mix that with a few beers and you have a concoction that makes the show feel like a convention for village idiots.

One show I remember when there were five lads from Kent and they got so pissed they decided to all take their tops off at the bar and start having mock fights amongst themselves. Someone told me what was happening so I went over with a pal to sort it out. I was nice and polite and told them to behave themselves and have a good night, they apologized and that was that I thought. Then about an hour later I get told they are at it again.

Now at Caesars we had two exits at the back , one was the main exit and the other was a side door which we nicknamed - *Right hand alley'*
If you was just being a bit of an idiot then the security would throw you out the

main exit, but if you had really been a right fucking mug and upset a few people then we would be slinging you out into '*Right hand alley*'

Now it doesn't take a professor to figure out what's going to happen to you if you are unfortunate enough to be thrown out the latter.

Anyway, these idiots from Kent now decided to start bumping into people and throwing drinks about so me and a few of the firm flew over and grabbed them, and quick as you like, we dragged them into a *Right hand alley*, crash bang wallop and four Kent boys were taught a nice little South London lesson in how to behave in public.

Posters

The posters we had made for Caesars shows were bonkers some of them. We used to get the fighters' pictures and cut the heads off and stick them on movie posters like Reservoir Dogs or Snatch.

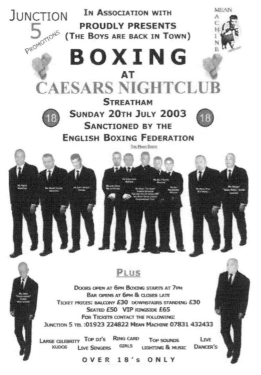

When I do think back on some of the things we did, it's a miracle the fighters boxed for us at all.

On the poster to the left, we stuck my brother Mitch's head on it and he wasn't even boxing. Dave Thursting as well, but we didn't care. (Thinking about it, Dave's picture was every bloody poster in 2004, lol)

We would also put stuff on the poster like,
"Idiots Are Not Allowed!"

One poster we had once was absolutely hilarious. We had a heavyweight contest where both lads were quite overweight. So we decided to make a new title called 'The London Kebab Title' we stuck the posters all over the place and it was hilarious. The fighters at first had the hump, but in the end, they saw the funny side.

On the night when they got into the ring, the crowd were in fits of laughter when Ricky announces the fight for the Kebab title. He then took it further and said, "In the blue corner we have DONOR and in the red corner we have SHISH!

After-Parties

The after-parties at Caesars were bloody legendary.

After every show, we would always end up back at my house. Carloads of fighters and thugs would completely cram the cul de sac and emerge from their cars with bags of booze. The music was turned up high, and the front door was wide open.

(My neighbours must have loved me!)

We would usually arrive around 2.00 am and stay till the booze and fun ran out. The summer shows were the best as I had a massive decking area outside the French doors with gazebos, sofas, and tables. We would all sit out in the garden as the sun came up, drinking, dancing, and enjoying ourselves.

One funny story was at a time I owned two houses, so I rented this house out to my good pal Steve Slater and his girlfriend.

Anyway, I got drunk at the show and told everyone to come back to the house as I still had the key.

Steve was in bed asleep with his girl when I turned up uninvited with about a hundred people. The music went straight on; the fridge got raided! And the BBQ got fired up.

I can still remember Steve's face when he came downstairs in his boxer shorts, straight into a full-blown rave.

It was a bloody good laugh; Steve still jokes of how he came into the living room to find a 7ft2 black fella swinging his Staffordshire bull terrier around his head in the front room.

Good memories and sorry to say, Steve moved out before the next show x

We all enjoyed his taste in burgers and sausages.

Another time I came home after a show with the entourage and my wife wasn't well, so she stayed at home

Anyway, she went to sleep on the couch in the front room and then woke up to about fifty people in the house and loads of ring card girls sitting and dancing around her. (She wasn't very pleased!!!)

MeanMachine go on the road …. To Ireland

In 2012 MeanMachine promotions packed our bags and took a bunch of fighters slap bang right into the heart of bandit country to Donegal in Ireland. It started a few years earlier, while I was in Thailand training at a Muay Thai camp, and I met a boxer from Buncrana, Donegal, a kid named John Hutchinson. We were both the only two boxers in the Thai camp, so we sort of found each other and started to train together and hang out after the gym.

A few years later, we met up again when John travelled over to the UK and boxed on one of our shows at the Oceana's club in Kingston.

After the fight, I talked to one of his crowd, and he suggested that sometime in the future we travel to Ireland for and England vs Ireland competition. It sounded interesting, so we put the wheels in motion.

A few months later, together with John Feld, the president of our World Sports Organisation, we were on the plane with seven of our fighters, Trevor Smith and his father, Joe gunner smith, Khalid Miah, Rocky Muscus, Daryl Sommers, Little Paddy Bryne. Louis Harrison and Lee Barrow.

We flew into the George Best airport in Belfast and were collected in a minibus and driven to our hotel in Buncrana. It was a lovely place just on the border. The boxing show was the following night so we had a quiet night in the hotel, just a meal, and sit down in the bar downstairs with the organisers of the show who were explaining to us what was happening the next day.

We all woke early and had some breakfast before it was time for the weigh at the hotel. All the boys weighed in and made weight, then we had a rest and was picked up in the minibus at 6.00 PM to get to the venue.

The boys went to their changing room to sort themselves out, while me and John had a wander around, feeling the atmosphere as it started to fill up. To be honest with you, it felt a bit hostile as we right in IRA country, and all the posters were Ireland vs England Boxing event for the annual WSO Anglo/Irish shield. (The idea was to have a team come to England the following years and then back to Ireland the year after. – An annual event)

While we were talking to the organisers, we found out that we were waiting around because the MC hadn't turned up for the evening. John Feld, who often thought of himself as an actor, commentator, and singer? Then volunteered to fill in for the absent MC.

I tried to make an excuse for him as John is a very well-spoken Jewish Englishman, and we were in the bloody heart of bandit country. I couldn't think of anything worse or more of an invitation to go missing than John getting up there in his snobby voice and arrogant demeanour to antagonise the native Irishmen.

However, John was really insistent despite my concerns, so it was agreed that he would take the job and MC the evening.

I walked away shaking my head and honestly thinking 'God help us'"

Now, if I thought things were looking bad (and remember I had two secret professional boxers with me which I kept a secret from the Irish), things did get worse ….. A lot bloody worse!.

I walked out to the start of the evening and John is in the ring and in his English public schoolboy accent he greets the crowd,

"My Lords, Ladies, and Gentlemen … Welcome to the annual World Sports Organisation - Anglo / Irish shield between England and Ireland'" he said, which got a few claps and a few boos.

I was looking around the room and the faces I saw looking at him in the ring were in that of bemusement, it was like "Who the fucking hell is this ENGLISH guy?"

People really were looking around, thinking, what the fuck is this!

I'm just thinking of getting the bloody first fight on.

What happened next almost knocked me over! In all his insanity and for whatever reason, I haven't got a clue; John decides to address the crowd again.

"I feel very honoured to be here tonight and as a thank you I would like to give you all a gift from me."

'What's he fucking doing now,' I'm thinking. What on earth is he up to, but a moment later to my absolute dread I found out, and it was something I would not have guessed in a million fucking years.

John puts down his notes in the centre of the ring, clears his throat, and starts the most English rendition of Danny Boy I have ever heard.

I had a cigarette in my mouth, and it dropped out as I just stood there fucking horrified. I couldn't believe it! He is going to get us all fucking killed.

John is now in the ring singing and sounding like Prince Charles singing the fucking unofficial Irish national anthem.

The crowd just sat there not knowing if this was a joke, a piss-take or some nut in the ring.

"What the fucking hell is he doing?" Daryl Sommers asked as he walked over to me.

"Getting us all fucking murdered!" I replied in disbelief.

But it got even worse as halfway through the song as believe it or not he forgot some of the words and started to fucking hum the words he forgot.

It was absolutely bonkers, so bonkers and so off the cuff and odd, it just had to be sincere.

One of the organisers came over to me smiling,

"He's doing okay," in said not knowing what else to fucking say,

"Ar he's doing fine lad, but we should have put him on last, so to get rid of all the drunks!"

After what seemed like an agonising hour, John finishes his take on Danny boy and bows to the crowd who are just fucking speechless! Honestly, the look on everyone's face was priceless.

John then smiles at everyone, and finally we can start the evening and get the first fight underway.

First up was Paddy Byrne, Paddy had been boxing for us for a few years as a journeyman. When he heard we were going to Ireland, he fancied coming as he had Irish blood in his family. Paddy puts up a really good fight but lost a decision to their fighter Paddy Swain. (Paddy vs Paddy)

Next fight was Lee Barrow for us who won his fight on points against Patrick Freil, squaring the series 1 -1

Lee's teammate Louis Harrison was next, and he stopped the Irish lad Chris Kelly in the 1st round, now making it now 2 -1 for the English lads.

Next was Khalid Miah, who was a very decent amateur boxer and was on the verge of turning professional, Khalid had a very slick style, a bit like Naseem Hamed and he dominated his fight to make it now 3 – 1 to us.

Next was one of my professional boxers, Rocky Muscus against one of their top boys, Tom Harkin, (Dom was also just about to sign a contract with me, so I had a word in Rocky's ear to go easy) the fight was a tough fight which ended in a points win for their lad Dom. The series was now 3 – 2 to us.

Trevor Smith was up next who had come with his father, my old pal Joe smith, Trev was a decent boxer and was matched against one of their stars, a kid called Mark McMahon. It was a good fight, and Trevor won on points which now made the score 4 – 2 to us, and with only one fight left, we had already won the shield.

I could sense the crowd was feeling disappointed as they realised that the Irish lads had already lost the shield, but next was their best fighter against my fighter who was a professional boxer using another name. Their boy was a very experienced amateur who was the Ulster champion and Irish boxing team representative.

He was definitely their main boxer, whom most of the crowd had come to support.

We had already won the Anglo/Irish shield, so I sat my fighter Daryl down in a quiet corner and had a quick word just before he was called into the ring.

"Daryl, you're going to have to lose this one, mate." I said to him sadly

"Leave it out Joe, I'm looking forward to putting on a good performance!" he answered, looking disappointed.

"I know you are, but this has to go their way, mate, we have just won the shield, let them win the main event, that way everyone goes home happy. If you beat their top boy, then who knows how tonight might end up." I replied.

Daryl wasn't happy, but he understood, and he did as he was told, it was a good three round scrap. Daryl followed the script to perfection and even wobbled their lad with a decent left hook. The crowd was going crazy, cheering their lad, singing his name, and really enjoying the fight. They got their win and the place erupted in cheers.

When the main event finished, all the team England was called into the ring and presented with the shield, and it was a lovely gesture when all the crowd rose to their feet to give all the boys a well-deserved round of applause.

It had been a good show and a successful introduction to the Anglo / Irish shield. The Irish were a little disappointed at not winning the shield, but their win in the main event evened things out, and they all went home singing and happy.

Once the crowd had gone home, we gathered our kit and waited to be picked up and driven back to the hotel.

We were still owed about £500, so I went looking for the organisers to sort out the rest of our money. When I found them, I was given an excuse and they said they would bring the difference of what's owed to the hotel in the morning before we left.

Me and Team UK with the Anglo /Irish shield

Not what I wanted to hear! I have done enough shows to see when someone is under pressure and struggling to pay the bills, I could see it on the organisers face, and I didn't want him going on the piss tonight without paying us and *accidentally* forgetting to wake up in time to see us. We were leaving by midday tomorrow to catch a flight back to London, so this needed to be sorted out tonight.

Long story short, I strongly suggested to one of the organisers that we drive into town to the hole in the wall machine and draw out what was owed.

We then went back to the hotel where the lady owner had laid on a small party for us. There was a singer and a small buffet, and all the boys had a well-deserved party. John Feld decided to sing again, which had everyone laughing and joking, remembering his annihilation of Danny Boy earlier in the evening. One of the stand out moments I will always remember is all the lads singing - 'We are the champions by Queen' on the karaoke machine. It was great to see everyone having a good time. It had been a hectic few days, and they deserved it.

CHAPTER 12
THE CAESARS GANG

Over the years, dozens of people have worked alongside us, helping to stage the shows. Some of which were my partners Like Ricky English, Warren, and Teddy, while others were an integral part of the machine that helped everything run smoothly.

In this chapter, I will give credit to those who have stuck by us and have been with us and owe a massive slice of all the fantastic memories we shared.

Ricky English

Ricky – Manny Clark – Colin Wilby – Joe Pyle Jr at Press conference – The Embassy club 2009

Me and Ricky go back years, I first met Ricky when I was a school kid, when we moved down to Lower Morden. Ricky was a few years older than me, and he was the toughest kid around the area.

In those days, I was still walking around in army greens from the army surplus shop, and I didn't care less about fashion. It was good days in those days growing up, we became good pals, and we still are today.

Ricky has always been involved in boxing, his uncle George used to be my coach when I was a kid training at the Hillcrest amateur boxing club.

Ricky was a very good amateur fighter as well.

In the early 2000s, I was doing professional promotions, and I had heard that Ricky was staging unlicensed shows in and around the Watford area.

He knew I was doing events at Caesars (professional shows), and when I walked away from the pro's we met up, and he told me all about what he had been doing.

It sounded exciting, so we agreed to run a show at Caesars.

Our first show was a massive success, we had over 1600 people in there and had some great bouts on, plus we both walked away with a nice little earner.

Loads of local lads signed up to box (we used to have application forms at ringside) and would make announcements throughout the night that if anyone wanted to fight on a future show, they would come to ringside and fill a form out. Is was a good move as after every show, we always had around a dozen forms and leads to call. (Unless Teddy Bam Bam got his hands on them first, lol)

We were a very good team, we both knew the boxing game like the back of our hands, and we bounced off each other well.

Before the show, we would make sure all the boxers arrived nice and early to sort out their ticket money and get their medicals from the doctor.

I hated this part, so Ricky usually took care of sorting this out while I made sure the venue was being set up correctly. A few times we doubled up on troublesome fighters, those who tried it on with their ticket money. Believe me, over the years we have heard every bloody excuse going, lost tickets, tickets being collected on the door, fighters saying their crowd is paying when they arrive, one idiot even tried to tell us he got nicked and the old bill have his tickets. Ricky said to him,

"When did you get nicked?"

"It was about a week ago." The fighter replied.

"So the old bill has our tickets, and you've had a week to tell us about it, and you've said fuck all until an hour before the show starts!" Ricky said back to him laughing,

"And you think me and Joe are going to swallow that fucking bollocks!" he added after looking at me.

Ricky also had a wicked and quick sense of humour, he was infectious when he was on form.

When he started to MC the events he was unbelievable, I have never seen anyone do it with his style. He would start the evening off by asking the crowd who they were there to see, he would say, "WHOSE HERE TO SEE COLIN WILBBBYYYY!" and Colin's crowd would all cheer. Sometimes he would call out a fighter's name and the fighter might only get a couple of people cheering, so Ricky would make a joke of it like, "Fucking hell … Billy no mates…)

Once he made all the announcements for the evening, he would call for the first fight to happen, the music would start, and the boxers would come into the ring. He would say their names and then sit ringside as the first round began.

Now at this stage, what other MCs would do is turn the microphone off and wait for the fight to end....... Not Ricky, he decided to give it a running commentary. It was nothing like you see on TV, but more of a gee-up for the boxers and crowd.

If a boxer landed a good shot, Ricky would shout out over the mike, "WHOAARRRR" or "WHAT A SHOT!" other times if a fight was boring or slow getting started he would shout, "COME ON, LETS GET THESE FUCKING TWO GOING!" the crowd loved him and he had them dangling in his hand.

He would also take the piss out fighters on the mike which was sometimes hilarious,

I remember him once saying to a fighter who was getting knocked about in the last round, "C'mon son, do something, your birds sitting ringside, you're definitely not getting your leg over tonight fighting like this."

Another time we had a right cocky fighter smothered in tattoos who didn't want his name being announced in the ring, so what do we fucking call you? Ricky asked him. "Call me the wild thing!"

"Mate, we can't call you wild thing, everyone will take the piss!" Ricky said, "Listen to me bro, all the mandem know me, just say *Wild Ting*, everybody knows me."

Anyway Ricky announces him laughing his head off, "And in the blue corner ... we have WILD THING!"

Everyone in the crowd was laughing and when the bell started for the first round, Wild Thing was fucking useless! He couldn't hold his hands up, never landed one punch and was knocked spark out in the 1st round.

"DOCTORS TO THE RING PLEASE!" Ricky shouted out over the mike worried for poor Wild Thing who was flat out on his back asleep.

The doctors and paramedics got and helped him out, and after a few minutes he got to his feet, looking nothing like his name.

 "Let's HAVE A ROUND OF APPLAUSE FOR WILD THING!" Ricky said, trying his hardest not to laugh. I was at ringside in hysteric fits of laughter, "Ricky, is wild thing okay?" I shouted out, only for Ricky to laugh back at me. Ricky had to turn away in laughter and then raised the winner's hand and turned to the wild thing, "Round of applause for Wild Thing!" he said to the crowd who were all laughing and shouting out.

Both boys got out the ring, and Ricky addressed the crowd,

"Well, ladies and gentlemen, you have just witnessed ...... Wild thing,"

Poor old wild thing was hobbling back to the dressing room, and when he heard what Ricky said, he turned and waved to the crowd, the soppy bastard, thinking he was being applauded.

Me and Ricky have had some laughs over the years and some great memories. I am godfather to his beautiful daughter Sadie.

I have been speaking to him lately, and we have decided to start doing the shows again in 2021, so let's hope we have many greater times ahead of us. One thing for sure is I can't wait to see him in action again.

A few words below from Ricky himself

From a young boy Joe Pyle Snr's name was a much loved One in my family household.

My dad Bill English trained him in his boxing gym at Rosehill ABC which he founded in the 1950's where he trained Joe from a young teenager.

I remember Joe Pyle Snr telling me that as a young boy he and his friends would all go to the St. Helier Arms pub in Carshalton on a Friday night and sit on the wall to watch the unbeaten bare knuckle fighter Bill English.

As a young man Joe was called up to do his national service with my uncle Ronnie English who was a national flyer weight champion. Joe was the army national middle weight champion. They shared a dormitory together during their National s service and remained friends till their dying days.

Whilst they were in the army My dad would call up and tell them Joe and Ronnie were due to box on a show that weekend so they were released to party all weekend. There was never no show!

I can remember from a young age Joe snr giving me his army boxing medal which I carried around with me for many years. later in life when Joe Pyle snr and I started off doing the unlicensed boxing shows together I gave him back his medal. Tears came to his eyes and he hugged me tightly and he fondly told me of his notorious fights whilst in the army.

When I was a teenager Joe moved to Morden and our back garden near enough backed onto each other.

One night I was walking down the street with all my mates when we bumped into a younger kid. We started taking to him and it turned out to be Joe Pyle jnr. We became friends from that day. Joe Jnr was always very mature for his age and we became inseparable for years.

Later in life when we were starting off as young men I became a boxing coach for the amateurs and later the pros. Joe became a professional boxing promotor. There was no money in either.

I started doing unlicensed boxing shows with Bobby Frankham and we were earning big money.

One night I got a call from Joe snr and Joe jnr proposing we join forces and do unlicensed boxing shows together at Caesars night club in Streatham.

On our first show we matched 14 fights, we had some good fights, some shit fights and some fucking tear ups. The audience was full of gangsters, boxers and music celebrities. It was an event!!

It was all about making money and we made some fucking big money.

Over the years we looked after some of our big ticket sellers with easy fights.

1. because they didn't want to fucking train.

2. Some of them couldn't fight and three some could. It was always about money and pleasing the crowd.

One night at Caesar I was in the ring when it all kicked off big time. People were fighting everywhere. Tables chairs bottles were being thrown all over the place. My first thought was "we are going to be robbed". I jumped out the ring and made my way through the crowd to the office where the money was in the safe. I pulled down the shutters got the staff and locked the doors. The police soon arrived 30 handed. I approached the man in charge and asked him "are you going to stop this" he replied "fuck that, I'll wait till they have run out of steam". I replied "you fucking wankers".

When it eventually calmed down I went outside and never seen so much blood, it was a blood bath.

Another memorable time at Caesars I was walking to the office when a car pulled up outside and shot at the main doors. I dived onto to the floor and could feel the wind of the bullets flying above my head.

Word went around they were looking for a cousin who was a friend of ours (no names mentioned). Soon after shows came to an end.

Caesar's will go down in history!

As the years go by Joe jnr and I are still the closest of friends and he is the godfather to my first daughter Sadie.

Our next venture together will be to get this Guvnor belt back to where it belongs.

Teddy Bam Bam

Ted is like a brother to me; he has been part of the firm for years and is one of us, but he can be a bloody handful at times and believe me, he can test the patience of a saint.

He is louder than life and lives life fast and likes to enjoy himself, but don't let that fool you; he is articulate, intelligent, and loyal.

Teddy loved the boxing, and in the early days when I started doing the shows with Ricky English, he said he had a few fighters that would box on the show or shows.

He was good to his word and always supplied us with a steady stream of boxers. Ted was like a silent partner to me and Ricky.

Boxing promotions was a funny game, and its tight having two partners involved, so having three equal partners is taxing. It's a lot of work to end up with one-third of the profit (if there is any profit!)

We worked out a deal with Ted on the tickets; he kept a percentage of the tickets he sold and also had a percentage of the ticket sales of the boxers he brought to the show.

It worked out well, and it was a good incentive for him to give his boys a kick up the arse to sell tickets.

I have also co-promoted with Ted and we staged some good shows down the years.

Teddy was the one who got our Unlicensed documentary up and running which is now featured on Amazon prime.

It was a big project and a great documentary with over two hours of fights and interviews.

Joey Pyle – James Flynn – Teddy Bam Bam

By the way, it was Ted who brought all the fucking Nazi boxers to the show! You couldn't make it up; honestly, Ted is black, and he is bringing me Nazi, racist combat 18 fighters.

Mitch – Warren Joe Pyle jr – Alan – Teddy Bam Bam

Warren Bammo (Wazza)

My fiery brother, Warren. If you look at any Caesars show on YouTube where it features a fight in the crowd, or things get out of hand in the ring, It is almost a certainty you will see Warren right in the thick of it trying to bring some order. The rows we had together in Caesars are so many I have forgotten half of them. Warren was like a second son to my father, and for years they were almost joined at the hip.

Bloody hell, we had some laughs at the shows, Warren and me were always messing about, always winding someone up.

He also used to look after a couple of local pubs and was always in the thick of it somewhere.

One night a fight happened over the far side of the venue and there was a bloody great crowd between us and where the fight broke out, Warren was trying to get over there to sort it out, but he couldn't get through all the people standing between us. So what does he do? He decides to table jump over to it. I'm standing there watching him jump from one bleeding table to the next like a bloody acrobat. That was Warren, though. Wherever something was happening, then guarantee, you would see him pop up breaking everyone apart.

We did do a couple of shows together, where he and his brother in law, Taylor, became a lot more involved. He was always with us and if I had to drift off into other pieces of work, Warren filled in for me.

He started getting a few boxers on his own, and before long we were setting up alternative shows. He staged a terrific show at a hotel in Heathrow, dinner show with a couple of championship fights. It was a proper good night.

Mitch Pyle

Like Warren, my brother Mitch has always been around us at the shows. He doesn't say much, but he was always on hand to sort out anything that needed sorting.

I have lost count the amount of times that together we have had to sort out a fight or argument in the crowd. One time I remember which was funny was when a group of football supporters were making a right nuisance of themselves.

It was near the end of the night, and typically these idiots had drunk way too much alcohol.

Caesar's owner Fred Batt came over to me and asked if I knew them as they were goading the security and generally driving everyone mad. I said they weren't my pals, so me and Mitch with the security took a walk over to them to have a word. I led the way and told them to behave, I said don't spoil a good night and just have some respect for the other guest, we don't want to sling you out so enjoy the rest of the evening.

The boys all agreed, and then as we are walking away suddenly, a pint of lager in a plastic glass is thrown at one of the security and hits him on the back.

Fuck it! I said, that's their fucking lot! So we move in to sling them out, next thing we are grabbing hold of them and pushing them all towards the back door, a few of my mates come over and we got them out, all except this big fat fucker who had a Millwall tattoo on his beer belly. This fella must have been twenty stone, and six-foot 4 and Mitch and Colin the head of security have got a hold of him trying to get him through the back door! The fella has grabbed the door and won't let go so were giving him a few digs in the stomach to get him out and the next thing I see him go down and drag Mitch and Colin with him, now everyone's on the floor trying to get this big fat lump upon his feet. I'm standing back now and laughing as Mitch is trying with all his strength to get him up, arms and legs are flying about everywhere and Mitch is sweating and straining and calling him names as he struggled to lift the idiot up, and then he looks at me and sees me laughing, "You bastard!" he says, "Go on son, get him out Mitch!" I said, winding him up.

Anyway we got him out and slammed the door shut, and then I'm looking at Mitch sweating like a pig and puffing like a racehorse.

"Next one is fucking yours!" he said.

Rob Davis (Mother)

Rob Davis was a very good pal of mine and larger than life, he was a big man, and he was always trying to look after everyone, or tell people what to do, we used to call him (Mother)

Rob was another one who was always in the thick of it when there was any crowd trouble. One night he even jumped in the ring when one of the fighters attacked the referee. He jumped in like a flash, grabbed hold of the bloke, pulled him over to the corner, pushed him back, and warned the poor fella that if he does it again, he's going home in the ambulance.

Rob used to make me laugh though. I was always getting him at it, winding him up.

He loved it at Caesars and was always at the shows bossing everyone about. I always fondly remember his face when I was fighting one night and he was walking me into the ring, Rob was more excited than me, and smiling from ear to ear; honestly, he was like a big kid on Christmas morning waiting to open his presents.

One show I promoted didn't end too well for Rob though. He ended up getting shot three times.

It was late on in the night, and I was collecting my belongings when I heard a loud bang followed by two others. Suddenly I heard screaming and then everybody started running, "Robs been shot!" someone shouted out to me. I ran over to him and he was flat out on the ground, so I knelt down where I saw he was drifting in and out of consciousness. I shouted out to Mitch to get on the door, just in case the ones who shot him tried to get back in.

I quickly felt around robs body to see where the shots were. Rob was groaning and there was some blood on the back of his head and on his lower back. I had already shouted out for someone to call an ambulance so I cradled his head and tried to keep him awake.

The ambulance shortly arrived, and it turned out he had been shot three times with a .22.

One bullet hit him in the forehead and travelled round his head under the skin and flew out the skin at the back!

Rob was okay though, he spent a couple of days in the hospital and was then out. He did make me laugh at the hospital when the old bill came in to see him. The hospital called them as it was a shooting incident. They asked Rob, who shot him and he replied, "it was Batman, officer!"

Whenever I think of Caesars I can't imagine thinking about it without thinking of Rob. (My dear friend and godfather to my daughter Angel Bonnie)

Charlie Breaker

Charlie was a good pal of everyone and had a pub in Norwood and Nunhead, we would always go and have a drink with Charlie, and it always ended up being a lock-in. When we started doing the shows at Caesars, he started getting a few of his locals to fight. Charlie himself was an ex bare-knuckle fighter and he loved the fights. He brought a few good lads to us, and they always put up a good show and sold loads of tickets.

As a thank you, we created a belt called the Charlie Breaker South London championship. He brought us some good fighters; Darren Taylor could have a row and boxed a few times winning Charlie's belt for us a few times.

Charlie now lives in Spain and runs a bar out there. One funny story was when we once held a charity night for Ronnie Biggs at his pub in Norwood. It was about ten o'clock at night, and someone runs in the pub saying there were traffic wardens outside the pub putting tickets on the cars. Ten at fucking night for fucks sake. We weren't having that! A few of us ran out the bar and chased the two bob mugs off up the road - the clip of what happened after was on YouTube where I'm talking about the robbing bastards. I was drunk, but it was a good night.

Wendy Propernaughty

Wendy is a good girl and pal, very loyal, and never once let any of us down. She would work her socks off for the shows and was always available at the end of the phone.

I first met Wendy when she was a manager for Carlton Leach, and I went to a UK premier at the Circus tavern for the Rise of the Footsoldier film with my brother Warren and Roy Shaw.

Wendy, along with her great friend Bill Hickey put that together, and it impressed me how professional the evening was.

It wasn't long after I 'poached' Wendy for our shows. Bill also started doing a few bits and bobs for me. Wendy took to the shows like a duck to water, and before long, she started recruiting and organising the ring card girls. A group of girls she named, The Mean Girls.

The next show we promoted, she turned up with 12 girls! At first I was thinking, "Who the fuck is going to pay for 12 girls!" Wendy just smiled and said, don't worry, I've sorted it.

As I said before in the promoting chapter, it's bloody hectic on the day of the show and the two hours before the doors open its stressful and you need people like Wendy who know their jobs (and other people's job) to take some of the load off of you.

I'm running off my feet, making sure everything is in place so the show starts on time but once the doors open and the crowd start coming in, everything gets even more frantic. Wendy would always help out with the crowd coming in. My auntie Lorraine was 'front of house' working the box office and together with Wendy they were bloody good at their job. I have seen people go to pieces with the stress at the box office. People are coming in and have no idea that you have only a certain amount of time to get over a 1000 people wrist-banded and searched and shown to their seats.

You need people on the door who are polite, friendly, but assertive. The line has to keep on moving and moving fast! People will turn up and say I put them on the guest list, so Wendy or Lorraine would have to then search the list, and if their name wasn't on it, they then had to listen to the person complaining but be patient and polite as they didn't know who they might be speaking to. And get rid of the person so the line would keep moving.

It's a tough job! But with Wendy next to Lorraine, I was comfortable in the fact that the job was being done correctly, so it freed me up to do other things.

What Wendy did with the card girls was amazing! She created a whole new brand.

The crowd loved them and they were good girls who had fun with everyone. They were a lot more professional than the girls we had been using before. I'm pretty sure, but I think we were the first promotional outfit that had our own brand of card girls! I do remember that shortly after what Wendy did it didn't take long for the copycats to come out the woodwork.

I really cannot praise Wendy high enough, she was a very important member of MeanMachine but much more than that, she was a good friend and even to this day we remain good friends and together with Tessa and Ian , I look at her as part of the family.

Auntie Lorraine

Lorraine was my auntie on my dad's side and she would always do the box office at the shows, I also got her to organize the raffles and auctions. She was really good at her job and she also worked the box office at my professional shows I promoted with Johnny Edwards.

The box office was a tough little number where you had to deal with hundreds of the public and a lesson we learnt the hard way … was to keep me away from the front of house.

Lorraine was great at this as she knew full well that I could be an easy target for people, or mates who would turn up and want a free ticket.

What you have to remember at a boxing show, to us the people who promote it, it is our **job** but the public see it as a night out, a piss up.

We're working, we had bills to pay so we couldn't just let dozens and dozens of people in for free.

Me and Ricky would have an agreement before each show and come up with a free guest list (usually around ten people each) which was for family and very close friends or VIPS. Anyone over that amount would have to pay.

Now there were plenty of times where I was caught on the box office by an old mate who would be trying to blag a free ticket. I didn't want to be rude and I'm usually rushed off my feet with one eye on the clock and noting the queue is being held up so I would just say okay, I'll knock a tenner of the tickets or something like that or okay you come in free and your two mates pay.

Lorraine would usually give me a scowl as she was just about to get full price, so it was agreed that I stay away from the crowd coming in. if someone came up to Lorraine and said they should be on the guest list then she would say to them, you're not on the guest list, so buy a ticket and see Joe inside, if there has been a mistake then he will give you the money back.

Once this was set up it worked well! Reading this you might think me giving a free ticket away here or there, wont damage the show but multiply it by ten or twenty free tickets and its losing the show hundreds of pounds.

Lorraine also had a knack of making a joke with everybody coming through the doors, she would calm people down and wind them up, which was needed as some of them often got flash and rude. Most people didn't know it was my auntie so they would walk in expecting to be jack the lad but she wouldn't have any of it.

A few times we have had to go and give someone a pull if they was abusive, Warren was never too far away from the box office and he never stood for any nonsense.

Sadly, my dear auntie has passed away and to this day she was the best at doing her job. Lorraine was up for a laugh as well and always ended up back at the after parties where she would be keeping an eye out for me, (making sure I was behaving lol)

I miss Lorraine as do all the other people who worked with her.

Rest in peace xx (and I bet your up there doing the door with St Peter x)

Colin Burns

Colin and his late brother (Dave) was the head of security at Caesars and over the years we had some mad bloody nights. He used to make me laugh at some shows where he turned up looking like a storm trooper ready for work.

Colin was a tough fucker, a football nut and a member of West Ham's ICF. We had some turn outs at Caesars over the years. Crowd trouble was part and parcel of the night so it was important there was a good security team on hand. I had a good team of my own but we were more security for ourselves and the VIPs. Colin was the security of the venue.

Colin was always smiling and he used to laugh when I arrived in the office and took out the baseball bats to hide under the counter. He also boxed for us a couple of times, one night he came into the ring with Carlton Leach and all the ICF boys. He won the South London heavyweight title and it was a good show. I still speak to Colin now and I enjoyed working with him.

Chris Thomas

Chris is worth a mention even though he worked for me after Caesars, at Tolworth and Kingston. He came a to a few shows at Caesars with Warren where he used to do some jobs for him but one time I was doing a show and my usual whip couldn't make it so Chris volunteered to do it. Now being a whip is a difficult job and if you don't do it right it gives me a right headache and can fuck the show up. So it's understandable that I was hesitant.

Thank god though on the night little Chris was great! Even the some of the trainers and fighters were praising him to me. And from that day her became a regular crew member of MeanMachine.

There was one funny night though where he turned up drunk and hadn't slept the night before. He was fucking gone, and I bollocked him the moment he walked in. "Look at the fucking state of you! You going to be able to do your fucking job!" I said pulling him to one side.

"Yeah, give me the fucking gloves Joe, don't worry about it!" he slurred back. Anyway I sent someone to get him a couple of strong coffees (lol) and somehow he pulled it off. He did get on my nerves a couple of times, driving me mad with cobblers, but credit to him, he did his job.

Steve Yorath

when we first started putting on shows at Caesars , Steve was paramount to us staging the shows. Steve comes from Bristol and had a string of fighters 'opponents' we could rely on.

Every show we would call Steve and tell him what boys we had, weights and experience etc. and he would get them matched and then turn up on the day with a mini bus full of boxers.

Steve was an ex professional himself so he would also box and Steve boxed everyone, Sven, Buckland, Welsh Phill, Garry Sayer, Joe Kacz. Stacy Dunn, Firby. He was hard as iron and on some nights he would even be the referee for us.

Great boxing man is Steve and without a doubt a legend in the unlicensed game.

James Flynn

James was out of Luton and just like Yorath he had a good stable of boys he would always bring down to the show. Over the years we had some laughs with James and he could also fight. He won a few fights on our shows and always gave a good account of himself.

He ran his own gym in Luton, so he always had boxers ready and on-call. He never came from the same boxing background as Yorath, but he made up the numbers when we needed them.

The Mean Girls – Joe Pyle Jr – Steve Holdsworth – Warren Bammo

Steve Holdsworth

I had known Steve since the early days of my promoting in the professionals. Steve was once a promoter himself but he fell out of love with the business side and he became a boxing commentator on Eurosport TV. Steve would also film shows and referee at times. He really knew the game and he has helped me out a few times with his quick thinking and knowledge. Steve has worked loads of my shows over the years and he was good value for money every time.

Some people just have that managerial instinct, Steve was one of them and as soon as he arrived he knew what was needed doing and he always helped out, even with things he wasn't getting paid for.

He is a good man, a real boxing man.

CHAPTER 13

THE 'ART' OF PROMOTING

I have seen so many people think that promoting a boxing show is an easy job, so many come and go … it's not easy!

It's a fucking headache at the best of times, I have never staged a show where everything goes smoothly and to plan. There are always things that pop up to test your patience.

The main headache is the people you have to deal with.

Dealing with people or the public its Russian roulette if they are as disciplined or professional as you, some are great, but some don't have a clue about the things you are juggling to make the show run smooth. They have no empathy and are so fucking self-centred you have to kick them up the arse to make them do what they have promised to do or they are being paid to do.

Remember you are dealing with people and money, (Boling water scenario)

One of the things that pisses you off the most, is the ticket money and trying to collect it off the boxers.

Some are fantastic, they turn up on the day of the show and have all their paperwork sorted for you, they write down the number of tickets sold and the tickets to be returned are in a separate envelope and they have the cash, counted and ready to give you.

Others are a fucking mess! I have lost count the number of times I say to the fighters; I need all your money sorted out by the latest 6;00pm on the day of the show. It's so important to get this sorted out so I can concentrate getting the show up and running and to start on time. Because come 7;00 o'clock, I will be pulled ragged all over the place.

When the doors open, its bloody hectic, I will have people coming at me for all kinds of questions, sometimes I'll be talking to someone and there will be three or four people waiting behind him to ask me something.

"Where is the ice Joe?"

"Are we still starting time?"

"Where's the doctor?" "Where do I take my music to," "The filming guy can't connect to the WiFi?" "The toilets broke," "Joe, my mates outside and he can't park his fucking car!!!"

Then I'll have trainers moaning about the running order and he wants his boy on earlier, and then I'll have someone asking me if I can put someone on the guest list, then the whip comes up and says are we still starting at 8;00? AGAIN! Then someone can't find their seats, then another comes and says his friend isn't on the guest list, fighters asking for more tickets as they have had a phone call. Argument's in the crowd! People moaning about where their seats are. It's endless and it doesn't stop all fucking night long.

The ticket money drives you mad! I try to explain that it takes time to work out all the tickets and over the years we have tried having meetings the day before to sort this out, but this isn't great for everyone. Some fighters might come from North London and they say to me they would rather be driving about getting last minute sales rather than drag themselves all the way over to South London to wait in line to sort their tickets out.

We have tried getting the boxers in early, telling them to be at the venue by 2 o'clock on the day, but they always turn up late, we have tried fining them, but it takes up too much time having to listen to them fucking moaning, tried telling them that if you turn up late then you will be boxing last! Again, it adds time listening to all the bollocks like they have a birthday party tomorrow and have to leave early. It goes on and on and on!

What people need to understand is the time it takes to sort out these things. Let's say we have 16 fights on and sixteen home boys all selling tickets to their friends and supporters. Each one of these sixteen boxers has to sit down and sort out what they have sold and what they haven't sold, and what their percentage of the ticket sales is, that means counting tickets and ticket stubs, writing it all out and working it out, and then counting all the money out.

So let us say that is ten minutes with each boy, now multiply that by 16. That is 160 minutes (2 hours 40 minutes)

Almost three hours before the show we need to sit in peace and sort out the money. On top of that, the money we have to pay out, has to be counted and then divided and put into envelopes to pay the opponents and all the show staff like doctors, whips, ambulance, card girls, waitresses, refs, house seconds, MC, DJ etc.

Then, once all the money is in we have to sort the running order out which always changes on unlicensed shows. (And on a lot of pro shows) the running list is the order in which the boxers are fighting and that needs to be printed out numerous times so there are copies for the MC, the DJ, then took to the changing rooms so the boxers know when they on.

The doors have opened at 7 o'clock and the crowd is already starting to fill up the venue, so now I got extra problems coming in, people can't find their seats, people knocking on the door asking for me just to say hello and have a general chat. Security saying people have parked and blocked the ambulance in. It's an endless wave of dealing with people and we only have a couple of hours or three at most to deal with **all of this**!

And it doesn't matter how many people you employ to take some of this away from you, you are the promoter so everyone wants to ask you what to do. It's your job to know and supervise everybody's else job.

One show I had we employed a new whip, now a whip is a very important job as the whip looks after the fighters, he shows them to their changing rooms, tells them when they are boxing and he makes sure they are gloved up and ready to fight when called to the ring.

If you have a bad whip working for you then the show is a bloody disaster. This one time, we had to get a new whip and he was a nightmare. I gave him the fight list, which had all the home boys on one side and the away boys on the other. It's his job to organize the changing rooms, but I was half an hour into the show and there are away boys sharing the changing rooms with the homeboys, some were even fucking fighting each other.

The trainers are moaning about it, coming to me and asking what's going on but now it's too late to deal with it. Next thing the whip can't find the gloves (remember this is his job) the show has started and now he's driving me mad asking where are the gloves? Something he should have done at least an hour before the show starts.

Next thing he comes down to me with the running list in his hand and tells me someone is moaning about fighting second to last. So I tell him the list has been done now and that is that, we can't change it now!

"Joe, he won't stop moaning mate,"

"Tell him it's fucking tough! If he thinks I am arranging the whole running order again and writing out new lists for the MC, the Dj and everyone else, he is fucking dreaming!" I said, trying to point out the fact it's too late and I don't have time for this cobblers.

Off he goes, only to come back ten minutes later with the same problem telling me the lad is still moaning.

"Look it's your job to sort this out! It's what I'm paying you for, tell him it can't be changed and if he doesn't like it then he doesn't fucking box… Deal with it!" I said now getting pissed off.

After telling him that you would think this would be the end of it, it wasn't, he carried on driving me mad all fucking night long. Why on earth he said he was a whip, I don't know? He never had a fucking clue how to do the job.

Going back to the tickets, it's a nightmare having to deal with idiots all night long, I have lost count the amount of times I'm running about with a list in my pocket of people who owe money.

Some fighters are so unorganised, it's a joke, one fighter springs to mind, who owed £500 and he said he would collect the money once his crowd arrived to their table and would then bring it over. So we let him go with it and give him the benefit of the doubt. The time is now gone nine o'clock, and the show is already three fights in, his table is filled and still there is no sign of him or the money, so I send someone up to the changing room and ask for the money and get the message he will be down in five to sort it out... Five minutes go and no show, so again, I send a message back, saying, if he doesn't come down and sort it out, then he is not boxing.

Finally, after about fifteen minutes he appears and says he hasn't collected it in yet.

"Look, I need the fucking money paying now! Its nearly ten a fucking clock. Go and get it off the table and bring it back here now!" I said angrily, now getting pissed off.

The boxer does what I tell him and only comes back with £220,

"There is £220 there and I'll get the rest before I box, mate,"

"Why is there only £220? The fucking table is full!" I snapped back at him."

"Sorry, joe, it's just a nightmare getting the money off them!" he says.
"A nightmare! So what they are sitting there thinking they are coming to the show for nothing!"
"Not like that joe, they're my brothers and family!" he answered back to my disbelief.
"What fucking difference does that make!" I said in disbelief, "So if I let every fighter's brother and family in for nothing there would two hundred fucking freebies in here."
"Look mate, I'll just have to owe you the rest,"
"Shall we ask your opponent tonight if we can owe him the money then?" I said now getting right pissed off.
I then called Warren over so he could hear what I was going to say to the fighter next,
"Alright, this is what we will do, you go back to them and tell them if they don't pay you what's owed then they will be thrown out and you won't be boxing."
"Joe, please mate, I'll owe you the money." He pleaded.
"Alright, this is what I'm going to do then, I'll pay your opponent what you have paid in already, you can tell them they can stay but because they haven't paid you, then you won't be boxing tonight,"
"Joe, why you being like this mate, C'mon give me some slack here, please,"
"That's the two options on the fucking table! Take it or leave it!"

With that he fucked off back to the table, but this is the kind of shit you have to deal with. Dealing with idiots all day and night. On this occasion the boxers brother even came over looking to act the tough guy!
"I've heard my brother isn't boxing! We've come all the way from North London to fucking support him!" he says trying to act hard and sound tough.
"That's right, he ain't fucking boxing, he isn't boxing because you lot haven't paid him for your fucking tickets!" Warren snapped back.
Anyway, we did get our money and the lad boxed, but it was so fucking not needed! All this drama, but this was regular, it happened every show no matter what you did to prevent it.
This cobblers doesn't just go on in the unlicensed show, it also happens all the time on professional events as well.
One time I was promoting a show at York Hall and a fighter turns up way short of what he knew he had to bring in.
On professional boxing shows its similar to the unlicensed shows, only it's more money as the costs are higher. Boxers get given a set amount of tickets to sell and they have to return with the opponent's money and then the house money and then what's left is, **his money** (the boxer)
The typical deal in the pro's is £1200 for the opponent and then £1000 for the house. You give him £3000 worth of tickets so whatever he sells over the opponent and house money, is his. All fighters know this and they know if they don't bring in the opponent and house money, then it is almost certain they

won't be boxing.

This fighter I won't say his name asks to fight on my show and he knows the rules and I reiterate them as I know he has let another promoter down in the past, I really stressed the point that he had to come in with the money and he promised me he would. I knew it was a risk, but we had lost a couple of fights due to injury so we needed an extra fight.

On the day of the show all the boxers have turned up and sorted out their ticket money all except this kid which straight away set alarm bells ringing. He eventually turns up just as the doors are opening which is a complete piss take. The doctors are waiting around to give him his medical and so are we. I'm down by the ringside sorting a few things when I get a call by my partner John Edwards to come to the back of the stage. I make my way there to find the fighter and John, who has an angry look on his face. I then talk to the fighter and listen to him saying all he has is the opponent's money, and no house money, which he knows full well is a piss-take, especially as I had called his manager a week before to see how he was doing with his tickets, and was told everything is okay.

'He will definitely be showing up with his money.'

John, however, is fuming and tells the boxer he isn't fighting.

I tell the boxer to go away and let me speak with John alone.

As the fighter arrived really late, his opponent has already weighed in, so even if the fight doesn't happen, then we have to pay him anyway. I don't know if the boxer did this on purpose, but that is the way it is in the professionals.

Me and John discusses this and I call the fighter back over,

"Okay, you can fight, but I want half the house money as you haven't sold the tickets,"

The boxer wasn't happy with this as he would be paying £500 to fight, but we had a good opponent for him, in fact it was one of the worst journeymen in the country and an absolute guaranteed win. Plus the fact we had been lied to a week before about there being no problems.

Reluctantly the fighter agreed and said he would go to the hole in the wall machine and we would be paid before he fights.

This might sound harsh, but you have to remember that promoting a professional show at York hall is going to cost around £16000 on expenses alone.

If the kids manager would have told me a week before he was having difficulty with the tickets, then I would have said okay, lets sort something out, but I know the game too well.

See this kid was due to box a couple of weeks later and I had a suspicion he had not tried too hard to shift his tickets for our show as he wanted most of his crowd at the next. Again, that is a piss take and I also knew this boxer had a very good business outside of boxing and was far from skint!

We give him the benefit of the doubt and I trust him, but I say the money Has to be paid (before) he boxes. The show starts and we have had a couple of fights and I'm still waiting for the money. He is on next, so I rush up to the changing room where I find him, gloved up and warming up on the pads with his trainer, there is about five minutes to go before he enters the ring.

"Take your gloves off!" I said as I walked into the changing room with the whip and John

"Take your gloves off … your now fighting last!" I added as I nodded to the whip to grab his gloves. The fighters start moaning and then his trainer comes over pleading, I tell his trainer the same again and that the fights on last and then the trainer asks if I can hold on a minute where he then goes into his training bag and pulls out an envelope with guess what was in it! …. £500. I gave him a look to say, you sneaky bastard! He had it all along and I bet the moment he won the fight, they would have fucked off as quick as possible with my £500 stuffed securely into the trainer's bag.

That's just a couple of stories about promoting. It's a tough and frustrating game at times and you have to have broad shoulders to be a good promoter. You have to able to deal with people and deal with them efficiently and quickly! Ninety-nine percent of problems happen on the day of the show, when you are at your busiest and most vulnerable, and the problems don't stop, they keep popping up from everywhere, you have to be able to make a decision on the spot, sometimes the unpopular decisions, but you have to deal with them there and then.

I have seen people who try to promote boxing shows, absolutely fold on the night! They're stressed out to the max trying to doing everything themselves. One time I went to a pal of mines show, it was his first show and he decided to have this crazy idea that people had to buy tokens to get drinks. I have seen this system work in the past and it can work, but you have to run it well or you have absolute chaos.

So I'm at the show and its 7;30 and the doors are closed, it was advertised to open at 7;00 so outside there is a line of people waiting to get into a single box office. The security is being driven mad and everyone outside is doing their nut! I go over to my mate who is sweating like fuck and tell him he has to open the doors, start getting people inside. But he isn't ready and won't open them until he's ready, so another fifteen minutes go by and I just take control and get the security to open the door, the crowd start coming in and the box office is bloody terrible! It's taken five minutes to sort out one person, (people inside the box office are arguing in front of the public) and the way he had it set up was for people to hand in their tickets and he exchanges them for wristbands and then buy the drinks tokens there as well. I walk over and say this is taking too long! Get the security to hand out the wristbands and set up a separate station to issue the tokens for the drinks. (I said, you can't have one person doing all three fucking jobs!)

After another fifteen minutes, I get this up and running and people are starting to get through the doors faster, but he set up the drinks station wrong and if people wanted a bloody drink they had to re-enter the queue, the same queue they had just stood in for twenty minutes. It was chaos!

I tried to say that to the promoter that no one was getting a bloody drink, but he didn't trust the girl who was at the drinks station to handle any money.

It was crazy! And that night he learned the hard way.

Another time someone I knew wanted to promote a show, but his financials were so optimistic! I took a look and sighed loudly, "You better have deep pockets!" I said to him.

It was crazy and the show was so heavy on the payout side, I warned him to cancel the show! He insisted it would go ahead only to cancel a couple of weeks before it was scheduled to happen as it suddenly dawned on him that he was going to lose thousands out of his own pocket if it went ahead.

By far the worst thing in promoting is losing a big fight after the show has been announced and going ahead. It's fucking horrible when you have spent weeks planning a show, doing posters, visiting venues, press conferences, checking paperwork, submitting fight cards, getting sponsors and having the venue dressed in the sponsor's colours, booking personnel, designing the ring canvas, designing fight programs. You do all this and then one week before the show your main event falls through.

The boxer is injured and cannot fight! So that's that and there is no way you are getting a decent replacement at such short notice. What hurts even more is if the fighter you lost is a big ticket seller!

One show I promoted at York Hall we lost the main event eight days before the show! It was for a southern area title and both boys were big ticket sellers. We lost five hundred tickets the week before a show!

In the space of one week we went from having an unbelievable show planned, to a show with no main event and we are now in a position where we will lose six thousand pounds on the night from our own pockets.

So now what do we do? Shall we pull the show?

If we do that then we upset all the other boxers on the show and all the people booked to work on the night, the venue will get the hump! I have three of my boxers on the show whom I manage. Three boxers who have been in the gym working like mad training and selling tickets. One fighter in particular, George, was scheduled to box on the show before which DID get cancelled a week before, he then had to go around refunding all the tickets he sold to his supporters. Now imagine if this happened to him again! He wouldn't be able to sell one ticket next time out!

So now we are under pressure and I decide we are going ahead with the show! I got seven days to try to narrow that six grand down! I immediately start designing a program for the show and hustle everyone I can think of to buy advertising space in the program. (I manage to get £4000 in ads) next I cut a couple of fights down to four rounds from six round fights. (Save another

£800) next I get on the phones and call everyone I can think of to come and buy tickets.

I am doing all this and I'm still arranging the show. I was waking up at seven in the morning and working until 12 or one at night, nonstop!

We did manage to go ahead with the show and walked away with just a very small loss. Did we get any thanks? Did we fuck! All we got was crucified for having a show half empty and what the boxing press said, a show with no atmosphere!

One headline said, "What was Joe Pyle thinking?"

Not a mention of how we lost the main event a week before because the fighter failed his brain scan! Not a mention saying we must have worked our balls off so the lads who could box, didn't get let down! No, they forget that and just moaned that the show had no atmosphere.

They forget to mention I spent six weeks working every day for nothing!

Boxing promoting! It can be a lot of fun but at times it's a thankless task.

CHAPTER 14
THE UNDERWORLD AND BOXING

Villains, faces, gangsters, they have always loved the boxing, it seems to be endemic that the two of them go hand in hand. Maybe it's because the vast majority of fighters come from the streets, the same streets of poverty as where the crooks up. You don't get many crooks mixing with cricketers or rugby union players. Those are the sports from the universities, the sports for posh kids, but boxing comes from the streets. Gyms are scattered in all the inner city boroughs. I guarantee you go to any of the rough parts of London and sure enough there will be a boxing gym close by.

It's strange as well the amount of famous villains who were professional ex boxers. My father was, so were Ron, Reg and Charlie Kray, Freddie Foreman, Roy Shaw.

Going back even further and you had Darby Sabini and his sidekick Bert Marsh both pro's.

Boxing has always had that air of menace about it. From fixing fights to the gangsters and hoods sitting in the ringside seats.

In America you had the mob who was always involved in the fights, especially fixing them and for years the New York athletic commission was dominated by the influence of the mafia.

I was talking to someone the other day and he mentioned that one of the main attractions of the Caesars shows was who was seated on the stage (the VIP seats)

And it's true as on any given show the stage was packed with well-known villains or faces. My father and Roy Shaw were always at the shows, then you had regulars like Tony Lambrianou, Freddie Foreman, Charlie Richardson, Howard Marks, Paul Ferris, Tommy Wisby, Wilf Pine, Dave Courtney.

One of our former fighters who turned professional Ryan…. Wrote this when being interviewed in the Boxing News.

I met Joey Pyle and had my first unlicensed fight at Caesars in south London at 21 years old. It was a crazy place and was full of gangsters and always kicked off during and after the fight.

That was what Caesars were all about! It had a fearsome reputation and as Colin Wilby our British light heavyweight champion said, **"Until you fight at Caesars, you're nothing!"**

Every show was different and you never truly knew who you could be sitting next to. Fred foreman was always at our shows and was always a gentleman to the fans in attendance.

One night in particular, though I saw the other side of him when a drunken pest was driving him mad, it started out good enough with the bloke just asking Fred for a signature, but then as the fellow had more drinks he kept driving Fred mad by offering him drinks and asking for pictures. It was like every five minutes this idiot would pop up asking Fred another question. Rob Davis noticed this and asked the fellow to leave Fred alone, which he did for an hour or so, but he then crept back on the stage and started asking Fred if he had upset him and could he buy Fred a drink. I was standing close by and went straight over to tell him to clear off but before I got there Fred grabbed his arm and pushed him away. Seconds later the idiot was grabbed and thrown out the building very fast, but I noticed a look on Fred's face. It's a look I have seen on so many of the well-known villains faces. The look of menace and the eyes that let you know not to fuck about.

Roy & Lenny and the London Mob.

When Roy Shaw destroyed Donny Adams in 1975 it was only six years after the Krays were sentenced to life. London in those days was still dominated by the old gangs.

Only six years! That is nothing, and the Krays were big names. Roy Shaw himself hadn't been out long.

In 1975, London was like a different world! One instance is West Ham won the FA cup!

The IRA was shooting and bombing everyone. If you drove through London in those days you would most likely come across the Graffiti on bridges and walls saying 'George Davis is innocent' from people campaigning on the armed robber's behalf of his wrongful conviction.

London in those days was still a close knit community and still warmed to the local tearaway and villain.

Roy Shaw was a villain! He was an armed robber and a legend when he was in prison. There is an old story about when he was in Wandsworth prison.

There was a part of the prison which led to all the wings called the central star. Back in the day you weren't allowed to walk over the grid and the screws were right fanatical about it. Anyone walking across it would be grabbed and disciplined and sometimes that would mean a good hiding by half a dozen screws.

When Roy heard about it, he wasn't having any of it, one morning he came out his cell and walked straight over to the middle of the grid, dropped his trousers and shit all over it, right in front of the screws standing around looking at him in disbelief.

Wandsworth prison had a reputation for being the hardest nick in the country. Other prisons would threaten to send you there if you misbehaved and be rest assured if you did fuck about at another nick and they ghosted you out to

Wandsworth then you were certain to get a Wandsworth welcome. That would start with a few of the screws having a word in your ear and telling that you are in wanno now and you won't be taking liberties here.

Roy went right through the prison system and he was uncontrollable, ultimately he was nutted off to Broadmoor where they drugged him up so much it almost killed him.

When Roy was released, he already had that reputation and everyone knew him so when he started fighting in the ring it was full of London's gangland in the audience.

Lenny was also brought up in that environment, he never had the criminal background as Roy did, but he mixed shoulders with a lot of well-known faces. His cousin Bobby Warren was jailed years before along with Frankie Fraser for carving up the legendary gang boss, Jack Spot.

One night I was boxing at Caesars, it was my first fight in years and I only did it because my father was ill and I wanted to give him something to look forward to. I knew he was not long for this world so I wanted him to see his boy box one last time before he went.

I was thinking about getting my fight on early and ending the fight quick but my dad decided to invite everyone!

Three tables of VIP mobsters all sitting on the stage waiting to watch me box! I wasn't nervous at all in the build-up, but when they told me my dad's arrived with half of London's underworld, I did start to feel the butterflies.

A few fights were on before me so I relaxed until it was my time to do the business!

I could hear my music start to play. (Things can only get better -D Ream) I was buzzing and now I couldn't wait to get out there.

I was wound up all day and already sunk a couple of vodkas, so I wanted a quick win to get back to all my mates and family on the stage and get some more booze in me.

I started walking to the ring and looked up at the stage, I remember thinking, *fucking hell,* if the old bill sets off a bomb in here tonight, they would end half of London's underworld.

Everyone was there to watch me fight. My father and uncle, Roy Shaw, Wilf Pine, Charlie Richardson, Freddie Foreman, Paul Ferris 'the wee man' from Glasgow had even come down to watch me and be with my father. Alan Paramasivan, Dave Courtney, Albert Chapman from Birmingham, a few of the Welsh boys. Even Ori Spado (the mob Boss of Hollywood) had flown over from Los Angeles.

I got in the ring and glared at my opponent.

(One round if you're fucking lucky) I said to him.

I went back to corner to Paul Bartley who had my gum shield.

"Calm down Joe," he said to me.

I looked at Rob Davis standing at ringside,

"Order me a Budweiser, I won't be in in here long," I said giving him a wink......Ricky English announced me and my opponent, Burt Reynolds.

We went to the centre of the ring and I could see he was really nervous, (Who wouldn't be with half of the UKs top underworld figures all supporting me.)

The first bell went and I flew out and caught him with a leading right, shocking him and sending him backwards where he covered up on the ropes. I didn't stop punching until he went down.

The ref took up the count and slowly he got to his feet at nine. So back I went, just throwing bombs! He went down again, but again, he fucking got back up. I knocked him down a further three times and he kept on getting back up.

I was getting knackered now just hitting him.

I punched him back into a corner,

"Stay down you c**t! Do you want me to fucking kill you?!"

The bell then went to end the round and I was fucking exhausted, honestly!

You hit a punch bag for two minutes nonstop with every punch thrown with all your might. See how fucked you are after two minutes.

My trainer and good pal, Paul Bartley pulled me back to the corner, he could see I was blowing.

"Just fucking calm down Joe.. Take your time, pick your shots and the knockout will come!" he said.

"Paul, I'm fucked mate...." "I gasped, trying to get some air, "if I don't knock him out in the next minute, that's me done." I added.

Round two went and I came out a bit slower, I let Burt throw a few jabs and I slipped them. I was waiting for him to throw another jab, so I could slip it and counter with a hard right, I offered him an opening and sure enough he threw another jab... CRASH! I hit him with a beautiful right counter, which sent him straight down... AGAIN! The ref started counting and he once again got up at nine but thankfully his legs were gone. The ref asked him to walk forward, but he staggered badly and fell back into the ropes. The referee then called it off!

"Thank fuck!" I said silently, I was exhausted and hardly had the energy to raise my arm in celebration. Paul got into the ring and lifted me up and then I saw my father on the stage, he was smiling from ear to ear.

"THAT'S FOR YOU DAD!" I shouted out to him.

I then got out the ring still had my gloves on and went straight to the bar and ordered a pint. I was taking my gloves off as they served it to me.

That was a great evening and all the chaps on the stage enjoyed watching me fight again. I sat down next to Paul Ferris, my father and Ori and really enjoyed my pint.

"Took your fucking time didn't you, Joe!" My father said to me smiling.

Chucky – Joe Pyle Jr – Ori Spado – Joe Pyle Sr – Anthony Spado (before my fight)

CHAPTER 15
THE FACEBOOK REVOLUTION
(THE GOOD –THE BAD- THE UGLY)

Facebook, that magnificent, monster of the internet.
Launched in 2004 it didn't take long to take over everyone's daily lives.
Before Facebook we had to rely on websites and Myspace was also popular.
But the internet is nowhere near what it is today.
Go back to 2004 and there was no YouTube! Can you imagine that, no
Facebook or YouTube, it seems like the stone age.
In 2004, we staged shows at Caesars and the way you sold tickets for these
events in those days was through the boxers or posters put up around the area.
Boxers had to work hard to shift tickets in those days (they still do now) but
without the help from Facebook,) which was in theory your very own website
or advertising platform) things were a lot more difficult for the lads and the
shows.
When I think back at it now I wonder just how we managed to have sell out
shows.
Today it is so much easier to get information out there in front of people. The
old days was word of mouth or if someone saw the poster and thought it looks
interesting.
But to be honest with you, not many people just turned up at Caesars
wondering what it will be like. Caesars had a fearsome reputation on the manor
and an even scarier reputation when it came to the boxing nights. People
wouldn't go there unless they knew someone fighting or of a group of their
mates were going.
In the early 2000s we created our very own website, Meanmachine.biz but a
website is not like Facebook!
People go on Facebook as its unique where all your friends in theory have their
own website, they choose to put whatever they want on their individual pages,
so someone could just be random scrolling about and then accidentally stumble
across a post from us or one of the fighters.
It was and still is today (if used correctly) a fantastic place to network and boost
your profile ad showcase your abilities.

Me and Ricky also loved a bit of controversy, we loved getting two fighters
publically having a go at each other. Before Facebook we got lads into the ring
to make challenges, but when Facebook came along and the fighters started
getting their own pages, well, let's just say me and Ricky often did a bit of
stirring (with a fucking big spoon lol)
It was easy to generate a bit of interest, you just typed a few words and hey
presto! Two fighters were suddenly in a bitter feud.

Facebook through the years has really helped evolve boxing, especially now with its Facebook live broadcasts, all the top promoters use it as part of their marketing. It's a very cheap way of advertising and it gets to the masses very quickly.

If you use social media wisely then it is a very good friend, but it does have a flip side which is very dangerous. A few wrong comments here and there and you can suddenly find yourself being in a situation that is akin to a modern day lynching!
I have seen people absolutely crucified over mistakes.
Some genuine mistakes yet I have seen people slagging off like they are some holy crusade.
Another thing to take note of is if you make certain claims on Facebook then beware, because somewhere or sometime down the line you will get found out.
I have seen so many lies and so many false claims it has at times made me burst into laughter and at times rage.
The groups are the worst.
Some groups are so biased that they forego any sense of rationality or truth.
Try to state a truth in one of these groups and very quickly you find a horde of lust blinded individuals claiming you know nothing and are causing trouble or why are you on our group, or sometimes you find yourself being blocked!
Its bizarre behaviour really,
The groups I see on unlicensed boxing and villain groups are the worst I have seen. Don't get me wrong, some are really good, I enjoy Tony Turner's crime group as I enjoy posts from Mark Bowman and Carole Martin.
But they are the exception as a lot of others I see post some things that I know hundred percent is just complete cobblers.
Then there are the facts that people have read in books and post what they have read and are convinced it is the solemn truth.
Let me tell you what a very famous man who had a (No.1) best-selling book once told me. (And it wasn't my father)
"Joey, books are 70% truth and 30% bollocks!"
I won't say who told me, but believe me, do not believe everything you read in books! If it sounds exaggerated, then it usually is.

There was a funny story once about what I call *The Facebook promoters.*
This guy, he came to a few shows at Caesars and kept sticking his nose into everything. Everywhere me and Ricky was he would pop up and ask questions. Ricky noticed it first and then after I started to see it and I spotted him hovering around outside the changing rooms, I gave him a pull and asked him what was he fucking doing backstage.
He made some bullshit excuse so I told him to go back into the crowd and not to come backstage again. A little while after, my brother Warren told me he had just heard that some fella had been going into the changing rooms and giving

out his cards to the fighters, telling them he was a boxing promoter and they should give him a call and he will get them on one of his shows.

I went fucking mad when I heard that, so we went to the changing room and ended up getting one of the cards with his number on it. I then thought about the fella who I told to piss off earlier, the one who was always sticking his nose in. So I grabbed Warren and Mitch and we found him by the bar. I pulled out the card and rang the number and saw this idiot reach into his pocket and grab his phone.

"Hello'" he said

"C**T!" I said, before walking quickly over to him where we grabbed him by the arm and pulled him through the crowd backstage to the changing rooms.

"What do you think you are fucking doing! You come to my show and nick my fucking fighters, you cheeky c**t!" I said to him as Warren pushed him against the wall.

"What's the matter, Joe, what have I done wrong?" he said now almost in tears

"You're trying to poach my fighters, you liberty taking mug!"

"Joe what have I done, mate, I'm putting my own show on soon and I was just seeing if they wanted to fight on it, what's the problem, mate? I'll be getting your fighters more fights" he said, unbelievably not realising what he had done is wrong.

"You want to put my fighters on your fucking show, all the hard work I have done is just so you can fucking walk along and take advantage of it!"

"Mate, what have I done wrong, what have I done wrong!"

"Done wrong, you c**t, you're lucky you're not knocked out!" Warren said to him threatening to punch him on the jaw.

What we had here was a typical Facebook promoter! He had been to a couple of shows and put a few posts up saying he might put a show on and had a few of his mates saying for him to do it and that they would go. Now this idiot doesn't know the game, he doesn't think it's wrong attend a show and start asking fighters under another promoter to box on his show.

But in boxing, this is like breaking a sacrament! It's so wrong and such a liberty. The fella was lucky I realised he knew no different or he would have definitely ended up getting a clump.

You see, this is what Facebook created, it created a lot of idiots who thought its easy money to promote shows.

I have learnt from experience, sometimes hard experience, everything there is to know about online marketing.

On Facebook you can create an event, and people have three options - attend, not going or interested. Let's say 200 people say they are going, well expect ten percent if you're lucky to turn up! It is not as easy as most people think.

Anyway, this fella got thrown out that night and told not to come back or don't dare contact any of our fighters. He subsequently found himself a few fighters and he put on his own promotion. He got a venue and got his tickets and poster printed and then gave the tickets out to the boxers, he then sat back until fight night expecting all the boxers to turn up and say they had sold all their tickets and give him wads of cash!

Surprise, surprise, the boxers as usual turned up giving him every excuse in the book about bad ticket sales etc.! He couldn't pay the bills

He ran out the back door, leaving loads of people unpaid.

A Facebook promoter!!

That was the idiots first and last show.

One of the things we have always looked out for, are new possibilities to promote and market our shows. I'm proud to say that I think, MeanMachine Promotions were the first unlicensed boxing organisation to really utilise the power of Facebook and then YouTube.

When Facebook Live first became available in 2016, I was the first ever promoter to stage ringside interviews using this format. (Worldwide!)

It worked really well and we had some fantastic viewing figures. I was running professional shows again and quickly after what we did, all the other promoters followed suit. Now it's common place for even Frank Warren and Eddie Hearn to stage weigh-ins, press conferences and public workouts all using Facebook Live.

We also launched our own Facebook channel 'Boxing LIVE' which was an offshoot of the live streaming it was very successful and still is where we proudly boast over 32,000 members.

Looking back at things I would say, on the whole, Facebook has been very good for the boxing game. It has opened up a whole new way of looking at fighters and also given the general public more access to these fighters.

Talking about access that is another thing that over the years we have had a few arguments over. Today it is so easy for a rival promoter or manager to start talking to someone else's boxer.

Before social media, we had what we called 'gym rats' sneaky snidy bastards who would float around the gyms trying to slip into the boxers by promising all kinds of bollocks behind their manager or promoters back. You still get them now, but with Facebook it's so easy to message a fighter and try to put doubts in his head about the setup he currently has.

Another thing that winds me is how people on Facebook use these groups to earn money!

Don't get me wrong, but if someone is talking about their family or was involved in what went on, then fair play to them, they deserve to get money more than the parasites who never met these people or was involved in any of the things they done.

One fella once phoned me up after putting out a post that he was doing a book on someone, who I knew very well.

"Joey, hope you're well pal, listen I'm doing a book on *** **** what I need from you is a few stories."

"Hold on a minute, who are you?" I interrupted.

"I'm doing this book and the family have given me permission"

"Stop right there! Don't you dare mention me or my father in that book!" I interrupted him.

"What the fuck has it got to do with you what we fucking done! Who the fuck are you to profit from the sacrifices and hard work that we put in!"

I'm sure you can see where the rest of this conversation went.

It does annoy me as certain things belong to us!

The things my father did and went through, were for his family. Not for someone to 'milk' who never met or knew him. If anyone should profit from his pain and suffering, then it should be his grandchildren or family. Why should some random fella feel he has the right to earn a living or make a name for himself on the back of someone else.

There is too much of this on Facebook. Too many strangers earning off the sweat and pain of others.

It is a minefield and is heavily biased. People do believe what is written and posted in groups or pages.

I see stuff which absolutely staggers me, stories that it is so far from the truth. I suppose that's should be expected in today's day and age, but what makes you laugh is if you challenge the lie, then you can be on the wrong end of hundreds of strangers all defending the lie.

There is one person on Facebook I am sure everyone has seen him who is completely bonkers! The claims he makes are truly out of Alice in wonderland! He actually looks like the Mad hatter! He states he has links to the mafia, the Colombian cartels, the Vatican and Vladimir Putin, yet he lives in an ex council house that was bequeathed him and drives a car for disability given to him from his benefits and the NHS. Still, all these people believe him.

Facebook fantasy land!!

MEAN MACHINE
MM
PROMOTIONS
EST. 2004

CHAPTER 16
UNLICENSED BOXING TODAY & THE FUTURE

Unlicensed boxing today is an industry all by itself and It has branched out in spectacular fashion.

Think of the irony that a few years ago the old bill were bending over backwards to stop these events, but now you can go to an unlicensed show where it's the Police vs the Fire Brigade!

Today they go under the guise of calling it a charity boxing event, but it's still an unlicensed boxing event.

White collar boxing is another moniker which has gained enormous exposure and interest. Blue chip companies box off against each other wearing 16oz pillows on their hands. These are big events staged at hotels like the Grosvenor or the Dorchester in central London.

I went to one of these once where the audience was full of millionaires and a few billionaires.

They had a charity auction and it raised over five hundred grand on the night (over half a million)

What unlicensed boxing done was opened a huge market for people who want to learn boxing and possibly have the chance to box in front of their friends and family in an exhibition style contest.

Before unlicensed boxing, if you wanted to fight, then you had to turn professional or join an amateur club. (Both have age limits)

Imagine you are a 33-year-old man, did a bit of boxing as a kid and now you want to just stay fit and maybe have a small contest for a bit of fun, sometime in the future, what were your options?

Do you want to go and join an amateur club and train twice a week with a bunch of teenagers, (some might like it, but if it isn't for you then your options are limited)?

I think that unlicensed boxing is only going to grow bigger in the UK.

Interest in boxing as a keep fit hobby is now bigger than it has ever been. You go to any gym and they offer boxing classes. Women have also become much more involved. Ten years ago, it was almost unheard of to have a female boxing coach. Now they are everywhere.

Over the last few months during lockdown over the Covid 19 pandemic, it is not uncommon to drive past a park and see boxing classes taking place under the sun.

With more and more people learning how to box, then ultimately it will have the result of more people wanting to test themselves inside the ropes.

There are lots of white collar outfits that target these keep fitters, I have seen boot camps and training camps structured with the end result boxing at an event.

The last three years we have also seen the emergence of bare knuckle boxing! Its televised now and staged at venues like the O2 at Greenwich. It's unbelievable because Brae knuckle boxing was unheard of a few years ago. There was no way you could stage an event with fighting and no gloves. Look at the agro we had over the Welsh Phill and Decca Heggie intended fight. (We were even threatened with arrest!)

It's a getting bigger and bigger and the way it is going; it won't be long until it's a mainstream sport with celebrity champions.

I might possibly have a look at promoting it in the future.

Unlicensed boxing now is a HUGE business. I am talking in the millions if the right people fight each other. On February the 4th, 2018, two men fought each in front of a sold out Copper Box Arena in what was a white collar contest. Almost eight thousand people paid to see this fight with an online audience of millions.

Who were they?

YouTube online gamers – **KSI vs Joe Weller**

Whilst it might have been something of a ridiculous contest - two non-boxers going head to head because they argued on the internet - it certainly proved popular.

Who the hell are they? You say. Well, let me tell you that 13 million people watched their online press conference! That is unbelievable figures, but it shows you the endless possibility. This wasn't Mike Tyson boxing or Tyson Fury, it was a white collar (Unlicensed) event featuring two young men who had never fought before, but had an argument online and decided to settle their differences in the boxing ring.

Every ticket was sold – (7500) but they had a waiting list for tickets of over 20,000.! (Twenty thousand)

The fight was watched live by 21 million people, with another 25 million watching the repeat. Those are astounding figures, mind boggling.

(Tyson Fury vs Deontay Wilder 2, generated 1 million buys!)

White collar boxing is now an industry all by itself. It has raised tens of millions and is a worldwide phenomenon.

Alan Lacey, founder of the International White Collar Boxing Association, has led the way in the UK and has staged hundreds of events. White collar boxing has even found its way on to live TV, BBC1 aired a show called 'Celebrity boxing' and raised over one million for charity.

It's big business! Wall street bankers from New York fighting city bankers at five star hotels in London. That's a lot of organising, but well worth the rewards.

As for what we do at MeanMachine Promotions and what will happen in the future is anyone's guess. Writing this book has whetted the appetite to create more memories, so in 2021, once this bloody coronavirus sorts itself out, we are looking to get the promotions up and running again.

In fact, As I am writing this we are already in talks for a massive 'Guv'nor comeback fight!

The interest in the book has reignited the interest in the title, and we are pleased to say that many of our old fighters like,

Sven Hamer,

Welsh Phill,

Peter Stoten

and Garry Sayer, are all interested in fighting once more for MeanMachine Promotions.

I'm sure many of you reading this book are aware of a few people who have tried to copy our title, and made their own belt. However, IT ISN'T THE GUVNOR TITLE!

They have backtracked now, and said it's a totally separate Guv'nor title, but they have used the notoriety of our title to garner interest and publicity.

But at the end of the day, It's just a copycat title, which doesn't have any of the history attached.

I suppose we should be flattered that they copied us, but it does give you the hump and think how disrespectful this was to the fighters who did actually hold the title of, **The Guv'nor.**

I received a message from one of these people saying there title is the Norman Buckland Guv'nor title, not the Guv'nor title.

I replied, laughing,

"I know!" Of course I know! It cannot be our title as I never promoted it.

To be completely honest, I couldn't care less what other people do, everyone has a right to earn a living, but it's their constant posts on social media, saying…

Their title is the REAL Guvnor title! It's pathetic really! Promoters don't do this to other Promoters and boxers don't disrespect other boxers. (At least this is true 99% of the time.)

It's absolutely ludicrous! Everyone with half a brain can see what they are doing. It's like me creating a hamburger and saying this is the REAL Big Mac! You might think it is the bollocks and the real thing, but to the whole world, it's definitely not a Big Mac!

Norman Buckland, who we wrote about in the chapter above is going around saying he is The Godfather of Guvnors. (That is so fucking disrespectful to all the other fighters – Roy Shaw or Lenny McLean against Norman Buckland – who wins?? I know where I would put my money!)

It has got so much now that some of the old fighters are challenging Norman to fight. Welsh Phill has said he would fight Norman and donate the money to charity.

Sven Hamer has invited Gary Firby to a rematch to fight for the Guv'nor title. The title Gary once fought for and lost.

Gary has said he swallowed in the first fight because he thought he wouldn't win on a points decision.

Well, the rematch is there if he wants it! Sven is willing to fight anytime, winner takes all, or we can sort out purses.

The one thing about being called The Guv'nor is that it isn't just a belt or a title. It is a position where a man is willing to fight anyone!

The Guv'nor cannot refuse a challenge! Roy, Lenny, Sven, Garry, Welsh Phill, Decca, Tyrone, Joe Kacz, they all made challenges and defended against challengers.

You cannot pick and choose your fights and call yourself the Guv'nor. It doesn't work that way – you can kid yourself, but you can't kid everyone.

What also baffles me and makes me laugh is we were the ones who promoted the shows and created the titles, we were the ones who created a platform for these men to fight on, and it was us who invited the likes of Roy Shaw along to the shows, to present them with the belt.

But now! Some of the people we stood by, have created another belt copying OUR name and been slagging us off for months. NOW! We have said, "Hold on a minute, what's your problem?"

And by asking that question, we are now the bad guys??

We didn't start this copycat new belt, we never started slagging other people's belts off! We never started all the shouting. We were minding our own business, going about our own business.

Now we have defended what has been said, suddenly we are the bad guys (work that one out???)

So we're not getting into any more stupid rows and arguments over something which is just irrelevant to us, all we will say is the following.

MeanMachine and the Guv'nor title will be returning and running our shows in 2021.

Sven Hamer is willing to fight Gary Firby where for the Guvnor title we created. We are looking forward to putting on some really good shows again and getting the Guvnor title back into action.

Hopefully Gary Firby will fight Sven Hamer and it will be a good show.

Sven coming out of retirement to defend the title is what the Guvnor title is all about!

I personally Like Gary, he is a good fighter, and boxed on a few of our shows at Caesars and won one of our titles… let's hope sometime soon we get this fight on. It has certainly stoked the interest of the public.

CHALLENGE TO GARY FIRBY

I haven't fought for 8 years but I will come out of retirement
one last time to see who The Guv'nor is.
Im challenging Gary Firby to a winner take all fight.
Forget all the shouting! Time to do the talking in the ring.
To be the Guv'nor, you have to earn it!
Lets do this and bring this title back to where It belongs.
In all my years of fighting, I never refused a challenge.
Gary, you call yourself the Guv'nor .
Now prove it in the ring with me!

CHAPTER 17
QUESTIONS & ANSWERS

Q. Gavin Swinscoe Who is the most dangerous person you have met. not the hardest the .out dangerous

A. Roy Shaw is definitely up there as a cobble fighter, he was wicked, he would fight dirty and do anything he had to do to win. If I'm judging someone as dangerous then I'm judging them by their wickedness. Frankie Fraser in his day was vicious. I have known countless dangerous men, my father, Freddie Foreman etc. some men are dangerous when they have to be and others have a reckless streak like Fraser. Johnny Nash was dangerous but he knew when to be and when not to be.

Q. Andy Smyth in a round robin competition where all eras collide at their best, who in your opinion would be the last man standing and the guv'nor of all the guv'nors past and present?

A. This is interesting! Sven Hamer on his day would definitely be in the final I think against him would either be Roy or Lenny.

Q. Christopher Keogh Which of the fighters featured if they had gone the legitimate route do you think could have made it to the top in their weight class?

A. Some of the fighters who have boxed for us have gone professional. Sven Hamer was a professional and then started boxing for MeanMachine. Pete Stoten would have made a decent professional, so would Steve Dossett. Mikey Bourne is another, I tried to get him to turn professional but it didn't work out. It's a shame as I think Mike was definitely British title challenger level, maybe beyond if he really got stuck in to the pro game. He had the talent and the punch.

Q. Peter Spensley What is your fondest memory with your dad (boxing wise)

A. Boxing wise that would be training with him. My earliest memories were at a gym in Carshalton called the cottage of Content. My dad used to get me and we would go to the gym around 4;30 and both have a workout. He would take me on the pads and show me how to move etc. other great memories I have are when he would take me to the shows with him. The Albert hall was a great venue to watch boxing. I remember the day when Roy boxed Ron stander at alexander palace and I had a great day.

Q. Leigh Hulk Hill Did Lenny or Roy ever refuse a fight with anybody they deemed too dangerous?

A. Not what I know of mate, fighters (fight) if the money was on the table then both would have fought anyone.

Q. David Mckay What is the true account of the supposed fight with Lenny and the fighter put up by the mob in New York.

A. Not for me to say! I don't know anything about it?

Q. Tommy Brown Roy told me he would not fight Johnny Waldron and cliff fields

A. Roy would have fought anyone if the money was on the table. I know he was being kind to Cliff Fields when he wrote the forward for his book. Both Cliff and Johnny were decent professionals but nothing spectacular (no disrespect) I certainly wouldn't say they were as good or experienced as Ron Stander.

Q. Lee Pearson They always say there's someone tougher around the corner... But was this the case when Roy and Lenny was around and if so who was it?

A. From what I know they took challenges from anyone who challenged them, there were a couple of fights that never happened, Sykes vs Mclean and Bindon vs Mclean. But that was just *life* stopping the fights from happening, Not anyone refusing. Dave Pearce was a very tough fighter and was coming on the scene but never did. He was the professional British heavyweight champion and in my opinion would have beaten everyone on the same night.

Q. Pat Dymond Why is nobody allowed to see footage of first fight between McLean Shaw where Shaw beats him?

A. it wasn't that no one was allowed, it has just been lost? Even the photographs of the fight. It is a mystery and one I wish I asked my father about.

Q. Ian Shaw Do you think Charles Bronson would have figured in the guv'nor title had he not been imprisoned for so many years?

A. No sorry! Charlie would have been destroyed by them. He was a fit, strong man but from what I have seen he is very limited with boxing gloves on.

Q. Andy Pollards What's the best bit of advice you or ya dad gave someone that had an effect on the outcome of the fight

A. When I was writing this book an old boxer of mine got in touch and told me something I said to him before the fight, this is what he said.
The reason I've messaged is because I wanted to share with you a quote you shared with me. I was stood with you by the ring early in the day, prior to the night beginning, you asked me if I was nervous, obviously I said 'yes', I said 'boxing is an art'... Your reply is something I always remember... 'In boxing if you haven't got the Art that begins with a (**A**,) you better hope you have the Heart that begins with **H**'. I very memorable quote for me

Q. Jim Buckett In your opinion which two fighters regardless of era or size would have made the best spectators fight.

A. one fight springs to mind that almost came off and would have been explosive, Welsh Phill vs Norman Buckland. I don't think it would have last too long (one of them would get disqualified) but it would have been exciting. I think Phill would have been too aggressive for him but sadly we didn't get to find out.

Q. Anthony Roberts BOXING WISE WHO WAS THE MOST SKILLFUL FIGHTER YOU EVER SAW IN THE UNLICENSED SHOWS

A. That one is easy mate, it when Floyd Havard boxing a couple of times on my shows at Caesars. Pure class! He almost took the head off his opponent with his right jab. Steve Holdsworth was the referee that night and he came over to me after and said "I am completely honoured to have shared the same ring with such a great boxer."
Caesars was always a mad house but I have never seen it like it was when Floyd was fighting, the crowd were mesmerized by his skill and gave him one of the best and most sincere round of applause I have ever heard at the venue.

Q. Brendan Moloney Would Tyson Fury beat every unlicensed boxer or do you think anyone in the unlicensed world would beat him

A. Yes mate! Tyson is leaps and bounds above anyone in unlicensed boxing.

Q. Dave English How do u qualify to be/challenge the guvnor? Is it a london title, just your promotion, just heavy weight?

A. good question, I have explained most of this in the chapters beforehand. The Guv'nor title was always different, it's always been the heavyweights so it's always been the big boys. When we did it at Caesars, the Guv'nor title was always our British title. There are no set rules attached to it. If someone wanted to challenge for it then we took a look at the fight and either said yes or no.
In the 2000s we formed our own governing body the EBF so all our titles were an EBF title, (The EBF British title, The EBF southern area title etc.)
Gary Firby was our EBF northern area champion so we matched him against Sven Hamer who was the EBF British Champion *the Guv'nor* Sven won in two rounds.
The next fight for Sven he defended his title against a tough street fighter doorman who challenged him.
It was a fight by fight basis. We made the fights that we thought the public wanted to see.

Q. Dave English Were the northern lads likes Duffy, Sykes, Graham ever challenged by the London lads likes of Lenny and Roy?

A. No! why would they challenge them? They never held the title so any challenger would be made by the challenger and not the champion.

Q. Cueball Robbie What advice would you give future generations coming into boxing?

A. There is an old saying in boxing, which says, Boxing is a mugs game! believe me it's not! If you're a mug, then you will get hurt! My advice to anyone is you have to live the life, be prepared to make boxing your number one priority and also fitness is the key. If you are unfit and you are in the ring under the lights with someone opposite you trying to take your head off, it's a horrible place to be.

Q. Mark Napier Had he stayed out would Charlie Bronson have become an unlicensed legend?

A. No I don't think so. I have seen him box and he doesn't look very good, I don't think he was big enough also.

Q. Mickey Oliver Wasn't cliff fields the real govnour?? He beat both Roy and Lenny apparently. There a interview on YouTube Roy admitting cliff the real guvnor. Is cliff in your book??? Cliff wasn't even good enough to be pro-British champion no. I did see a flyer years ago when Roy was set to fight ali there was talks of it then bbbc striped Roy of his license

A. Okay, first of all Cliff fields beat Lenny (twice) he never fought Roy Shaw. Cliff won a few fights on the unlicensed scene but he was limited as a professional fighter. When Roy said he was the guvnor, it was for cliffs book and cliff was very ill at the time. Roy was being kind and make no mistake, if the money was there then Roy would have fought him.
the Ali thing was a joke poster just to get some publicity, there was never any talk of a fight, just a bit of banter.

Q. **Russell Bradley** Who owned Caesars at the time and what sort of character where they.?

A. Fred Batt, there is a section in the book about him in the chapter Caesars.

Q. **Rob Brenton** Who would have won the Paul Sykes Vs Lenny fight?

A. all fantasy match-ups are difficult as you have to factor in different alternatives. For instance, are we talking about a Lenny like he was against Roy or a Lenny a few years later when he was 20 odd stone?
personally I would say Sykes wins as he was a professional boxer and a good pro. He would have an enormous advantage of 'Ringcraft' and years of experience over Lenny. (But as in all heavyweight fights – one punch can change a fight!)

Q. **Neil Thomas** Who is/was the hardest man you know (appreciate you know lots) someone who wasn't a boxer/bare knuckle but was fearless and respected?

A. there are a few I can think of, Roy would be up there as he was very dangerous years ago. Frankie Fraser was vicious back in his day, he was a small man but a tool merchant, he would open you up as soon as look at you.
my father and Johnny Nash were two men who could really have a fight on the cobbles, both two big powerful fellas. There were a lot of tough men out there, but what I always say is, the man who lands the first clean shot should win the fight! If you get hit right by a big fella and it breaks your jaw, then there is not much you can do. Other fellas who were dangerous were Teddy Dennis, Freddie Foreman and Brian Emmett. Peter Tilley, Terry Plummer, Nosher Powell, Vic dark, Johnny Mcfadyn, my late cousin Pat McCann, there is a long list!

Q. **Simon Presland** If you could choose any two fighters passed away or alive who would you love to see fight?

A. Dave Pearce vs Paul Sykes would have been a good fight, and also Lenny McLean vs Johnny Bindon (which almost happened) would have been interesting.

Q. Ben Poole Who's the biggest disappoint in and out of the ring

A. Norman Buckland! I like Norman and respect anyone who gets through the ropes but he retired before having a defining fight. We spent a lot of time building him up and designing posters and stuff, we were marketing the hell out of him. Then just as we were looking at a big fight for him, he announced he was retiring? And over the last few years he has seemed to have gone off his head? He continually goes on social media putting down the guvnor title (the title he held and says he covets?) plus he has gone on to create another belt and puts us down to promote his belt! I don't understand why he feels he has to do it. We helped him to get the name Guv'nor Norman as he calls himself. Its strange that he now condemns the very same title he says he hold so dear. Some of his recent outburst have been disrespectful to the other fighters who boxed for the title. He once said he was 'the Godfather of the Guvnors' yet he is the only one who held the title and never fought a challenger? Its bizarre the way he has decided to act. He boxed three journeymen and then retired before accepting a challenge from welsh Phill and Garry Sayer??

Q. Glen Martin Would Bartley Gorman have beaten them all.

A. I have never seen Bartley box with gloves on, so I have no reason to think he would have beaten them. Donny the bull Adams claimed he was the king of the gypsies. Why didn't Bartley challenge Donny?

Q. Rich Austen Who is the one fighter that you always wanted to get to fight for you on one of your shows but it never happened for one reason or another or a fighter that was just in the wrong era that you would've loved to have showcased.
Ps Sorry I'm retired lol

A. I would have loved to have promoted both Roy and Lenny (two men who are a promoters dream) Sven Hamer vs mark Potter would have been a big fight and also I would have like to have seen Welsh Phill vs Norman Buckland.
ex professional and British and European boxer Floyd Havard boxed at Caesars and I was trying to get a fight on with fellow Welshman Barry Jones (the former world champion) who some say won the title because Floyd retired? That would have been one amazing fight!

Q. Stuart Parkin If the Guvnor title was to go mainstream do you think it would lose its prestige or do you think it would be a benefit from a possible wider audience?

A. What do you mean by 'Mainstream' ? are we asking of it became a televised event on terrestrial TV? If so, then No, I think it could be something very big! It's not like other titles where the best skilled fighter wins, it's a title for who is the craziest1 the toughest and the one with the biggest heart.

Q. William Deigan Do you think some of the unlicensed boxers, including the big names and small,
Had the chance to go the full way in legit boxing?

A. two boxers spring to mind, Mike Bourne from Essex was a very good fighter, strong and very heavy handed. He had his first fight for MeanMachine in Canvey and then went on to have thirty more fights and was undefeated. Pete the assassin Stoten is another. Pete has been fighting all his life and he would have definitely made a very decent professional.

Q. Mark Bowman I'd be interested to hear some more info on Harry Starbuck and Stevie Colombo ? Met both fellas and both proper characters, Harry was very well respected across S London and Steve was pretty unique too

A. Harry was a big name around Abbeywood and Woolwich in south east London, I met him a few times and he was nice fella, I've headache was a right handful if you upset him but people did and still do speak highly of him. Colombo was indeed a real character, he was tough as nails and came out of Hungary just after WW2, I seen him fight loads of times and recent years I used to bump into him around Bermondsey and the Old Kent Road where he always had something on him to sell1 he always had bags with shirts or t shirts. I liked Steve and had some good times with him and his best pal Davey Lane.

Q. Jim Ewing Who in your opinion would have been a great guvnor title holder...but they never actually fought for it?

A. Billy Isaac would have been one. He was menacing outside the ring so he had that persona that goes with the title. Billy was an ex professional so he could fight in the ring. I also think Mark potter and Dominic Negus would have been worthy of a guvnor status.

Q. Spencer Guainiere Who put the hours in the gym and who liked to party pre fight

A. as a rule of thumb its usually the ex-pros who put the hours in the the gym in the unlicensed world. They're used to the endless hours of training and lifestyle.

Roy Shaw was a good trainer but he also liked to party. Bill the bomb liked a party. As you know mate partying and boxing don't mix!

Q. Mark Golightly Do you think Bill the bomb would have beat Lenny and Roy?

A. It's a fair question, but another fantasy match up question. Bill was a decent professional, so it's back to the argument – ex pro vs unlicensed boxer. I think I would favour Bill to win against both as he had the ring craft knowledge.

Q. Garry Cadd What was the most brutal fight and who between?? Xx

A. There has been a few! Roy Shaw vs Lenny Mclean 2 was brutal. Tough fight. On my shows, Steve Dosset vs Marc Woolf was a tough fight and so was Sven Hamer vs Joe Kacz.

Q. Wayne Elson Who had the hardest punch Lenny or Shaw

A. Both could punch! Lenny was the heavier so I would go with Lenny.

Q. Jamie Hallett Who made the most money in one fight

A. I would say Roy Shaw when he boxed Donny the Bull Adams, the side bets were huge and the place was sold out.

Q. Andy Lee Who would you have on the cobbles standing next to you Lenny or Roy

A. Both! No seriously, I would feel safe with either of them next to me, but if I had to choose then I would edge towards Roy because he had that little bit more of wickedness and naughtiness on the cobbles.

CHAPTER 18
TRIBUTES

WENDY

To my dear friend, bruva from annuva, my Boss, Mr. Joe Pyle

One of the most powerful influential person ino. The original Thomas Shelby.
Firstly, I'd like to start by wishing you all the best in everything you do and
Everything you've achieved. You deserve health wealth and most importantly
happiness in your life!

It was a great honour for me to become part of MeanMachine boxing
promotions in 2007 working in a man's world as big as the boxing circuit wasn't
easy but by god what a world to be allowed into.

Unlicensed boxing at Caesars in Streatham was the place to be the vibe was
electric, the aura as u walked thru them doors I never met the Krays or went to
their clubs but I should imagine it felt exactly the same, I've done many shows
Kingston and my own show in Canvey and Heathrow Hotel but nothing
compares, and yes ino there's probably bigger shows now and probably better
promotions that think there better than us ha-ha. BUT I can guarantee if u was
ever lucky enough to be a part of Caesars or to be looked after by both joe's snr
and jnr you will agree there was no other and will never be a buzz like it
FACT!!

So in 2009 the 'Mean Girls' were brought in by me as manager 20 ring card girls
on my books to walk joes finest into the ring, which entailed hours n hours of
photoshoots, finding them, interviewing, buying hot pants, scouting everywhere

all-day in the middle of Romford market, training them, then onto matching up boxers finding photographers, film guys, bodyguard ,and getting medals for shows, selling tickets, and blasting out flyers, as well as running my own home and family life straight off the back of being Carlton Leach's manager for 5 years on tour with Rise of the Footsoldier,

Don't know how I done it but I pulled it off, I've always been a bit of rebel a ruff diamond with a loaded criminal record for battery affray assault GBH so I guess I fitted in nicely with the so called big boys, but still to this day people always ask me what's it like a little lady in a firm I correct them by saying me & joe have never quoted firm or LL&R same as ino there is no such thing as gangster now = but that's another book ☺ these guys are just human being to me I been round joes house when he's with his children and I've had him round mine I see nothing more than a loyal good decent kind friend and a bloody good boxing promoter, and I quote: "The Real F*****g guvnor in my eyes!

10 years ago we filmed Thugs Mugs And Violence together and I then saw joes full potential as an actor when he changed his whole script to suit him the producer went within ha-ha well wot else could he do , I knew then Joe had a book inside him and definitely a film, unfortunately all our hard work never got released but I have no doubt in my mind that Joes talents will eventually shine on our screens, in 2011, I was very blessed when I received a phone call from joe asking me to go to an office set up for me in Ilford to work on putting together the Joe Pyle snr foundation magazine that was a real pleasure in honour of his late father who unfortunately I never got the chance to meet, but I must say joe I'm sure he'd be proper proud of you now and how far you've come and Don't u forget that.

unfortunately, on 31st May 2015 I tried to take my own life I hit a low point whilst exhausted yet who was at the end of the phone on my hospital bed as soon as I was resuscitated my dear lifelong brother - WEND he said ohhh I'm in trouble now. His exact words were you're a silly girl you're a major part of the boxing with me. I need you. And don't u dare think you're not! Promise me your get well and don't u dare do this again, u fink I don't get days were I wanna give up? Get better then I come see you. Down went the phone. That was the kick up the Jacksy I needed to which I'm eternally grateful.to this day I have the upmost respect even on my recent daughters Tessa birthday party he made an appearance u made a big impact on her life she still talks about being allowed to be a ring girl which gave her a massive confident boost.

So it gives me the greatest of pleasure to have worked by your side and a Massive thankyou from the bottom of my heart and I will continue for as long as u need me to help you promote or work with you for many more years to come

All the best and go smash this book - my main man "often imitated, never equalled, the one n only Joe Pyle, Love you

Wendy Propernaughty x

CHRISTIAN SIMPSON

I didn't want to rush what I wanted to write as I wanted it to come from my heart. Here is below what I have just completed and finished writing for your book. I hope you are happy with it. God Bless Always from your friend Christian x

I would like to start by saying I feel honoured to be doing a 'forward' among others for a gentleman, a friend and a honest man, who has a lot of respect on a international level, not only in the world of professional boxing and as well as in the unlicensed boxing industry but also in the music business.

The first time I met Joe Pyle Jrn was through his father, the late, great Joe Pyle Snr, back in the 1990's.

It was a time, when being in their company, you could notice that the great man, Joe Snr was at the time, passing on the responsibilities of his family, upon his son Joe Jnr.

It's hard to put into words, but as each year went on, Joe Snr would in his own time, start to take a back seat and that's when Joe Jrn, started to shine as he still does to this very day in everything, he puts his mind to and all that he has achieved.

During those earlier years, between the three of us, having our own direct separate connections, on a professional working level, within the music industry, we, three would meet up at many show business events or when a international or a British high profile music artist, would be performing live, during a world or UK tour.

Joe Snr and Joey Jrn, would be in music artist's management positions and I would be in my role as close protection for certain music artists and bands.

It was only until 1999, that discussion took place, where with proudness, both gentlemen, asked me to take on the role as security director on behalf of Joe Jrn at some of the most glamorous boxing events, that have ever been staged in the UK.

The list of venues, were the likes of the most prestigious 5 star hotels in London.

Not only were the boxers, legendary in their own rights and up and coming boxing legends of the future.

There also were always major stars from television, film, sport and the music industry.

All were nothing less than A-Listers in their own chosen careers.

To name, only a few such as Roger Daltrey from The Who, Ali Campbell and Astro from UB40, Snooker World Champion Ronnie O'Suvillan, Ronnie Woods from the Rolling Stones, Snooker legend Jimmy White, World Heavyweight Boxing Champion Mike Tyson, Music Artists Wyclef Jean and Mark Morrison, multiple film award winner actor Ray Winstone, British award winning film screen writer Nick Moorcroft and so many more.

Mixing among and happily to do so, with the faces of many a leading crime family, from throughout England as well as from Ireland and Northern Ireland, Wales and Scotland.

Never ever was there any trouble and with Joe Jrn, by now having a solid firm around him, everyone who attended such shows from city bankers to casino whales (high rollers) to investment bankers and even certain Italian America gentlemen from across the pond, New York as well as Las Vegas.

Everyone were there to show their support and respect to Joe Pyle Jrn and his family.

Which was very important to both Joe Jrn as well as his father as they would always ensure, that the element of family was always a huge part of these spectacular boxing events.

As many of their own family, all also would be in working roles for such events to make the events, run smoothly.

That's when you just could see and feel, such a great sense of how strong, caring and staunchly respected, that this family was.

And that their history, speaks for itself, from many years previously, from when Joe Snr first, himself started in the boxing industry with the likes of legends such as Alex Stein and Roy Shaw to name, only two such legends in the unlicensed boxing industry.

As the years, went on Joe Jrn found a regular more suitable venue, that then become the main venue for future events, that being Caesars in Streatham, South London.

There already was a very solid and capable security team in place so I was able to by then, enjoy the events as a invited guests and still of course, being on hand, if Joe or his father needed me.

Both father and son, always had a loyal firm around them so at all times, they could get on with the show and never have any problem to worry about.

As as well, the very same level of calmness in both their personal lives, through the respect, that both earned over the years by always being fair and reasonable businessmen.

The passing of Joe Snr, is a void, that no other man, can ever replace as such men as Joe Snr as well as my Godfather Freddie Foreman or the Nash Family, are gentlemen, that are from an era, which can never again be matched.

When Joe Snr sadly passed away, Joe Jrn didn't try to become his father as by then, Joe Jrn had already earned on his merits in the way, he personally conducted business, from how he was a family man to his own and a genuine friend to his friends, he had become in a natural process, the head of his family.

His desire and motivation to continue in the boxing game as a boxer's manager, and boxing promotor, went onto even greater heights on a personal and professional level for Joe Jrn as equally did his involvement in the music business, still to this current day.

I am proud to call Joe Pyle Jrn, my friend for now over 25 years.

And I will always back him in his corner, even though I'm not a fighting man, like many of his other close friends are but I would still always stand by his side, through any difficulties times, and not just through the good times.

He knows that himself and so do those, who it matters to.

I wish Joe, the very best of success with this fantastic book and I do hope a film project or a documentary, comes his way soon.

It is a family, that deserves a film to be made about them as so does the unlicensed boxing industry, on the behalf of many individuals, from across England, Wales, Scotland, Ireland and Northern Ireland, who train so hard with such an intense discipline and have the balls and guts and strength to step into boxing rings, up and down the country.

With huge courage to give it their all for their towns, their counties and their families, time after time.

Displaying their natural abilities as warriors, boxers and staunch fighting men. Supported through their careers to become the greatest, by such gentlemen as Joe Jrn and his late father and many others.

God Bless from Christian Simpson.

***

ALAN KITSON

It a pleasure and aN honour to have boxed for mean machine promotions at the iconic Caesars in Streatham. I was only supposed to have one fight to get something on tape as I was already teaching boxing but never had nothing on tape from my amateur days to show the lads I was teaching. It was just to show the lads I could box which I'm proud to say MeanMachine gave me the opportunity to do all that and more. I ended up having four fights with them and boxed for the title. In my time with MeanMashine I fell in love with the boxing game made some amazing mates and I'm more than proud to have been a part of some amazing all round entertainment. I have nothing but love respect and appreciation for everyone involved, past, present and future. They were great days an amazing Time in my life that is still inspiring me to this day

Ko Kitson

***

GARRY SAYER

I first started going to Caesar' unlicensed boxing to watch one of my good friends Colin will be fight got to know Joe and I signed up for a fight was in a boxer just could have a row My first fight was such a good had experience If you hadn't been to Caesars you wouldn't understand the atmosphere drove the crowds when you come out cheers with your name. Such good times so many laughs met so many good people as I was coming up the ranks several fights before challenge Big joe Kacz Who was the governor at the time which ended up me and Joe going out of the ring and the flight being put off a few months later I won the title of the governor and had many challenges my biggest defence of the title was going to be was going to be against Billy Isaacs absolute beast of a man we was both meant to be fighting on the same show before we thought each other Roy shore Remembrance show to fight before I was meant to fight me and Billy had a fight before in the crowd got broken up Just like to say a big thanks to Joe and all his support when from unlicensed boxing To K-1 cage fighting and won 2 titles at UCMMI Always having support from Joe fighting for the main machines was like a big family and a great part of my life and become in the governor not only did you defend the title in the ring it was out of the ring as well many fights on the cobbles

Garry Sayer

***

SUKI DHAMI
I first met Joe Pyle in 1997 at his boxing gym on Streatham. I had been to his legendary shows at Caesars where u would see all the faces of London. The atmosphere was electric and were some great fights in and out of the ring. I wanted to showcase my talent on his show so I had a chat with Joe and he decided to put me on one of his summer shows at Caesars. Joe was always a gentlemen easy to deal with and I had no regrets. As the evening approached I felt a few nerves but no fear. The dressing room pumping with adrenaline and testosterone along with ten men who all had a survival instinct within them ready to go war, only no one had troops to go with them. Joe matched me up evenly with a solid southpaw. After stepping through the ropes we had a great first round and it was one of the best fights of the show. I won by no in the second round and the crowd went wild. Joe was the first man to congratulate me and Wendy head of the ring girls. The afterpartys were legendary getting in at 9am.Thanks to MeanMachine I have great memories to treasure. thankyou Joe Pyle.

Suki Hitman Dhami

***

MICHAEL COLEMAN
I'm honoured to be asked by best mate Joe about all the top boxing events I've been to of which there are many. Not only is Joe Legendary but his events too which were started by his also extremely respected father Joey Pyle senior.
Both Joe and his father boxed along with many of the fraternity who also were and are legendary with each one commanding respect and names in their own right.
Joe's events ' Mean Machine ' are always a big affair, an event and ones that everyone goes too and no one misses out on. It's a guaranteed top night full of entertainment, top people from all over and glitzy sell out events!

273

People probably don't actually realise the effort Joe puts in to make each night Legendary and he's a perfectionist when it comes to this and works tirelessly for weeks prior to the event to get everything just right.

The venue must be right, the boxers have to be right and then matched for a fair fight. It always amazes me how professional it all is as the ring is surrounded by tables just outside it full of adjudicators, commentators, medical personnel, Judges and more.

Joe has to get there very early and boxers fighting are weighed in and given a medical and have to be in the peak of health as otherwise they won't be allowed to fight. The safety and health of the boxers is paramount always.

We've been all over for Joe's events including gorgeous hotels where we've had delicious three course meals and worn black tie evening wear. It's always great to see everyone and always a highly social affair and great catching up with everyone and always meeting more also good people. People travel from all over as different boxers come from different areas and many travel hours for the prestige of fighting at one of Joes events.

People usually pick their favourite for each fight and everyone really goes for it willing them to win. Its enthralling to watch especially as there's all weights fighting and a featherweight is a completely different fight to a heavyweight and no boxer is the same and sometimes the underdog can really surprise everyone. You have to have great admiration for each fighter going up there in front of everyone and the stamina and fitness involved is huge. After there's usually an after party so everyone's usually out till the early hours and as well as the boxing, it's a top social highlight for everyone.

I think it's safe to say that the real long standing home of ' Mean Machine ' is the very Legendary South London club ' Caesars ' on Streatham High Road. A venue that goes way back and a place my father went when he was young as a prior incarnation ' The Locarno Ballroom.'

Since I was young, you couldn't miss Caesars with its actual massive silver sculpture of four Roman chariot horses over the entrance canopy with mirrors behind it and a black Bentley outside with ' Caesars ' on the number plate.

Joe and Joey Pyle senior certainly have built a firm steadfast staple and legacy in the boxing game which many have now followed. The unlicensed arena which they created and the absolute Legendary much coveted ' Governor ' title which has brought such titans like Roy Shaw, Lenny Mclean, Stormin Norman, Sven Hammer and Gary Sayer.

Its fantastic Joes writing this all down to share with us so we can all enjoy and hear about it from the man himself, the Guvnor of Unlicensed boxing! Thanks Joe for being such a top mate and gent which is always very much appreciated and taking me into your family. Enjoy the book, love Michael **Michael Coleman.**

***

STEVE WRAITH

I have known Joe for over 25 years now. We first met at a Casino in Leicester Square. He was with his Dad; I was with my good friend Christian Simpson. Also present that night were Freddie Foreman, Frankie Fraser, Tony Lambrianou, Dave Courtney, and Tommy Wisbey. We weren't planning a job! It was a social night and a bit surreal for young Geordie lad. We had a. great night and I hit it off with Joe from day one. We both. loved boxing so had a lot to talk about that night. Mike Tyson was the main man back in those days and we both admired him. Over the years I'd catch up with Joe on my visits down South. We used to frequent the 'Monday Club' together in the Carlton at The Elephant and Castle with all the faces. When Joe branched into the boxing he asked Metrocentre if I had any fighters up in Newcastle to put on. I did. Gary Firby got his chance on Joe's shows at the Hammersmith and at Caesars and he always pulled a crowd. He won the 'Guvnor' belt against Steve Yorath and was presented it by Roy Shaw. Joe launched the first doorman union 'FEDS' in the early noughties and I was by his side with that venture to. We both had a good relationship with the Krays of course, visiting them both frequently. Not many can say that. Our friendship has grown over the years and in recent years we have launched books together and worked closely in the world of professional boxing. Joe is a loyal man, a man of his word, and doesn't suffer fools gladly. Most importantly he is my friend. Love and respect as always Joe.
Steve Wraith

***

JAMIE O'KEEFE

It's a true honour to be asked to add a piece to this book. I've known Joe many years and we have worked on few things together over that time.
I remember once when we were out together and I was standing by his side when he fronted up to about 15 blokes who were hyped up on alcohol and drugs mouthing off. Without going into detail, he nipped that in the bud. He is the real Mcoy.
I don't like fakes or wannabees which is one of the reasons I admire Joe and have bundles of respect for him.
Then there's Roy Shaw who I have known for decades. Years ago we would go and have lunch together when he visited his dear old mum weekly in Dagenham. That was about 40 years ago. Over the years Roy gave his time unconditionally to his friends, and even sent flowers to my mother's funeral as did Reggie Kray. It was this side of Roy that not many saw, he didn't like to let his guard down. I was once releasing one of my books and Roy came to promote his book. Those that attended were just in awe of him. It just showed the other side of Roy. The last time we were together was in his bungalow shortly before he passed. He had just experienced a road rage incident and

banged the guy out. Roy drove straight home but he wanted to go back to see if the guy was ok. He found him slumped over the steering wheel still out for the count but still breathing. So that's the two sides of Roy Shaw. I miss Roy a lot and was honoured that I was one of the few people actually invited to his funeral to say my goodbyes. As I sprinkled the earth on Roy's coffin I felt the deep loss and impact he had on my own life and many others. Roy was one in a million.

***

DAN CONNOR
I had my first fight at Caesars after I had just boxed in the novice ABAs, Ricky English rang me and asked if I fancied earning a few quid, so I jumped in a cab over to Caesars and won the fight by TKO vs Liam Bucko, I used to love fighting at Caesar's, the smell of the burgers and onions when you walked in made me love the place, I had a few fights there early on before I turned pro and made some good memories, see some wicked fights as well, Lee Bates vs Scott Mcdonald was a cracker, used to love Colin Wilby's 'Banged our' entrance tune , was a pleasure to work with Joe and Rick and they were some of my best boxing memories to date
Danny Cassius Connor

***

MICKEY O'SULLIVAN
Joe Pyle was a top fella! lovely bloke! my one regret was not boxing there more!! best venue I'd ever boxed at and the crowd was menacing lol think I sold about 30 so I got about £200, maybe 250 I believe but didn't do it for the money. I do it just for the love of boxing! I boxed a lot as an amateur around Europe and England then I boxed white collar, unlicensed, and pro, iv boxed countless times at places all over but Caesars was the best venue I'd ever boxed at. I boxed a fella named James cox I just showed bit more to body and head on the night so won! A lad who I ko'd in amateurs ended up fighting for the British title I won't mention any names but would love to fight under mean machine again! but at 35 we're see.
Mickey O'Sullivan

***

To Joey P

I just want to wish you all the best with the new book, a can't wait to read it and get a signed copy and a see there's a cracker of a wee picture of me and you sitting marking plans, I remember that night lol there's been a few, I remember when I picked Howard marks up from Leeds and we came down for a show we ended up all night in the hotel and we kept that going for 3 days and ended in the Liverpool Adelphi hotel or the time we had some meetings going on and me you and Billy Issacs ended up out on the town and I was in the bad books for a week when I got back up the road, yourself and your brothers warren, Mitch and Alan always made us feel part of the family and put time aside for us proper gentlemen. Every time you invited me down south me and the lads had a ball you looked after us and showed us a great night always with good company. I understand why you call it the family; whether it was Boxing events in Caesers palace or boxing in hotels or at DCs castle it's always a great night. So from your brother from Glasgow a wish you every success and am sure we will see plenty more of JP. Oi oi
Jason Murray

CHAPTER 19
THE GUVNOR OF THEM ALL
JOEY PYLE SNR

This will probably be the hardest chapter in the entire book that I have to write. It's difficult on two fronts, firstly he was my father, and I love and miss him every day, and secondly, it's difficult to do a tribute chapter because he (is) my father. I don't want to come across as sounding conceited or biased or blowing the trumpet.

I wasn't even thinking about writing this chapter until earlier tonight when Welsh Phill rang me to discuss a few things and his words were,

'Joe, it's important this book is about you and your dad, you both made all of us, and your book must be about that, you are both the real guvnors.

It's tough knowing where to start about my father. He was just dad to me, he never tried to be something, he was just himself. He had an uncanny knack of knowing the exact thing to do at the exact time; it was effortless for him to wave his hand and make a decision.

Don't get me wrong, I've seen times when it was hard for him, like having to prepare a case when he was nicked (that would test the patience and nerve of anyone) especially if you lose then the result was going to be spending possible all your remaining life living in a concrete cell!

Ever since I was a young boy, I have seen these big powerful men around my father, yet he controlled them all. I have never seen anyone control my father (the closest I have ever seen doing that, was his father, my grandfather) he could be in a house, an office or down the pub, my father sat central and held court over everyone.

I have never once seen him look out of place. No matter where it was or who he was with, he dominated the setting and those around him.

He was a people's person with the unique ability to be assertive without coming across as arrogant or bossy. To be in his company was fun, exciting, he would light up the room with just a smile, put everyone around him at ease, and you just couldn't help wanting more, he was infectious.

He truly was a leader of men who led from the front and by example.

A kind nature and a caring one, he always had time for people and he enjoyed company. On the other hand, I have seen him turn when needed to, and when he did, he did not need many words to make his point. It was a quiet word in your ear and a look, and you got the message straight away, believe me. I have seen that look in his eyes many times and I have seen some big men (Big names) be on the end of it and seen them almost half in size before it.

I've heard over the years, people talking cobblers like they were Joey Pyle's (minder) I'm telling you now, he never needed a minder. He was a big strong, powerful man himself; he was just under six feet and around 15-16 stone and solid as a rock.

(what I say next I hate saying as it makes me sound like a kid in a playschool yard) but regardless, it needs to be said.

My father could unquestionably hold his own on the cobbles! He was an ex-professional boxer and was always training in the boxing gym, he could throw his punches, and if he hit you and caught you right, then it hurt, you stayed hit! 15 stone of weight on the end of a fist is going to do some damage.

I have heard people say about Roy and Lenny being the best at street fighting, but i'm telling you, they would both have their work cut out in a fistfight with my father. When I was a kid, and my father chased Johnny Bindon up the road, poor Johnny must have broken the 100m world record!

(it was one of those things and they ended up being close mates in the end.) But that wasn't what my father was all about. He had that strength in his (locker), and it was only used if absolutely necessary.

If I had to write down all the qualities about my father, then one would stand out and be very close to the top of the list. It was the way he treated his friends. And also the respect he received back from his pals. He would always tell me to value 'friendship'; it was very dear to him, and I know he loved most of his pals like family.

For example, Alex Steene loved my father, and If I close my eyes, I can still see him saying to me, "Joey, your dad is the king of kings! He is the king of them all!"

Roy Shaw was another who didn't hide his love for my father, they had a unique bond, and nothing ever got between it. Roy's love for him was almost sacred. At the funeral, me and Roy were at the front carrying the coffin and Roy was struggling to stay composed, I gave him a nod to say 'Don't worry we will do this' and he looked back at me with tears in his eyes and said: "he was the bollocks, Joe." It was one of the things that stood out for me at the funeral; that day, Roy Shaw had to draw all his strength just to hold himself together.

Ori Spado, my father's dear friend from across the pond, has so much respect for him. Ori has known and mixed with them all, people like John Gotti, Russell Bufalino, Sonny Francese, and even Frank Costello, yet Ori holds my father above them all! I have lost count the times he has told me that my father would have been a big boss if he had lived in the states.

Wilf Pine was a very respected gentleman, he is undoubtedly one the unsung heroes who quietly behind the scenes took care of so many things for people, but Wilf only ever had one boss, one man he only ever truly looked up to. He would often say to me and to others in that loud voice of his that, "Joey Pyle was the boss of them all, the boss of bosses!"

At my father's funeral, he said the words, "Joe was different class to everyone else, he was different gravy, and you will never see that recipe again."

I loved Wilf, he reminded me of Alex Steene in certain ways, both prominent strong characters, but they both had no hesitation or shame when it came to pronouncing their loyalty and affection for my father.

Below are a few words I have found written about my father from his friends.

Charlie Richardson – The Last Gangster
I'm sure that you can see why I enlisted Fred Dineage to sniff out the finer details of the relationship between the Krays and Richardson's. I have a good idea who 'the Voice' was - and it carried no idle threat.
I believe Fred talked to Joey Pyle, one of the most feared men ever to walk the streets of London.

Roy Shaw – writing the foreword for Tel Curries book, Left Hooks and Dangerous Crooks.
He was also friends with my best friend of all time , 'the main man' or 'Boss' Joey Pyle snr and you really had to come recommended to be in joes company let alone be a trusted friend of the man.

Tel Currie – Left Hooks and dangerous crooks
The day after joe died I wrote the following tribute for the internet.
since yesterday many of the UKs toughest men have found themselves weeping uncontrollably. People with solid reputation as hard and dangerous men said goodbye while trying and failing to choke back floods of tears as they told another man they loved him. The one they had come to say their final farewells to was of course the great Joey Pyle.
of course we all knew joe had been ill for a while, but strangely it was still a huge shock. It seems nothing can prepare you completely for the bad news even if you know it's coming. The benefit show we all did for him almost a year ago to the day. I remember having some trepidation about whether joe would make it to the show.
true to form though, joe fought on for a year despite the debilitating illness he was living with, and never gave up. I have said it before and I will say it again, joey Pyle did a lot more good in his eventful life than he ever did bad. Sure, he did some naughty things but he also worked tirelessly for sick and underprivileged children among many other good causes. He would frequently visit Zoe's Place children's hospice with the other chaps and was so touched and inspired by these amazing kids that he wrote a book called *Looking at Life* and gave every single penny it made to Zoe's while simultaneously exposing those huge companies that had made vast fortunes from children's products but refused to give anything back. Joe continued with this work until his strength finally deserted him. His loyalty and generosity to his friends was also huge. While others talked about it, Joe just did it and there were very successful benefit nights for Ronnie Biggs, Charlie Bronson, Wendy Lambrianou and many others. Joe was always being asked to help out somebody or something and I personally never saw him turn anyone down.
As far as the chaps are concerned, I would certainly say Joe was the most popular and I truly mean that. There were many reasons for this, not least Joe's

larger than life personality. Perhaps the biggest factor was that despite being close to the Nash family, Joe wasn't connected to anyone firm so became friendly with all of them. For example, he was great friends with the Krays and the Richardsons so could pop down the East End and see Ronnie & Reggie or into South London for a drink with Charlie and Eddie.

He was good friends with both Roy Shaw and Lenny Mclean, Freddie Foreman and Jack Mcvitie. Within the so called underworld, Joe had no enemies to speak of. He always saw the advantages in peace over mindless violence for violence sake. He would also stick up for the underdog despite the fact it may have upset some faces. For example, he always said that Jack Mcvitie deserved a far more dignified end than he got: "Jack died like a grass, a slag and he was no grass. He deserved a far more dignified end than a room full of people jumping on him to try and impress the twins."

Roy Shaw will tell you straight that Joey Pyle literally saved his life three or four times over. It was because of Joe's involvement that Roy finally saw the light of day after barely surviving hell on earth, drugged up with the liquid cosh, hallucinating in pitch darkness in the dungeons below Broadmoor. Without Joe, would Roy have died a slow painful death in the bowels of hell, a forgotten man? Roy will answer yes!

Joe stood by Dave Courtney at a time when it would of been far easier for him just to blank Dave. Joe didn't. Many did though, only to drift back because Joe was sticking with him.

It was Joe that Charlie Bronson called Dad after his own father passed away. There was no criminal link there, it was just that Charlie looked up to Joe, learned from him and was inspired by him. Charlie is just one of those hard men that are not ashamed to have shed many tears since yesterday. The amount of quality people I have spoken to since yesterday has been truly mind blowing and, no, they are not all rascals.

The vacuum that will be left by Joe will be impossible to fill; in fact it's not worth even trying. He was a one off, unique. He was also the glue that kept many people who on the face of it had nothing in common together. "How's Joe?" was a classic ice breaker and got people over awkward conversation lapses. If you think I am overplaying the importance of Joe, it's obvious you never even knew him. I could go on and on and on but I shall leave it there.

Kate Kray – Hard Bastards

JOEY Pyle is the archetypal gangster - like the film Godfather Don Corleone. He would not look out of place in movies like The Long Good Friday or Goodfellas.

Joey has ruled the roost in the underworld for more than four decades. He is the original Teflon Don - nothing sticks. Every man I interviewed knew or had heard of Joey Pyle.

He is the most respected of them all. I've never heard anyone say a bad word about him. Whether that's through fear or admiration, I'm not really sure.

The beauty of Joey Pyle is that he can mix in any circle. Royalty, MPs or murderers, he's at ease with them all. He is a man of few words, a shrewd businessman. His presence is enough to make you take a step back.

You're only in Joey's company if invited. Remove his sunglasses and they reveal twinkling blue eyes that are soft around women and as cold as ice to men. Joey can sort any problem with a word or a wave of his hand, but only a fool would mistake his kindness as weakness.

Charles Bronson - Loonyology

after the visit I got back to my cage, and was told that Joey Pyle had passed away. My whole world fell in. it was like losing my dad all over again. How many many more friends and family have I got to lose on this fucking sentence. And to top it all I still can't got a funeral.

to say I'll miss Joe Pyle is an understatement. He was a true friend. Joe was a second dad to me and he looked after me and bits of biz. When I needed something done it was done. Nothing was too much for joe – nothing! Any problem no matter how big or small, he would sort it for me, why/ well he was Joe Pyle, the true governor and don't let anyone tell you different – cos I'm telling you - he was the daddy of all daddy's. I'm not interested in the mafia or who or what it represents. But JOE PYLE to me was the ORIGINAL godfather – the best the UK has ever seen and will ever see.

Lew Yates – Wild thing

Shaw's close friend Joe Pyle (a south London gangster with more connections than the national grid) saw the fight as a unique money making opportunity. Pyle became Shaw's confident, promoter and manager. The Krays and the Richardson's and men like buster Edwards or Freddie foreman may be better known to the public, but by the end of the 60s all these men and their hangers on were either in prison or living abroad in exile. Amongst the criminal fraternity Joe Pyle was equally notorious and equally feared and equally respected. If something major was being planned by a criminal gang, Pyle would know about it. From the events leading up to the murder of jack the hat by the Kray gang and the great train robbery to the American mafias attempts to overtake London's casino scene. Pyle witnessed it all. Yet despite a few close calls – including a spell in prison on a murder charge that would have seen him hanged if found guilty – Pyle remained at liberty throughout. He was and without a doubt remains, a very, very shrewd operator. Together Pyle and Shaw made a very formidable partnership.

Paul Ferris – Vendetta

Joey Pyle – The Don of Dons and his son go from strength to strength in legitimate business

***

282

The list is endless and very flattering for me to read, I still speak to my father's friends the ones who are still alive on a weekly basis and that friendship they had with him still exists with me today.

I am very proud of my father and some days I see his qualities in my three sons, Sonny – Joe, Manny, and Cassius.
They have a long shadow to live in but they have to draw strength from the pride they carry the name.
It's not about money or how many house and boats you have...It's about what kind of man you are.
We are born into this world because of our fathers and forefathers, what mark we make on this world is what we have learned from their wisdom and noted from their mistakes.

Rest in Peace My Father
No matter what happens in this life, one thing can never change,
I have been, and always will be .. Your Son.

ABOUT THE AUTHOR

Joseph (Joey) Pyle is a very complex and deep individual. Born into a London family of criminal 'Royalty,' he has led a full and very colourful life.

He has mixed and worked with every top criminal in the UK, The Krays, Richardson, Freddie Foreman, Frankie Fraser, Charlie Bronson, Roy Shaw, Lenny Mclean, Howard Marks, Ronnie Biggs, Bruce Reynolds, Paul Ferris.... To name just a few.

Joe was one of the youngest professional boxing promoters in history (UK) and was the youngest promoter ever to stage a professional boxing world title contest in the UK.

Boxing is Joe's first love, but outside of boxing, his life has been eclectic, frantic, and unique.

President of his own union at just 29-year-old, he courted politicians in the houses of parliament while at the same time was the director of two PLC companies, plus managed internationally famed pop artist such as Mark Morrison and Brian Harvey. He was partners with Suge Knight of Death Row Records, and Ori Spado (Mafia associate - dubbed the Mob Boss of Hollywood, and also Danny Sims (Bob Marley's manager)

He has spent time in prison in the UK, Spain, Cyprus, and Angola (part of the process - Joe remarks)

His phone book is a who's who of the underworld and the celebrity world where he mixes with the same ease and poise.

One of the complexities of his mind is his love for poetry. Joe has been compared to Lord Tennyson and Tony Soprano - it's a bizarre mix, one which Joe wears well.

If you ask him what is next, he will smile and casually reply, "Who knows what will happen - I'm in god's hand

I grew up amongst it all, I was there, I saw it.

I lived it, and breathed it, it's in my blood.

From an early age I have always loved boxing.

I have promoted over 200 events and staged over a 1000 fights.

I founded MeanMachine promotions, the Guvnor of unlicensed boxing.
Created the Guvnor title.

I have Seen it all and been a part of it.

Those the we call the Guvnors were either my friends or family or those I put on that pedestal.

This book answers all the questions, and describe the controversy.

Thank you

I would like to thank
My Esther, (For showing patience & Support x) Wendy, Ian Mills, Brian
Emmett Jr, Michael Coleman, Alby and Charlie Baxter, Teddy Bam Bam,
Ori Spado, Fred Batt, Alan D, Steve Slater, Jim Bucket, Clive Black, My Mother,
Christian Morgan, Sean Attwood, James Esposito, Johnny Edwards, Ricky
English (Always my business partner) Wayne Feltham, Warren Bammo,
Mitch Pyle, Ted Pyle, James Eastwood,
& My Children
Sophie, Angel, Sonny, Manny, Honey, Cassius and Nate.
And last but not least
Little Ralph x

UNLICENSED
Who's the Guv'nor

THE END

Or
JUST THE BEGINNING

INFO & LINKS

If you enjoyed this book and purchased it on Amazon, could you please leave a positive review.

Please also subscribe to our website

www.the-guvnor.co.uk

and our YouTube channel

UNLICENSED BOXING THE GUVNOR

Contact

info@the-guvnor.co.uk

OTHER TITLES
From JOE PYLE

LIKE FATHER LIKE SON - A Journey of Minds
Is the combined poetry work of Joe Pyle snr and jnr.
Both keen lovers of verse, this book is a compilation of Joe Pyle
Snr's book - Looking at Life and Joe Pyle Jnr's book - From Villain
to verse-maker.

The work also contains a few unknown stories as well a few excerpts from the script
of the motion picture currently in post-production about the life of Joe Pyle Snr.
There are also extra poems that never made it into their original poetry books, one
of which is a poem Snr wrote for Ronnie Kray when he was in Parkhurst prison.
I have also included a few chapters of my time in South Africa, a fun time which
turned very dark. It is a tale of my life which few people know, but I have included
it in this book as there have been talks about the possibility of a future movie being
created from it.

A collection of poems/thoughts and quotes from the mind of Joey Pyle Jnr.

From a prison cell to the house of parliament as the president of his own union.
From gaols in Angola, South Africa and Spain to penthouses in Los Angeles, New
York, and Bangkok. Joey Pyle has seen and done what most dare not to think
about.

He has known and worked with almost every top table villain in London and holds
a phone book full of private numbers of some of the most famous celebrities in the
music/acting and boxing worlds.

This book is a brief insight into his spirit, his way of thinking and his lust for the
passions of this sometimes stinking rotten world. Joey Pyle has been compared to
Tony Soprano, Lord Tennyson and Gene Wolfe!

Is he a villain, a businessman or a poet? You decide…

https://www.amazon.co.uk/gp/product/B088BJPJLR

JOE PYLE SNR

JOE PYLE JNR

A Journey of Minds

LIKE FATHER LIKE SON

If you want to walk in the Sunshine with me
First you have to stand besides me in the rain

Printed in Great Britain
by Amazon

47943090R00176